The World

THE According to SIMPSONS

What Our Favorite TV Family Says about Life, Love and the Pursuit of the Perfect Donut

STEVEN KESLOWITZ

SOURCEBOOKS, INC.®
NAPERVILLE, ILLINOIS

"It was very interesting how many issues were addressed in *(The World According to The Simpsons)*. This book was easier to relate to (than *The Simpsons and Philosophy,* and *The Gospel According to The Simpsons)* and very example-driven. It's a quick, fun read."
~ Josh Belkin, Tufts University

"*[The World According to The Simpsons]* examines the political, social, and philosophical aspects of *The Simpsons* and how the series covers all aspects of human existence. The book also takes into account recent developments and how this amazingly insightful satirical cartoon responds to them in some of the most creative and unusual ways...The book has some of the most impressive writing that I've ever seen."
~ News Editor, *The Excelsior*

"*[The World According to The Simpsons]* is a book that offers a detailed insight into some of the strange similarities between *[Springfield and our own society]*. This book makes *The Simpsons* seem incredibly sophisticated as it points out parallels between fiction and reality using satire. For example, Mr. Burns is quoted as saying, 'One dollar for eternal happiness? I'd be happier with the dollar.'"
~ *The Shore Weekly Record* (Australia)

Published by Sourcebooks, Inc.
P.O. Box 4410, Naperville, Illinois 60567–4410
(630) 961–3900
Fax: (630) 961–2168
www.sourcebooks.com

Library of Congress Cataloging-in-Publication Data
Keslowitz, Steven.
  [Simpsons and society]
  The world according to the Simpsons : what our favorite TV family says about life, love, and the pursuit of the perfect donut / Steven Keslowitz.
    p. cm.
  Originally published: Tucson : Hats Off Books, 2004, under the title: The Simpsons and society.
  Includes bibliographical references and index.
  ISBN-13: 978-1-4022-0655-9 (alk. paper)
  ISBN-10: 1-4022-0655-0 (alk. paper)
  1. Simpsons (Television program) I. Title.

PN1992.77.S58K47 2006
791.45'72--dc22
                                    2005037943

Printed and bound in the United States of America.
VP 10 9 8 7 6 5 4 3 2 1

In memory of
Bleeding Gums Murphy:

now that you're gone,
we're singing the blues.

Contents

Foreword

KING DUNCAN: *Who wrote this feeble dialogue anyway?*
MALCOLM: *Shakespeare, sir.*
KING DUNCAN: *Fire this "Shakespeare" fellow.*
MALCOLM: *Um...he's dead, sir.*
KING DUNCAN: *Excellent.*
—from *MacHomer*, **Act I, Scene 7**

For ten years now, I have been performing a one-man show called *MacHomer: The Simpsons Do Macbeth*, which has been seen by more than half a million people worldwide. If we were to look more closely at that audience, I would guess that 10 percent are not familiar with *The Simpsons* at all, 30 percent have seen an episode here and there, and 50 percent are fans who at some point in their lives have watched it religiously. For the remaining 10 percent it seems that *The Simpsons* IS a religion. Indeed, I was once sent a Master's thesis detailing how Christianity paled when stacked up against the "Gospel According to Matt Groening!" The fact that so many people take this animated television sitcom so seriously is proof of its incredible influence on our turn-of-the-millennium culture. I have been fortunate enough to travel to four continents and over one hundred cities with *MacHomer*, and I am continually amazed at how far-reaching *The Simpsons* is. It seems that with globalization, for better or for worse, the middle-class suburban life depicted in Springfield has transcended North America and can now be identified with all over the world. Are we all destined to become homogeneous? Or, perhaps, Homer-geneous? (*COMIC BOOK GUY: Worst...pun...ever!*)

There's more to it, of course. *The Simpsons* has survived this long for many reasons, most of which have to do with the consistent strength of the writing. You can see it just by perusing the quotes throughout this book. It may not be Shakespearean, but I suspect the Bard would have loved *The Simpsons!* The fact that I can rely on these characters to pull off *Macbeth*, one of the world's bloodiest tragedies, is testament to the profundity of Matt Groening's creation. The inhabitants of Springfield are so well-conceived that they are possessed of what I call "tragic nobility." You are intended to laugh at them, their flaws, and their pathetic longings, but you also care deeply about them.

Haven't you ever found yourself shedding a happy tear at the end of an episode? That just doesn't happen when you watch other cartoons. We love *The Simpsons* characters more profoundly because we see ourselves in them; we understand them and what they are meant to represent. And that is why high school students, who almost inevitably find Shakespeare's writing boring and incomprehensible, really appreciate my performance. Those same "boring" words are filtered through Homer et al., and suddenly they get it. And more importantly, they *like* it.

Personally, I consider myself a fan, as opposed to a fanatic. I don't watch many new episodes anymore, although they still make me laugh when I do. But to most of my generation, *The Simpsons* was required viewing in college. The show was at the top of its game, seasons three through six, and hundreds would gather at the campus pub every Sunday night to take in a new episode. The crowd erupted with laughter at every good line and the energy was electric. And if I may draw a parallel, that same kind of energy must have permeated the Globe Theatre in London whenever Bill Shakespeare came out with a new play. Shakespeare was, like *The Simpsons* are now, the pop culture of four hundred years ago. He not only held up a mirror to reflect the state of society, he helped define what society was. That's what good writing does, whether it is satire, comic, or tragic: it effects change. For an in-depth analysis of how Shakespeare's writing has influenced society, please visit your local library. For an in-depth analysis of how *The Simpsons* has done so, look no further than this book. I leave you in the good hands of Mr. Steven Keslowitz. Mmm...scholarly!

~ Rick Miller

"Just once I'd like someone to call me 'Sir' without adding, 'You're making a scene.'"

~ Homer J. Simpson

Dedicated to my mom, my dad, my brother Justin, my turtle, Speedy, and of course, my parakeet, Homer. I love you all.

Seven (False) Myths About *The Simpsons*: D'oh!

- *The Simpsons* is "just a cartoon."

  The reality: *The Simpsons* is MORE than just a cartoon. The series presents iconic satire in a manner that is accessible to fans and scholars of all ages and backgrounds.

  No cartoon series addresses important issues in contemporary society with the unique critical lens that *The Simpsons* uses on a weekly basis.

- *The Simpsons* is one of the most liberally-slanted shows on television.

  The reality: Some have argued that *The Simpsons* has a liberal slant. While this seems to be the case, the writers address issues in an evenhanded and balanced manner. *The Simpsons'* political philosophy is best defined as "Simpsonian," not liberal or conservative.

- *The Simpsons* is destructive to the idea of the nuclear family.

  The reality: *The Simpsons* is one of the most family-oriented television shows on the air today. The family is shown to be the cornerstone of a happy life in an otherwise hectic and corrupt world.

- *The Simpsons* is anti-religion and iconoclastic.

The reality: *The Simpsons* is one of the most religion-based mainstream television programs on the air today. *The Simpsons* does not promote anarchy or the breakdown of governmental or private institutions.

- *The Simpsons* is a formidable opponent of capitalism.

  The reality: *The Simpsons* mocks certain abuses in the capitalist economic system but does so in a lighthearted manner and does so only to expose the ways in which certain individuals take advantage of our economic system. The system, by and large, is depicted as functional and conducive to a productive society. Furthermore, *The Simpsons* harshly attacks communism. In one episode, Fidel Castro is shown admitting that "we all knew this mumbo jumbo [communism] wouldn't fly."

- *The Simpsons* glorifies alcohol consumption.

  The reality: *The Simpsons* consistently shows the negative effects of excessive alcohol consumption. It one episode, for example, it was revealed that Homer's friend, Barney Gumble, was on a path to success before he began to get drunk all of the time. Once Barney curbed his drinking habit, however, he was able to achieve many of his goals, such as flying a helicopter. By portraying Barney as being unable to reach his goals in life while under the influence of beer, the show examines the negative effects of alcohol. The fact that Homer's most embarrassing moments often arise while he is drunk serves to reinforce this point. As Homer once exclaimed, "To alcohol: the cause of— and solution to—all of life's problems."

- *The Simpsons* is just another "smart" cartoon.

  The reality: *The Simpsons* is *the* SMARTEST television show of all-time.

The Simpsons: More Than "Just a Cartoon"

"Oh Marge, cartoons don't have any deep meaning. They're just stupid drawings that give you a cheap laugh."
~ **Homer Simpson, "Mr. Lisa Goes to Washington"**

A 2003 poll taken by the BBC asked respondents who they felt was the "greatest American of all time."

Here is the list of online responses as of June 13, 2003:

Bill Clinton	3.92 percent
Bob Dylan	6.15 percent
Benjamin Franklin	4.52 percent
Thomas Jefferson	6.43 percent
Martin Luther King Jr	10.06 percent
Abraham Lincoln	10.28 percent
Franklin D. Roosevelt	4.34 percent
Homer Simpson	40.83 percent
Mr. T	8.38 percent
George Washington	5.10 percent

Note that 40.83 percent of all respondents voted for Homer Simpson.

Another BBC Internet poll listed Homer as the viewers' choice for favorite U.S. television star. A third BBC poll recently revealed that Marge Simpson is the ideal mother. What do these polls say about America and its relationship with *The Simpsons?* Critics of *The Simpsons* would attribute America's ills (lack of ethics and morality) to the series. However, by responding that Homer Simpson is the most important American of all time, Americans—and the rest of the world—have come to realize that *The Simpsons* directly helps to engender the aura attributed to the United States.

Homer Simpson is a great philosophical thinker. Don't scoff: it's true. I challenge fans to find any figure over the past sixteen years who has come to as many important conclusions about pertinent issues in contemporary society as Homer has. Be it gun control, gay marriage, presidential politics, celebrity culture, consumerism, adultery, scandal, nuclear safety, obesity, alcoholism, religion, morality, popular culture, vegetarianism, poverty, or law enforcement, Homer has examined the ways in which society treats important issues and has made informed—yes, informed—opinions about what he sees in his society.

And this should not come as a surprise, despite the fact that Homer is a fictional character in a cartoon series. Homer Simpson lives in Springfield, Anywhere U.S.A., home of the Whopper, the Electoral College, and all things American. He represents everything that is both right and wrong with America. Although he is tempted by—and often succumbs to—indulgence in his most superficial desires, including, but not limited to, donuts, beer, television, gambling, and, perhaps most memorably, eating sixty-four slices of American cheese ("Mmm...sixty-four slices of American cheese"), he is a family man who presents himself as at least partially devoted to his two or three children (depending on whether he can remember that Maggie exists) and a loving husband. He is a product of the age of television, con-sumerism, and the celebrity-obsessed culture to which he belongs.

Homer is not exactly a religious man, but he does go to church (it's a great place to listen to the football games on the radio while that "church-guy" is talking) and has pledged his allegiance to "Jebus" on several occasions. Fearing imminent death, Homer once exclaimed, "Jesus, Allah, Buddha, I love you all!," and explained afterward that he was simply covering all of the bases. Funny, yes. But more importantly, this was a classic moment of philosophical inquiry emanating directly from the hectic head of Homer.

Everyone Loves The Simpsons

People's love of the show can be seen within the show itself. *The Simpsons* has had the most guest stars of any series of all time. As noted by Michael Solomon in *TV Guide*, "You haven't truly arrived until you merit an appearance on *The Simpsons*." The guest stars come from all walks of life—from Bret "The Hitman" Hart to Elton John to Stephen Hawking. *The Simpsons* attracts so many guest stars because of its satirical nature: a guest star must expect to be made fun of when they decide to star in a *Simpsons* episode. Still, guest stars often repeatedly star on the show (Kelsey Grammer, for example) because they understand that the show is extremely well-written. For example, as Matt Groening stated, "A lot of talented writers work on the show, half of them Harvard geeks. And you know, when you study the semiotics of *Through the Looking Glass* or watch every episode of *Star Trek*, you've got to make it pay off, so you throw a lot of study references into whatever you do later in life."

Guest stars are attracted to *The Simpsons* because it is not an "average" cartoon. Case in point: of all the musicians asked to guest star on the series, only Bruce Springsteen turned down the offer. World leaders are also attracted to *The Simpsons:* British Prime Minister Tony Blair recently appeared in an episode and has stated that he enjoys watching the series. Similarly, former U.S. Attorney General John Ashcroft reported on CBS *Sunday Morning* that he is an avid fan of *The Simpsons*. Even the Archbishop of Canterbury, Dr. Rowan Williams, has admitted to being a big fan of *The Simpsons*.

We can clearly see that the world loves *The Simpsons* and has embraced the show as a cultural and global phenomenon. The producers, writers, and actors have been able to create hundreds of magnificently powerful and insightful episodes of *The Simpsons*. The amount of energy and dedication that goes into producing each episode, combined with the enormous talent of the cast, has made *The Simpsons* one of the greatest and most loved television series of all time.

Why Study The Simpsons?

In *The Simpsons* episode entitled "Little Girl in the Big Ten," Lisa sneaks onto the campus at Springfield University and enters a large lecture hall. The course is based on the wildly popular *Itchy and Scratchy* cartoon series and is designed to explore the intricacies of the cartoon in an attempt to learn more about contemporary society. While this may at first seem like a farfetched idea, a number of colleges across the United States are currently offering courses based on America's favorite family, the Simpsons. One such course is called "*The Simpsons* and Society" and has been taught at Tufts University.

The course explores the ways in which *The Simpsons* reflects and influences various aspects of life in contemporary society. While some professors dismiss the notion that *The Simpsons* merits serious academic attention, many others disagree. Professor Paul Levinson of Fordham University was recently questioned in an NBC interview about the value of *The Simpsons* as a scholarly tool. When asked about "*The Simpsons* and Society" course and academic books written on the television series, he noted that, "To be serious, [material] doesn't have to be presented seriously.

The comedy [genre] goes back to the ancient Greeks and...[can be considered] as important as the Greek tragedies." So to fully appreciate the inherent academic value that the writers of *The Simpsons* incorporate into virtually all of the three hundred-plus episodes, viewers must disregard the fact that *The Simpsons* is a "cartoon" and give it a chance.

The purpose of scholarly studies of *The Simpsons* is to outline the important issues discussed on the series. The influence of *The Simpsons* lies in the power of its satire, and the power of its satire is derived from its inherent social and political commentary. It is important, for example, to understand that the characterization of Homer Simpson as America's "average" man speaks volumes about our society. Yes, Homer spends hours on his couch eating potato chips, but many Americans perform a similar action in their everyday lives. Homer Simpson, in many ways, serves as an exaggerated extension of human beings' penchant for laziness. When we look at Homer, we see a carnival mirror version of ourselves; we sincerely hope, however, that the mirrored image that we see does not reflect our true identity—or, for that matter, the direction where we, as individuals, are heading. In order to get a "feel" for how Simpsons humor transforms itself into academic satire, consider the following quote from the "Treehouse of Horror" episode in which the ghost of Snake, one of the criminals on *The Simpsons* who was executed earlier in the episode, kills from beyond the grave:

> **Lisa Simpson:** "I told you capital punishment isn't a deterrent."

Lisa's quote is satirical because pundits often debate about the efficacy of capital punishment as a deterrent for criminals. Capital punishment (Snake was executed in the electric chair) does not serve as a deterrent in this episode because Snake was indeed able to kill from beyond the grave. This is precisely how *The Simpsons* can take a nonsensical topic (Snake has posthumous killing power) and turn it into a satirical commentary on the effectiveness of capital punishment.

In a recent conversation that I had with Robert Thompson, the director of the Center for the Study of Popular Television at Syracuse University, he explained why he believes *The Simpsons* is so special. He noted that *"The Simpsons* is the best show in the history of television," and is "one of the great creations in the history of American comic art." He also noted that the show is "on the same level as [works by] Mark Twain and Will Rogers." Noting that Homer Simpson's "daily fight through life for the promise of another donut" is reminiscent of Job's actions in the Bible, he asserted that "Homer is one of the great creations of American literature." In terms of the use of *The Simpsons* as a teaching tool, Thompson noted that "the genius of using *The Simpsons* [in classrooms] is taking difficult concepts and using something students know intimately. *The Simpsons* is like a Trojan horse and is a useful tool in getting students to learn."

I also recently spoke with Matt Selman, co-executive producer of *The Simpsons*. He was delighted that academic studies such as this one are being written about *The Simpsons*. He told me that he tries to make the show funny and that the academic content that comes out of it is only a second priority. The brilliance of *The Simpsons* is due to its ability to maintain a fun tone, while exploring some of the most important and complex political, social, and philosophical issues in contemporary society. Each of the following themes present in contemporary society has, at some point, been examined on *The Simpsons*.

Section Three of this book addresses fundamental issues such as gun control, education, globalization, the age of television, Descartes' three-fold Method of Doubt, the modern industrialized employee, and a wide range of other important social issues. Please note the vital impact that *The Simpsons* has had on society pertaining to several academic areas of study (politics, mass media, American Exceptionalism, philosophy, and industrialization). Also note that the following individual essays focus on central academic themes and later tie these themes in with examples from *The Simpsons*. Since the writers of *The Simpsons* study society, it behooves us to analyze these issues and then explore how *The Simpsons* has treated each issue over the course of its prime-time run.

Why The Simpsons Rewards Repeat Consumption

The Simpsons is chock full of hidden elements that keep fans coming back for more. Episodes are generally broadcast several times a day across the United States and throughout various parts of the world—and with good reason. It is simply impossible to discern all of the allusions to popular and contemporary culture, and analyze the scathing social and political commentary by watching each episode only once.

The writing of the show is the major force behind its greatness. *The Simpsons* merits repeat consumption because the writers layer the show with a tremendous amount of intricate detail. In the opening sequence, for example, Maggie is scanned through the cash register at the supermarket as Marge is paying for groceries. This particular scene is extremely short, but fans have taped the sequence, pressed pause at the exact moment in which Maggie is scanned, and found that the register reads "$847.63." The reason for this particular price is that it was once stated as the cost required to raise a baby for one month in the United States.

Therefore, it is important to understand that a funny scene often contains more depth and meaning than appears on the surface. With *The Simpsons*, it is always a case of looking deeper and finding more. True *Simpsons* fans are never satisfied after watching each episode only one time. In "Last Exit to Springfield," Mr. Burns is angered when the workers at the Springfield Nuclear Power Plant coalesce and sing in protest outside. He suddenly appears frail, spiny, and especially wicked—more so than usual.

He is bewildered by their insubordination and tells Smithers, who is standing beside him:

> Look at them all, through the darkness I'm bringing.
> They're not sad at all. They're actually singing!
> They sing without juicers.
> They sing without blenders.
> They sing without flunjers, capdabblers, and smendlers!

What is particularly interesting about this scene is its reference to Dr. Seuss's infamously evil character, the Grinch. Burns's spiny, frail body and hand gestures appear to be quite similar to the Grinch's. Most telling, though, was Burns's choice to both rhyme and invent words that sound like something out of a Dr. Seuss book ("flunjers, capdabblers, and smendlers!"). A fan watching this episode for the very first time may very well not catch this direct reference and tribute to Dr. Seuss. However, if a viewer does not catch this particular reference, he will not be alienated from the main idea behind the show. *The Simpsons* is incredibly skilled at making direct references to elements of our culture—some more esoteric than others—without alienating members of the viewing audience who do not understand the reference. But when a viewer rewatches an episode, he or she will almost certainly find references that they did not latch onto during the first time they watched it. And thus, the use of a VCR or TiVo is required for watching *The Simpsons* seriously, if you want to take as much out from it as the writers put in. *The Simpsons* clearly rewards repeat consumption.

The Simpsons Is Pop Culture

Michael Jackson: Hi, I'm Michael Jackson of The Jacksons.
Homer: I'm Homer Simpson of the Simpsons.

The Simpsons has transformed the American way of life. Fans of the series view the show as a parody of the "average" American family. Indeed, *The Simpsons* does provide insight into the inner workings of the American household. However, the television audience may not realize that *The Simpsons* has actually shaped our very way of life.

Where do we see this impact? While *The Simpsons* often presents allusions to popular movies and television programs, the series has also created its own unique brand of popular culture. Bart Simpson's number one single "Do the Bartman," coupled with the enormous popularity of the show itself allowed *The Simpsons* to secure a place on *People* magazine's "200 Greatest Pop Culture Icons." From Bart's bad boy antics to Homer's laziness, the series has become a cornerstone of American life. Case in point: How many times do Americans commonly hear phrases such as "D'oh!" and "Don't have a cow, man" used outside of the series? The language invented on the series coupled with Simpsonian virtues has transformed the very nature of the American familial unit.

The Simpsons adds an important satirical element to television because it is rare to find a cartoon series in which the main characters voice their opinions about government, politics, or any other matter. And ever since this show exploded into the culture, satire in itself has become an American way of life. Any important event that occurs (excluding terrorist activities and mass murders) is immediately ridiculed by television programs and late-night comedians (Jay Leno still hasn't completely stopped talking about O.J.).

Lev Grossman of *TIME* magazine recently wrote that "all satire has a certain measure of futility built into it...The real targets of satire tend to be impervious to it...As Jonathan Swift notes, "Satire is a sort of glass, wherein beholders do generally discover everybody's face but their own". But I disagree with the aforementioned statements—the impact of satire is indeed universal and permeates American society. Some religious individuals laugh at the antics of Ned Flanders, while some convenience store owners chuckle at Apu's quirks. More importantly, however, is the impact of Simpsonian satire in the realm of politics. Sideshow Bob, the Republican criminal mastermind on the series who was arrested in a particular episode, noted: "I'll be back. You can't keep the Democrats out of the White House forever—and when they get in, I'll be back on the streets—with all my criminal buddies! Bah ha ha ha ha…" Democrats would not be impervious to such a statement. Because of the vast *Simpsons* audience, Bob's political views have a tremendous reach. Somewhere in Washington, a Democratic congressman must have toughened his stance on crime after hearing Bob's political commentary.

The Simpsons and American Thought

Cultural critic Chris Turner more accurately pinpoints the function and underlying goals of satire, noting that "satire has…ambitious goals: it starts from a belief that the ideas and things it mocks—usually ideas and things invested with authority—are wrong and that exposing this fact through satire will erode their authority and precipitate change. Satire is in this sense inherently optimistic." And *The Simpsons* gets the job done. Satire helps us realize the fact that authority figures in Springfield—as well as in contemporary society—are not always beyond reproach.

In *The Simpsons and Philosophy: The D'oh of Homer*, Paul A. Cantor cites an interesting example of how *The Simpsons* infiltrates the minds of Americans.

New York Senator Charles Schumer visited a high school to speak about the subject of school violence. One of the students responded to the question of gun control that arose:

"It reminds me of a *Simpsons* episode. Homer wanted to get a gun, but he had been in jail twice and in a mental institution. They labeled him as 'potentially dangerous.' So Homer asks what that means and the gun dealer says:

'It just means you need an extra week before you can get the gun.'" The student was better able to express himself by relating to a *Simpsons* episode. In fact, many fans of *The Simpsons* can relate some aspect of reality to life in Springfield. Often, fans become immersed in the episodes, all the while forgetting that *The Simpsons* is an animated program. So the next time you think about what features define the "average" American family, look no further than your TV set and watch *The Simpsons*. Television may have been intended to serve as an escape from our real lives, but *The Simpsons* has penetrated the previously impassable barrier that separates reality from cartoon. As the series has now reached its seventeenth season, it is time for us to consider all of the note-worthy contributions of *The Simpsons* to American society.

As Michael Starr of the *NY Post* stated, *"The Simpsons...is...* one of the most influential shows in pop-culture history."

There are many reasons that fans of *The Simpsons* have trans-formed the television series into an institution. (*The Simpsons* licensing constitutes a $1 billion industry.) In the following pages, I will discuss why *The Simpsons* is more than just a cartoon. This book will touch upon many aspects of Simpsonian-flavored life in contemporary society: family life, news, politics, and medicine. My goal is to provide the American viewing public with examples of the series' impact on contemporary society. (One quick example: the word "D'oh" was added to the Oxford English Dictionary.) So without further ado (please feel free to let out a Homeric "Woo-hoo"), it's time to see exactly why *The Simpsons* matters. Or, in the words of Kodos, "I say, we must move forward, not backward, upward not forward, and always twirling, twirling, twirling towards..."—Uh, just turn the page...

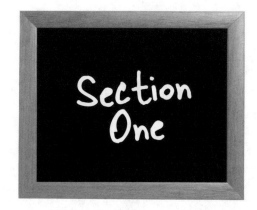

Section One

The Simpsons and Society

"Your moral authorities don't always have your best interests in mind." ~ Matt Groening

"Where there is power, there is resistance." ~ Michel Foucault

Marge: You know, Homer, it's very easy to criticize.
Homer: Fun, too.

"What would not a man give if he might converse with Orpheus and Musaeus and Hesiod and Homer?"
~ Socrates, *The Apology* (Did he mean "Homer Simpson?")

In Plato's *Apology*, Socrates is put on trial for supposedly "corrupting the youth" by means of his subversion of authority figures and institutions. Socrates is known as the "father of modern philosophy" precisely because he constantly questioned everyone's beliefs—including his own. His followers considered him to be wise, while his detractors viewed him as a foolish and potentially destabilizing agent of the established status quo. But Socrates did not view himself as wise—"I am very conscious that I am not wise at all," he noted—just wiser than everyone else. He goes on to give an example of a conversation he had with a man who had thought himself wise:

> "Well, although I do not suppose that either of us knows anything really beautiful and good, I am better off than he is—for he knows nothing, and thinks that he knows. I neither know nor think that I know. In this latter particular, then, I seem to have slightly the advantage of him."

But Socrates was smarter than he gave himself credit for. His relentless pursuit of the truth never truly amounted to corruption. Can the search for the truth ever manifest itself as a form of corruption? I think not—and neither does *The Simpsons*.

The Simpsons constantly searches for the truth in life. By subverting authority figures, corrupt institutions, and creating its own blend of unique ideals for society, *The Simpsons'* voice speaks out against evils and envisions a society where corrupt politicians are held accountable for their actions, where business people are honest and fair, and where the nuclear family is a central component of a healthy, well-functioning society.

The Simpsonian use of satire does portray corruption as an integral part of life in Springfield. But this is, of course, intentional. The goal of *The Simpsons* is to create awareness of the many problems in society so as to form solutions to correcting society's ills. Socrates would love *The Simpsons* precisely because its central focus is not to accept anything as truth simply because an authority figure or institution declared it so. *The Simpsons* has carried on the tradition of Socrates in that it holds to his ultimate ideal: "The unexamined life is not worth living." True, *The Simpsons* is funny, but its use of satire goes much deeper than humor. *The Simpsons* searches for truth in a town full of corruption and lies. And it teaches us to do the same. Let's take a closer look at some of the ways that *The Simpsons* comments on society.

Questioning Authority
"All of us are entitled to our own opinions, but not our own facts." ~ **Senator Daniel Patrick Moynihan**

"The whole reason we have elected officials is so we don't have to think all the time." ~ **Homer Simpson**

Socrates was clearly the Matt Groening of his day. In the *Apology*, he notes that "in my investigation in the service of the god I found that those who had the highest reputation were nearly the most deficient, while those who were thought to be inferior were more knowledgeable." Clearly, Socrates was extremely distrustful of authority. He was perturbed by the fact that the masses hung onto virtually every word spoken by those in power simply because they were arbitrarily deemed superior and more knowledgeable. Socrates would agree that perhaps a king was indeed superior to others in certain ways but argued that there was no reason to believe the king's view on matters outside the realm of his expertise such as religion, death, and moral philosophy.

The phenomenon that Socrates describes was examined in *The Simpsons* episode entitled "They Saved Lisa's Brain." In the episode, the most intelligent residents in Springfield (Lisa, Dr. Hibbert, Professor Frink, Principal Skinner, and Comic Book Guy) set out to create a Platonic utopia: "a real candyland...of the mind," as Chief Wiggum notes. Dr. Hibbert explains why the members of Mensa must take the reigns of power: "Why do we live in a town where the smart people have no power and the stupid people run everything? Maybe we should just move back to Alabama." The power distribution in Springfield is indeed a classic example of the most ill-suited persons holding positions of authority: Chief Wiggum and Mayor Quimby lack the intelligence, fortitude, and honesty to look out for the needs of the people of their city. The most intelligent residents of Springfield are right in line with the philosophy of Socrates. They do not want to accept the word of authority figures simply because those persons are the ones who hold the power.

Interestingly, however, the lesson in this episode takes a step back from the hardened lesson that those who are the most intelligent can do a better job of governing the city. Comic Book Guy, for example, proposes that breeding occur only once every seven years. Professor Frink spends his time creating a sarcasm detector. Each of the members of Mensa comes up with crazy ideas that don't sit well with the people of Springfield. Here, *The Simpsons* shows us that it is not always the most intelligent people who are the best suited to govern a society. In fact, *The Simpsons*, in a wink to Socrates, criticizes authority figures, but unlike the ideals Socrates sets forth in *The Republic*, does not offer a true alternative to the status quo. The goal of *The Simpsons* is to attack everyone and everything, and this is particularly evident in "They Saved Lisa's Brain." Dr. Stephen Hawking, the man widely perceived to be the "world's smartest man" appears towards the end of the episode and notes that "Sometimes the smartest of us can be the most childish." The lesson we can take from this episode is that power corrupts. The intelligence of those in power, while important, will not prevent corruption. As noted by Elphaba, the Wicked Witch of the West in Gregory MaGuire's fantasy novel, *Wicked*, "The wickedness of men is that their power breeds stupidity and blindness." While admittedly a bleak and perhaps excessively cynical assessment of the political sphere, this is the point that the writers of *The Simpsons*, by depicting those in power as blind and corrupt, have chosen to explore.

At the very end of the episode, Dr. Hawking sits down with Homer for a Duff at Moe's Tavern. He notes that he is fascinated with Homer's notion of a "donut-shaped universe." Funny, yes. But if we look deeper into what this conversation says about the relationship between ideas and intelligence, this conversation becomes an enlightening commentary on the way that highbrow culture interacts with lowbrow culture in contemporary society.

Surprisingly, Dr. Stephen Hawking is interested in the ideas of "jerk-ass" Homer J. Simpson. Sure, Hawking might be smarter, but that doesn't mean that he has all of the answers. Sometimes—and Socrates and Matt Groening would certainly agree with this assertion—great ideas can come from the strangest and least predictable sources. If we ignore the actual content of Homer's remark, we come to realize that perhaps a person whose intellect is not dissimilar to Homer's will eventually come up with a great idea.

The Simpsons shows us that the most intelligent are not necessarily the least misguided in their actions. Nor are the least intelligent always the best-suited to rule. Instead, we find that the writers of *The Simpsons* look at the world in a more complicated manner—probably more so than Socrates. We see a hint of nihilism in this episode—by the end of the episode, we are forced to relinquish our belief that the smartest are always the best-suited to rule. Similarly, the flaws in the current system are so deep that no quick fix is possible. We are, in effect, left to believe that power inevitably corrupts. Our previously held notions about those best fit to rule are thus placed into question.

Subverting Authority

One of the central themes of *The Simpsons* is its consistent and relentless subversion of authority. Springfield is a haven for corruption: Fat Tony heads the local mafia; Mayor Quimby spends the bulk of his time taking bribes; and Mr. Burns attempts to use his wealth and power to influence policy, knock down rivals, and hurt his employees. In "$pringfield," the town of Springfield is in financial crisis and the residents turn towards their mayor, Diamond Joe Quimby, to help solve the financial mess. Quimby offers the following: "I propose that I use what's left of the town treasury to move to a more prosperous town and run for mayor. And, uh, once elected, I will send for the rest of you." So instead of sticking with his constituency during these tough times, Quimby, Springfield's perennially corrupt mayor, attempts to flee the town, as he has so often done in other episodes—whether he finds refuge on a beach in Jamaica or another destination far, far away from Springfield. *The Simpsons* shows us that although there are times when our leaders do act in our best interests, there are also times when greed and the pursuit of personal interests tend to cause leaders to act in certain ways that do not translate into creating the "greatest amount of happiness for the greatest number of people."

The Simpsons also questions the efficacy of the educational system, the healthcare system, and government uses of power. Matt Groening has stated that his goal in creating *The Simpsons* is to subvert authority figures and established institutions. Radical, no?

Well, Socrates beat him to the punch. Again, Socrates was disheartened by the fact that words spoken by authority figures were considered to be true simply because they were uttered by those in power. A line from the fifteenth season *Simpsons* episode "Fraudcast News" clearly expresses Socrates' objective: after Lisa attempts to keep the newspaper she is printing separate from Burns' monopolistic media conglomerate (she notes to readers that, "You hold in your hand the last paper not controlled by the Burns Media empire. We are not afraid to say Montgomery Burns is a monopolistic, self-aggrandizing um, stinky pants!") , Homer notes that he is proud of his daughter, asserting, "All my daughter ever did was tell people to think for themselves. I may be her father, but when I grow up, I wanna be just like her— except still a dude." Socrates would surely support a free press and was open to new ideas. Socrates would commend Lisa for her defiance and refusal to become swallowed by Burns' media empire. Might, as Lisa shows us, does not always make right.

In Plato's *Republic*, Socrates outlines his vision for an ideal society and argues that the guardians of the city should not be wealthy or live in luxury. Those interested in money, Socrates argues, will be too focused on personal gain and will thus be more likely to ignore the needs of the people. Wealth, according to Socrates, should remain separate from power and authority.

Wealth and power in contemporary society, however, do work in tandem and generally lead to influence. Perhaps nobody on *The Simpsons* uses the power of the bribe more than Monty Burns. But Burns was not the first person in history to understand the importance of acquiring wealth and power. Frederich Nietzsche argued that those with wealth and power determine what is "just" and "unjust." He claimed that such distinctions were entirely arbitrary: the wealthy justify their actions by claiming that poor people are inferior. If the poor usurped power, however, Nietzsche argues, they would claim that the actions of the rich are considered "unjust." Those in power determine what is right and wrong, good and bad. Tevye, the protagonist in *Fiddler on the Roof*, echoed this tone when he exclaimed, "When you're rich, they think you really know!" Homer Simpson similarly observed that those in power hold a great deal of influence when he noted, "I'm a white male ages eighteen to forty-nine. Everyone listens to me no matter how dumb my suggestions are." But white males have had some very dumb suggestions.

The following is a list of "weird" laws created by lawmakers that are still technically enforceable in the United States:
- Selling donut holes in Leigh, New England, is forbidden. (Homer wouldn't like this law!)
- In Ottumwa, Iowa: It is unlawful for a man to wink at any woman that he does not know.
- In Gary, Indiana: People are prohibited from attending a cinema and from riding public transport within four hours of eating garlic.
- In Carmel, New York: A man cannot go outside while wearing a jacket and trousers that do not match.

With laws like these on the books, there certainly seems to be good reason to question the actions and motives of politicians in society.

To satirize this, Springfield has its share of stupid laws on the books as well. In one episode, Chief Wiggum was surprised to learn that it is illegal to put squirrels down your pants for the purposes of gambling. In another, Wiggum was similarly surprised that, as a person of high authority, he was entitled to a pig.

Therefore, both Socrates and *The Simpsons* teach us not to take any claims of truth or intent for granted. Authority figures may very well have some very good ideas that would, if implemented, serve to benefit society. But that is no reason to suppose that some of the laws that they create do not merit serious criticism. *The Simpsons* shows us that it is better to think for ourselves, rather than to blindly accept what we are told by those in power. It's not that *The Simpsons* supports some vision of anarchy; rather, it simply teaches us to question the actions and orders of those in power. In this way, we can serve as alert and active members of society.

By encouraging us to serve as alert members of society, both *The Simpsons* and Socrates help us hone our critical thinking and reasoning skills. In his formulation of the Sleeper Curve, cultural critic Steven Johnson argues that certain elements of our culture can help promote reasoning ability.

The Sleeper Curve

One could reasonably argue that both Socrates and *The Simpsons* are both prime examples of Steven Johnson's notion of the Sleeper Curve. In *Everything Bad is Good For You: How Today's Popular Culture Is Actually Making Us Smarter*, Johnson argues that popular elements of our culture are actually more intellectually stimulating than we generally tend to believe. He defines the Sleeper Curve as follows: "The most debased forms of mass diversion—video games and violent television dramas and juvenile sitcoms—turn out to be nutritional after all."

In a very real sense, this is precisely what has happened with both *The Simpsons* and the teachings of Socrates. Socrates' use of free speech and his relentless search for the truth were viewed with skepticism—his actions were viewed by his many critics as debased forms of mass diversion that in effect corrupted the youth. *The Simpsons* was also viewed by many critics as a debased form of entertainment that inevitably corrupts society. Today, however, we can see how the Sleeper Curve has indeed come into play: both Socrates and *The Simpsons* are the subjects of college courses across the United States. Socrates' brand of "debased mass diversion" is now viewed as the foundation of modern philosophy. Similarly, *The Simpsons*, though still criticized for reasons we'll address a bit later, has found a distinguished place among the best that television has ever had to offer. The teachings of both Socrates and *The Simpsons* were initially viewed as dangerous agents that would serve to corrupt the youth. It is quite evident, however, that both have had precisely the opposite impact on society.

Why does this occur? It is because these forces are feared and loved for the same reason: their search for the truth. It is interesting to observe that some of the most popular books, television shows, documentaries, and magazines deal with the issue of searching for the truth. The recent surge of many newsmagazine shows and documentaries, such as *20/20* and *Bowling for Columbine*, have become so popular I would contend precisely because they claim to strive for the truth (although viewers should certainly be careful not to accept everything they hear in the movies or on television as absolute truth). Barry Glassner's seminal book, *The Culture of Fear*, has become a national bestseller on the premise that we are fed lies by popular media. The book, in essence, serves not only as a commentary on the foibles of our culture but also as a guide that helps us to search for the truth lurking beneath the surface. Like *The Simpsons* and Socrates, *The Culture of Fear* teaches us that it would be wise to not accept everything we hear from figures of authority simply because the ideas come from people in positions of power. The popularity of philosophy courses at universities, television shows like *The Simpsons*, and books such as *The Culture of Fear* is due to their ability to force us to think for ourselves and not blindly accept everything that we hear on television or in newspapers. Society craves the truth, and those aspects of popular media that can successfully uncover lies will almost certainly find a home among the most popular forms of entertainment in contemporary society. And where society is most in search of the truth tends to manifest itself in controversial or "hot button" issues.

Hot Button Issues

Contrary to popular belief, *The Simpsons* generally does not take a particular stand on most of the issues that it addresses in specific episodes. With *The Simpsons*, the overriding agenda is to question *everything* and *everyone*. In the eyes of the writers, every group or individual is fair game for satire. But one of the great things about *The Simpsons* is that it will, in its attempt to find the truth lurking beneath the surface, attack both the proponents and opponents of a particular issue within the same twenty-two minute episode. A thorough analysis of "The Cartridge Family" (gun control), "There's Something about Marrying," and other politically-charged episodes serves as evidence for the idea that *The Simpsons* purposely does not take sides when broaching controversial issues.

In "Lisa's Angel," Ned Flanders ebulliently exclaims that "There are some things we don't want to know—important things!" But in fact, human nature generally works in the exact opposite way. We are curious creatures, and, like Socrates, are constantly searching for the truth. *The Simpsons*, as we shall see, provides us with a gateway for finding the truth.

The Simpsons is a television series that is tailor-made for democracies. Satire in general and *The Simpsons* in particular serve an important purpose in free societies. *The Simpsons* sort of provides a "check" on the powers that be and is an invaluable resource that highlights the importance of a free press in contemporary America. For authoritarian governments whose goal it is to repress free expression and control the information that people receive, *The Simpsons* would indeed be a nuisance, an annoying pest always asking questions, questioning established authority, and searching for the best possible ways to debate controversial issues.

Season sixteen addressed a number of hot button issues, including global warming, smuggling prescription drugs from Canada, the "Walmartization" of America (more on this later), and the controversy surrounding the Janet Jackson Super Bowl half-time show. Perhaps no episode, however, was as controversial as the Simpsonian discourse on gay marriage. In *The Simpsons* episode entitled, "There's Something about Marrying," Springfield legalized gay marriage, and Homer became a minister in order to profit financially from marrying gay and lesbian couples.

A cartoon taking on the hot button issue of gay marriage? Well, *The Simpsons*, as fans know, is undeniably far more advanced in its inherent structure and methodological approach to presenting issues than your average cartoon. Before the episode even aired, critics came out firing about the prospect of a cartoon (which, by their measure, is intended for and aimed at children) being broadcast on national television addressing such a delicate issue. The episode, however, was a Simpsonian classic, as it presented both sides to the gay marriage debate and educated viewers about the main arguments from both advocates and opponents of legalizing gay marriage, by addressing both civil rights arguments and slippery slope fears. *The Simpsons*, in classic form, purposely did not declare its own take on the issue at hand. *The Simpsons* does an excellent job of addressing controversial issues but does an even better job of portraying the views of two sides to a debate in an evenhanded manner.

The Simpsons' main contribution to American society is that it forces viewers to think. *Itchy and Scratchy* segments aside, *The Simpsons* presents fans with twenty-two minutes of "think TV" every week. The goal of *The Simpsons* is certainly not to eliminate religion (Mark Pinsky's *The Gospel According The Simpsons* certainly suggests otherwise), nor is its vision an anarchical or iconoclastic one. Instead, *The Simpsons* provides fans with a wonderfully crafted—some would say, at times, ingenious—starting point for debate. For a collective people who hold free speech close to our hearts, *The Simpsons'* contribution, in this sense, is immeasurable. This is not because it says whatever the hell it wants to say—but, conversely, because it outlines both sides of an issue, invariably irritating both ebullient proponents and ardent opponents of whatever particular issue it chooses to both document and chronicle. *The Simpsons* constantly attacks both conservatives and liberals, leaving nothing—and nobody unscathed. A prime example of this can be seen in how the series simultaneously both ridicules and supports vegetarians. By ridiculing vegans (Jesse: "I'm a level five vegan. I don't eat anything that casts a shadow."), and showing how meat eaters can be perceived as almost "vicious," (Homer struggling with Bart over the last pork chop is not a gentle nor pleasant scene, to say the least), for example, *The Simpsons* is effectively able to touch upon the viewpoints of virtually every member of society. When successful (as is most often the case), the producers will receive thousands of letters from agitated viewers about their displeasure pertaining to the political incorrectness of a particular episode. And the writers would have it no other way. Clearing the way for real debate about issues often starts with—but certainly does not end with—*The Simpsons.*

By opening up the floor for fair and open debate, *The Simpsons* introduces issues that are already at the forefront of the collective American psyche. By satirically mocking both sides of the issue, fans get to see a glimpse of something that they won't see on MSNBC or the FOX News channel. The absurdity of extremist positions is constantly attacked on *The Simpsons.* By showing that the extremist viewpoints of a debate are often absurd, *The Simpsons* helps us to isolate and concentrate on mainstream viewpoints. From there, we can formulate our own opinions about issues without being unduly influenced by the likes of Ann Coulter or Al Franken.

The Simpsons Generation
"The truth can't just be swept under the rug." ~ Lisa Simpson

My generation is a product of *The Simpsons*—heavily influenced not by a political voice spoken in overbearing tones but by the idea that it is important to speak openly about important issues in order to both discover and cure society's ills. My personal take on *The Simpsons* is that it is a cultural phenomenon unmatched by anything my generation has ever experienced. It is certainly possible to ignore the influence of *The Simpsons*, but it is more difficult to deny the very existence of this influence—on society in general and on my generation in particular. If you have absolutely no idea what I'm talking about here, you probably have not seen most of the classic *Simpsons* episodes.

The rest of this book will explain why *The Simpsons* is so important and will use examples from both *The Simpsons* and contemporary society to highlight the reasons that *The Simpsons* is such a dominant force in a global context. My point is not merely that *The Simpsons* is not as bad as some critics claim it is; rather, I make the case that *The Simpsons* provides society with a healthy dose of reality that encourages each and every one of us to consider the views and opinions of others.

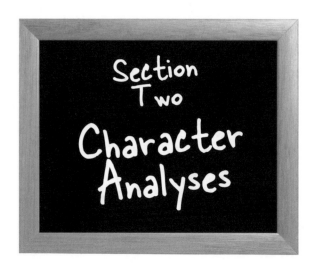

Section
Two

Character
Analyses

Is Homer a Good Father?

"I'd rather drink a beer than win father of the year."
~ Homer, in "Simpsoncalifragilisticexpiala-D'oh-cious"

"Ah, aliens! Don't eat me. I have a wife and kids...eat them!"
~ "Treehouse of Horror" episode in which Homer is abducted
   by Kang and Kodos

"Oh, why was I born a dad?" ~ Homer, in "I D'oh Bot"

S*impsons* fans are well aware of the fact that Homer Simpson is insightful. Each show invariably contains some of Homer's slices of life. For instance, in "Lisa's Pony," Homer lied to Marge but then defended himself by remarking, "Marge, it takes two to lie: one to lie, and one to listen." In another episode, Homer tells his children that "trying is the first step towards failure." Funny, but true. Homer's insightful humor does not distract viewers, however, from the fact that he clearly lacks the requisite intelligence to be deemed a budding intellectual (or even a man of average intelligence, for that matter). In fact, Homer often does some pretty stupid things—like putting nuclear waste on his own gums in "E-I-E-I D'Oh" and eating a ten-foot hoagie on a continuous basis for several weeks in "Selma's Choice." However, if we look past Homer's character flaws and witty remarks, we can explore the question of whether or not he is a good father.

Homer Simpson himself has admitted that he shows only "sporadic interest" in his children. But in order to more accurately determine whether or not Homer should be deemed a bad father, we must give a definition of a "good" father. A good father is one that is well-intentioned and cares about his children. Homer does have good intentions, and often does care about his three children—when he actually recalls that he has three children (he often forgets that Maggie exists). He also spends many hours of "quality" time with Bart, Lisa, and Maggie on the couch. In contemporary American society, many parents spend most of their time with their kids watching television. Homer can thus be considered the "average" American parent in that he bonds with his kids by means of watching television with them.

Homer Simpson: Model Parent?!

Is Homer a good father? Many say yes. In 2004, Homer Simpson was ranked fifth on TV Land's "TV's Top Dads" television special. In spite of Homer's flaws as a father, he does play the single most important role of the all-American dad: he is there for his family. And, as Marge once noted after Bart, Lisa, and Maggie had tied up the "babysitter bandit":

> "The way I see it, [if] you [successfully] raised three children who could knock out and hog-tie a perfect stranger, you must be doing something right."
> ~ "Some Enchanted Evening"

Although Homer is generally lazy when it comes to his work, there are times when he works assiduously to provide for his wife and children. For example, in the very first full-length *Simpsons* episode ("Simpsons Roasting on an Open Fire"), Homer takes a job as Santa Claus at the mall to obtain money to purchase Christmas gifts for his family. Thus, he demonstrates a fundamental love for his family. In fact, in this episode his love for his family surpasses his penchant for laziness.

In "Lisa's Pony," Homer takes a second job (at the Kwik-E-Mart) because he fears Lisa doesn't love him any more. His plan is to earn enough money to buy her a pony. Of course, he had brought this upon himself; he stopped in for a drink at Moe's and was late to Lisa's saxophone concert. And Marge did have to convince him that he should not give up on Lisa. Homer had previously said: "Maybe I should just cut my losses, give up on Lisa, and make a fresh start with Maggie." Obviously, Homer's ignorance often steers him off-course. Still, Homer eventually demonstrates his true love for Lisa by sacrificing virtually all of his leisure time in order to try to win her love. Homer's new work schedule? I'll let him explain:

> "I'll work from midnight to eight, come home, sleep for five minutes, eat breakfast, sleep six more minutes, shower, then I have ten minutes to bask in Lisa's love, then I'm off to the power plant fresh as a daisy."

Homer's willingness to give up television in order to win Lisa's love demonstrates that he is a devoted father. Homer also demonstrates his love for Lisa in the episode entitled "Homr." During this episode, Homer learns that he has had a crayon stuck in his brain since his childhood, and that this has lowered his intelligence. A doctor removes the crayon from Homer's brain and the result is that Homer becomes more intelligent. Homer takes note of his newfound intelligence: "Now, who's up for a trip to the library tomorrow? Notice I no longer say 'liberry' or 'tomorry.'"

Homer is now better able to understand Lisa's needs and bonds with her during the short period that he remains intelligent. Just before Homer returns to Moe and asks him to surgically implant the crayon back into his brain, Homer writes the following letter to Lisa:

> "Lisa, I'm taking the coward's way out. But before I do, I just want you to know: Being smart made me appreciate how amazing you really are."

This quote serves to emphasize my earlier point: Homer is well-intentioned. He wants to build strong relationships with his children, but his lack of intelligence often does not allow him to do so. However, once he became smart, he truly enjoyed spending time with Lisa.

Yet this alone does not make Homer a great dad. Immanuel Kant discusses the categorical imperative (which is defined as performing some action regardless of one's desire to carry out the action) as being of great importance in virtually all situations. In "Homr," Homer certainly demonstrates his love for Lisa. However, Kant's categorical imperative would not allow Homer to decide at what times he wishes to bond with Lisa. Instead, Kant would declare that Homer should "Do Y," which in this case should be to bond with his children. He should not bond with his children only when he decides to do so. Still, as mentioned above, Homer is often too ignorant to understand the needs of his children and thus cannot be held to the standards that Kant sets forth.

Homer's parenting techniques are also examined in "Bart the Daredevil." In this episode, Homer tries to deter Bart from jumping the Springfield Gorge. At the climax of the episode, Homer says to Bart: "I tried ordering you, I tried punishing you, and God help me, I even tried reasoning with you." Homer is obviously trying his best to be a good parent in this scene. His efforts take him as far as threatening to jump the gorge himself in order to show Bart how dangerous the jump is. Bart pleads with Homer not to do it and promises never to jump again. Thus, Homer's parenting techniques are completely sound in this scene. Of course, it wouldn't be a Simpsons episode without some comedy. Following Homer and Bart's exchange of words, Homer tells Bart "You know boy, I don't think I've ever felt as close to you as I do right..." and slips off the cliff.

Homer shows that he truly cares about the well-being of Bart and incurs injury as an indirect result of deterring Bart from jumping the gorge.

Other episodes also portray Homer as a good, well-intentioned father. In "Lisa's Sax," for example, Homer recalls the time he bought Lisa her first saxophone. At the time, money was tight for the Simpson family, and Homer was saving money in order to purchase an air conditioner. However, he decides to purchase Lisa her first saxophone instead of buying the air conditioner, thereby demonstrating his love for her while encouraging her future creativity and intellectual prowess. Homer is willing to stand up for his children in times of crisis and in the face of danger. These qualities certainly help to portray Homer as a good and decent father. For example, in "Two Bad Neighbors," Homer defends Bart against former President Bush after Bush spanks the boy. In season thirteen, Homer creates the police force "Springshield" mainly because Lisa's Malibu Stacy dolls were stolen from the Simpson home. In the episode "I, D'oh Bot," Homer attempts to gain the respect of Bart by building a working fighting robot. After he is unable to successfully do so, Homer steps inside of the nonfunctional robot, and risks both life and limb by engaging in numerous bouts with other fighting robots. This is all part of an effort designed to impress his son.

In many episodes, Homer acts as a decent man and as a thoughtful father. Yet, that's not the whole story.

Homer as the "Bad" Father

Bart [to Homer]: *We're fighting over who loves you more.*
Lisa [pushing Bart]: *You love him more*
Bart: *No, you love him more!*

There are also episodes in which Homer is portrayed as a sub-par father. For example, in "Three Men and a Comic Book," Marge tells Homer to check on the boys. Homer looks out the window, sees Bart and his friend choking each other, and says they're fine. In addition, he also encourages fierce competition between Bart and Lisa (certainly not a great idea). For example, in "Lisa on Ice," Homer attends the hockey game that features Bart's team versus Lisa's team. During a crucial point in the game, Homer says: "Oh, my God, Marge. A penalty shot, with only four seconds left. It's your child versus mine! The winner will be showered with praise; the loser will be taunted and booed until my throat is sore."

Another example of Homer's deficient parenting capabilities is found in the episode "Marge Be Not Proud." In this episode, Bart steals from the local Try-N-Save store. Homer attempts to punish him:

> "I've figured out the boy's punishment. First: he's grounded. No leaving the house, not even for school. Second: no eggnog. In fact, no nog, period. And third, absolutely no stealing for three months."

Obviously, this punishment lacks substance and quality. In fact, it is severely flawed. Once again, it is Homer's ignorance that binds him in situations such as these. Homer does not want Bart to steal ever again but cannot effectively verbalize this declaration. He might have the right idea, but he's lucky that his children have Marge as their mother.

Homer's worst display of parenting may be in the episode entitled "Homer Alone." In this episode, Homer is forced to take responsibility for Maggie, the youngest of the three Simpson children. During Homer's brief stint as the primary caretaker for Maggie, he does the following:

He uses a staple gun to fasten Maggie's diaper.

He sits on top of her while watching TV from the couch.

He prepares her 9 a.m. feeding at 11:45 a.m.

Maggie feels a close, parental bond with Marge and later sets out to look for her. Who could possibly blame her? Homer certainly does not act as the ideal father in this particular episode.

Finally, in "Barting Over," the series' three-hundredth episode, Bart is at odds with Homer because Homer spent all of the money that Bart had earned as a child making "Baby Stink Breath" commercials. Homer acts selfishly by squandering all of Bart's money, which Marge notes was supposed to be used toward Bart's college fund. Homer's selfish tendencies also prevent him from acting appropriately and being deemed a good father.

Trying to Be a Good Father

So where does this leave Homer in terms of being a good or bad father? Let's look a little deeper. Homer often attempts to be a good father but falls short in his efforts. For example, in "Saturdays of Thunder," Homer wants to learn more about Bart but doesn't really know where to begin. He takes the National Fatherhood Institute Test and fails. Later in the same episode, Homer attempts to find a way to become a good father. (Homer's plans often center on a quick fix method or approach.) He visits the National Fatherhood Institute where he speaks with a good father. Homer is given a copy of *Fatherhood* by Bill Cosby. Here is Homer's conversation with a good father:

> **Dave:** Mr. Simpson, if you want to be a good father, you have to spend time with your son.
> **Homer:** Well, that's easy for you to say, you...preachy...egg-headed...institute guy! How much do you see *your* son?
> [Homer then watches Dave bond with his son].

Certainly, Homer does not like hearing Dave say that becoming a good father takes years of effort. Still, Homer attempts to become a good father in this episode and helps Bart build his soapbox derby racer. Homer also begins to read Bill Cosby's book.

In other episodes, Homer realizes his shortcomings as a father. In "Simpsoncalifragilisticexpiala-D'oh-cious," for example, Homer sings, "I'd rather drink a beer than win father of the year." Perhaps this statement sums up Homer's position on fathering. He may want to be a good father, but, for the most part, he will not work hard for extended periods of time to achieve this end.

In "Saturdays of Thunder," Homer utilizes his "quick fix" approach to life when his parenting techniques are placed in question. As Marge tells him: "Homer, I've always said you were a good father. I've always defended you when people put you down...But I guess I was wrong. You are a bad father."

A few brief moments later, Homer successfully answers the questions on the Fatherhood Quotient exam. He is elated by the fact that he was able to answer the first three questions on the test: "Wow, I'm one question away from being a perfect father."

He decides to fool himself into believing that he truly discusses parenting with another father, specifically Ned Flanders, "I talked to Flanders about parenting—I'm a perfect father!" Homer then drives down to the soap-box derby racing championship and offers Bart some words of encouragement, "Do it for your old man, boy." After Bart wins the race, Bart caps the scene off: "I was riding alone out there. But someone was with me in spirit. This is for *you*, Dad."

In this scene, Homer and Bart are arguably as close as they have ever been during the course of the series. When Bart is scolded by Marge for being a sore winner after he laughs at Nelson (the loser in the race), Homer supports Bart's insensitive treatment of Nelson. It is here that we realize what message the writers are attempting to convey to the audience: a good father is loyal to his son at all times. The father/son bond is as significant in Simpsonian life as it is in contemporary American society. As the episode draws to a close and we hear a small segment of the song "Wind Beneath My Wings," we realize that although Homer may not be considered a good father by most standards, he does demonstrate true loyalty to his son. Homer's "quick fix" approach to parenting was surprisingly successful. Homer is a lucky guy because he is able to convince himself that he is a great father.

So at times Homer overtly displays great strides toward becoming a good father. But he still ultimately falls short of being deemed as such. He is bound to a life of laziness and stupidity— barriers which serve to hurt his chances of becoming a good father. This dual nature is best expressed through his relationship with Maggie.

The Forgotten One: Maggie
"I'll lavish my attention on Maggie—the forgotten Simpson."
~ Homer

Maggie is the oft-forgotten third child in the Simpson clan. By viewing life through her eyes, we can gain some insight into how she perceives Homer. In one particular episode, she does not care to be identified with being a member of the Simpson family until Marge comes and she crawls towards her. (Homer had also asked Maggie to come to him, but she would not do so.)

In another episode, Homer attempts to teach Maggie how to swim, and as a test of trust, the instructor tells all of the fathers to catch the babies when they jump into the pool of water. All of the other babies jump into the pool, while Maggie remains on the edge of the pool. She does not trust Homer to save her. However, in the same episode, Maggie saves Homer when he nearly drowns in the ocean. She may not have complete trust in Homer (it is kind of difficult to trust a man of subpar intelligence), but she certainly possesses a special love for him. In the episode "Lisa's First Word," Maggie uttered her first and only word: "Daddy." By referring to Homer as "Daddy," she demonstrates a special degree of respect for her father, unseen previously, as Bart often refers to his father as "Homer." (Interestingly, Lisa was able to pronounce "Bart," "David Hasselhoff," and "Homer," but did not say "Daddy" when she was a baby.) In this episode, we get the sense that Maggie may very well be Homer's special little girl. In "And Maggie Makes Three," Homer flashes back to a time when he was unhappy about his job, and explains that Maggie's birth served to cheer him up. It is then that we learn that all of Maggie's baby pictures are posted in Homer's office.

So ultimately, Homer may not be the ideal father, but he does love his children. In "One Fish, Two Fish . . ." Homer is told that he is going to die (he had eaten sushi that was believed to be poisoned). He says goodbye to his three children:

Goodbye, Maggie: Stay as sweet as you are.
Goodbye, Lisa: I know you'll make me proud.
Goodbye, Bart:...I like your sheets.

In "Homer's Triple Bypass," Marge allows Bart and Lisa to enter the operating room.

Homer: Kids, I wanna give you some words to remember me by, if something happens. Let's see...er...Oh, I'm no good at this.
[Lisa whispers into Homer's ear]
Homer: Bart, the saddest thing about this is I'm not going to see you grow up...[Lisa whispers into Homer's ear]
Homer:...because I know you're gonna turn out well, with or without your old man.
Bart: Thanks, Dad.
Homer: And Lisa . . .
[Bart whispers into Homer's ear]
Homer: I guess this is the time to tell you...
[Bart whispers into Homer's ear]

Homer:...that you're adopted and I don't like you.
[Realizes]
Bart!
[Bart whispers into Homer's ear]
Homer: But don't worry because you've got a big brother who loves you and will always look out for you.
Lisa: Oh, Dad. [Hugs him]

So how to describe Homer's parenting? As critic Jeff MacGregor pointedly notes, "It is Homer Simpson who drives the show. As a moving, ever expanding satire, he is at once the best and worst of American dadness." Or in the words of Homer Simpson: "That's the end of that chapter."

Bart: America's Bad Boy?

"I didn't do it. Nobody saw me do it. You can't prove anything."
~ Bart Simpson

"Even I wouldn't do that, and I'm America's bad boy."
~ Bart Simpson

"Oh, please. This is just senseless destruction without any of my usual social commentary."
~ Bart Simpson

P rank calls. A slingshot. Disrespect for authority. These are all unmistakable trademarks of the character of Bart Simpson. But is Bart really *that* bad? Or is the ten-year-old Simpson boy simply crying out for attention? In this chapter, we'll explore these questions, while also analyzing Bart's influence on children in contemporary society.

An Introduction to Bart Simpson

Bart Simpson is the punk icon that has defined a generation supposedly hell-bent on obnoxious behavior. T-shirts bearing his face were banned from some elementary schools in the United States during the early 1990s. Slogans on hats and shirts like

"Underachiever and Proud of It," "I'm Bart Simpson—Who the Hell Are You?", and "Don't Have a Cow, Man" were proudly worn by fans seeking to create a rebellious image for themselves. The period during the early 1990s, defined by the Gulf War, the George H.W. Bush presidency, the end of the Cold War, the disintegration of the Soviet Union, the unification of Germany, among other world events, was also defined by Bart Mania. Bart Mania swept through the United States, and his rebellious attitude and bad boy image took America by storm. Never before had we seen such an influential punk icon—in the form of a cartoon—that sparked such outrage. But Bart Mania certainly did not vanish because of public condemnation of his bad boy image. In fact, such public outrage helped to fuel Bart Mania—and eventually Simpsons Mania into becoming a global phenomenon.

By condemning Bart, cultural and religious conservatives devoted special attention to the spiky-haired kid from Springfield, and, soon enough, mainstream America began to recognize the humor in the antics of the boy. Sure, he was "bad," but there was a certain realistic sweetness about Bart that Americans began to fall in love with. When he did something wrong (i.e., steal a video game from the local Try-N-Save) he made it clear that he did not want to be known as the "black sheep," and attempted to salvage his image by doing something nice for his mother. Conservatives would have been wise to make amends with Bart because he would lead the way in bringing *The Simpsons* to the center of our popular culture universe.

Bart's pervasive influence was made clear when he graced the cover of *TIME* magazine on December 31, 1990, entitled "The Best of 1990." An astonished Bart was pictured next to the caption, "Yes, Bart, Even You Made the List." Bart Simpson would come to define America, and, in many ways, serve as a symbol of cultural unification for diverse peoples. Jewish children, for example, wore Bart Simpson yarmulkes. Bart Sanchez—a streetwise Latino version of Bart—was pictured on bootleg Bart

Simpson merchandise. There was even a black Bart depicted on merchandise, who denounced apartheid, and often possessed a ghetto attitude, proclaiming: "You Wouldn't Understand, It's a Black Thing." Bart was accepted by people of all cultural backgrounds, and he represented the essence of the American "melting pot" theory. People of diverse backgrounds may disagree about politics, traditions, and religion, but virtually every culture has its share of punks. And Bart Simpson represents the "bad boy" that links people of all cultures together. His rebelliousness against authority is a characteristic exhibited by people of all cultures during any given point in human history.

Is Bart Simpson the modern-day Socrates, questioning authority from every angle in search of a universal truth? Well, perhaps that would be going a bit too far: Bart does not exactly search for the truth. His actions, however, inadvertently provide keen insight into the way that miscreants function in society—and the inherent value of their existence in the first place.

"Don't Have a Cow, Man": The Nature of Deviancy

"We can all learn a lot from this young man here."
~ Brad Goodman's assessment of Bart's value to residents of Springfield

"If you wish to understand behavior, try to change it."
~ old adage

"The less routine, the more life." ~ Amos Bronson Alcott

Go ahead—do something crazy. By crazy, of course, I mean deviant. As Principal Skinner would undoubtedly tell us, Webster's Dictionary defines *deviancy* as "the act and/or condition of being deviant." So much for stiff authority figures telling the MTV generation how to properly define deviancy. So what is it, and why does it matter? Let's go to the experts, including one Bart Simpson.

A Lesson from the Scholars (Not the Stiff Principal Skinner-types)

David Lodge once noted that "Deviations can only be perceived against a norm." Normalcy and deviancy are relative terms and are invariably formulated in the eye of the beholder. Normalcy cannot be determined scientifically, and thus cannot be measured with any true degree of reliability. An example of the not-so-concrete distinction between deviancy and normalcy is outlined in "There's No Disgrace Like Home." Homer, upset with his family's apparent dysfunction, takes the Simpson clan to observe a "normal" family in action:

> **Homer:** Look at that, kids! No fighting, no yelling.
> **Bart:** No belching.
> **Lisa:** Their dad has a shirt on!
> **Marge:** Look! Napkins!
> **Bart:** These people are obviously freaks.

As evidenced by the above, it is often difficult to define normalcy, since perceptions of what is "normal" differ amongst nations, communities, and individuals. And, as pointedly noted by Lisa, all of us do share certain things in common, "The sad truth is all families are like ours," she declares. Deviancy is easier to define than normalcy, and for the purpose of the forthcoming discussion, deviancy can be defined as something that "differs from a norm or from the accepted standards of society."

Before we begin to discuss Bart Simpson's "deviant" behavior, it is important to note that many of us share something in common with our favorite ten-year old brat: we're all basically deviant. In "Practicing Deviancy—The Value of Being Different," Dr. Daniel H. Johnston of the Georgia Psychological

Association challenges us to take notice of this behavior. He suggests a number of common ways of practicing deviancy:
- Wear a new color. Make it bright.
- Buy a bold tie.
- Mismatch your socks, and see if anyone notices.
- Eat a new food. Something exotic.
- Go to a movie in the middle of the day.
- Change your hairstyle.
- Send yourself flowers.
- Run barefoot through a park.
- Skip instead of walk.

Engaging in such "deviant" behavior can benefit individuals and society in general. We all develop routines, as Dr. Johnston notes, but do we often enough consider *why* we engage in these routines? Were these routines created for some particular reason, or did we fall into certain patterns and habits simply because we're used to performing these practices? Complacency never leads to progress. In his essay "Bart Simpson: Prince of Irreverence," media critic Douglas Rushkoff carefully outlines this point: while Homer is easily manipulated by the media, Bart is always one step ahead—thinking actively, not passively, and often engaging in noncomplacent behavior. While all the Homer Simpsons out there eat what is fed to them by the mass media, Bart's sharp distrust of authority figures and institutions enables him to act in ways that are deviant but also progressive. In other words, Bart and his deviant ways can show us the path to progress.

Bart the Deviant: Bad for the Sake of Bad

Deviancy is often not tolerated in contemporary society nor in Springfield, as satirized in the season three episode "Stark Raving Dad." In this episode, Homer fears that wearing a pink shirt to work will cast him as an outsider. Homer expresses his fear of becoming a pariah and his inherent desire to conform, noting sadly, "I'm not popular enough to be different." (Indeed,

Homer is forced to undergo a psychological examination because he wears the pink shirt to work.)

Mass media has engendered models to which "normal" persons should, ideally, wish to conform. Yet, while Homer fears the effects of deviancy, Bart seems to live for the thrill of being unique. Bart builds his reputation by consistently subverting authority. Once others follow self-help guru Brad Goodman's advice and model their behavior to conform to Bart's behavior in "Bart's Inner Child," for example, Bart longs to regain his deviancy by now changing his own actions since they are now considered conformist. His conversation with Lisa addresses this point:

> **Bart:** Lis, everyone in town is acting like me. So why does it suck?
>
> **Lisa:** It's simple, Bart: you've defined yourself as a rebel, and in the absence of a repressive milieu your societal nature's been co-opted.
>
> **Bart:** [pause] I see.
>
> **Lisa:** Ever since that self-help guy came to town, you've lost your identity. You've fallen through the cracks of our quick fix, one-hour photo, instant oatmeal society.
>
> **Bart:** What's the answer?
>
> **Lisa:** Well, this is your chance to develop a new and better identity. May I suggest…good-natured doormat?
>
> **Bart:** Sounds good, sis. Just tell me what to do.

We see here that all Bart really seems to care about is being deviant. Lisa is right on the money: Bart finds himself in an undesirable situation precisely because society is now conforming to his actions, and he is no longer the deviant that has defined the Bart we all know and love. Bart is so infatuated with the idea of being deviant that he is willing to give up all of his subversive actions and become a "good-natured doormat." This exchange puts to rest any doubts of whether Bart is bad for the sake of being deviant. Evidently, if everyone were poorly behaved in society, Bart would seemingly choose to be well-behaved. For Bart, deviancy is an essential part of life; in fact, it is a strategy for dealing with life.

So how does this strategy apply to real life? Let's take a look at a recent example. In a June 2004 *TIME* magazine article entitled "Minding Their Manners," Sonja Steptoe quotes etiquette "experts" who teach proper decorum to youngsters. She notes that "such instruction [in proper decorum] is essential, say experts, for a generation raised on Bart Simpson and Britney Spears." Diane Diehl, who teaches an etiquette course to youngsters, notes that "Kids are being encouraged by pop culture to be disrespectful and self-destructive, and their parents are frightened and looking for help."

Diehl, however, carelessly dismisses the inherent value of popular culture. Popular culture is not a "forced" process; it develops in the way that society wants it to develop. Diehl's etiquette course, on the other hand, *is* forced. For a fee of $250, Diehl devotes four hours to teaching children proper manners.

This is exactly what Bart is rebelling against—a forced status quo that does not reflect the attitudes and desires of youngsters is not particularly healthy for society. Bart Simpson's bad boy antics reflect the desire of children to sporadically break free from the established status quo. So perhaps bad (or deviant) behavior in and of itself is not necessarily harmful.

The episode "Bart's Inner Child" further illustrates this point. Self-help guru Brad Goodman (voiced by Albert Brooks) praises Bart's outspoken demeanor and lack of proper manners.

After Bart makes a rude remark at the self-help session, Goodman calls Bart up to the stage and asks him why he made that particular remark. Bart's response was a classic:

"I do what I feel like."

Goodman's response:

"I couldn't have put it better myself!…People, this young

man here is the inner child I've been talking about!"

Goodman goes on to call Bart "emotionally healthy" and says that "[Bart] has fully developed ego integrity with well-defined boundaries." Even while receiving such praise, Bart is rude: he snores during Goodman's speech.

Goodman appreciates Bart's lack of decorum because he acts honestly within his own set boundaries. He is not bound by rules or concepts that seem useless or boring.

And, to a certain extent, this is an important virtue for children to have. While etiquette courses focus solely on discipline, Bart experiments with new ideas and sets new boundaries. Whether or not the boundaries he sets for himself are acceptable by society's standards is debatable, but the very idea of experimenting with new behaviors—and redefining certain boundaries—is not only important but also admirable. Nobody wants to grow up to be a "square" like Ned Flanders, who was disciplined at a young age and has a problem expressing his emotions when he becomes angry or upset about something. As Paul A. Cantor correctly notes, "this country was founded on disrespect for authority and an act of rebellion." Therefore, Bart's deviant behavior seems to simultaneously have roots in Americana and holds some positive value in contemporary society.

There have, of course, been many authority figures who have attempted to repress Bart's behavior. His parents, though largely ineffective at keeping him under their control, have, of course, attempted to teach him the "right" way to behave. Homer and Marge's parenting aside, however, certain professionals have tried to use other means to prevent Bart from freely expressing himself. In the season ten episode "Brother's Little Helper," for example, the Pharm Team laboratory researchers convince Homer and Marge that forcing Bart to take a new drug called Focusyn will help him perform better in school, concentrate, act respectfully towards others, and, in general, behave "correctly." But the drug will essentially control Bart's behavior, effectively creating a new, well-mannered Bart Simpson. The Pharm Team researchers explain the benefits of Focusyn:

> **Researcher # 1:** It's not about slavery. It's about help-ing kids concentrate. This pill reduces class clownism 44 percent.
> **Researcher # 2:** With 60 percent less sass-mouth.

Do we want to change Bart and create a different boy alto-gether? Probably not. Ridding the world of class clowns is not a goal that we should aspire to attain. Class clowns bring laughter into the world; the Pharm Team researchers offer the world a method of controlling people, thereby preventing them from developing naturally. Bart's bad behavior, as we have seen, is not something that necessarily needs to be repressed.

Many Simpsons episodes serve to develop Bart's character by showing him performing his "bad boy" antics. As noted, Bart's bad behavior reflects his penchant for expressing himself freely. We'll look at examples of this behavior.

Bart's Bad Behavior

Bart has been disrespectful to Homer on a number of occa-sions. For example, in "There's No Disgrace Like Home":

> **Mr. Burns:** And make yourself at home.
> **Bart:** Hear that, Dad? You can lie around in your underwear and scratch yourself.
> In another episode, Homer tells Bart the following: "Don't worry, son. You don't have to follow in my footsteps."
> **Bart's response:** "I don't even like to use the bath-room after you."

Bart is certainly not afraid to speak his mind. He often does and says whatever he feels like. And while this is admirable in a certain sense, it also can be disruptive at times.

Bart's bad behavior often manifests itself in various forms. In many early episodes, Bart cheats, lies, steals, and disobeys his parents. In the afore mentioned emotional episode entitled "Bart the Daredevil," for example, Bart disobeys Homer and leaves to jump Springfield Gorge. In "Bart the Genius," Bart demonstrates his propensity for slickness by switching exams with the class whiz, Martin Prince.

Bart also shows disrespect for both adults and God. In "Two Cars in Every Garage and Three Eyes on Every Fish," Bart says:

> "Dear God, we paid for all this stuff ourselves, so thanks for nothing."

In "Homer vs. Lisa and the Eighth Commandment," Bart says:

> "Man, I wish I could be an adult so I can break the rules."

Bart evidently does not have a good impression of the characteristics of the adult figures in his life.

But the greatest example of Bart misbehaving occurred in "Two Bad Neighbors," a monumental episode in the long run of *The Simpsons*. In this episode, Bart got on the nerves of former President George Bush with antics similar to those of Dennis the Menace. Antagonizing the president definitely tops the charts of childhood mishaps. Here, Bart engages in the following conversation with President Bush:

> **Bush:** Y'know, in my day, little boys didn't call their elders by their first names.
> **Bart:** Yeah, well, welcome to the twentieth century George.

An eight-year-old showing disrespect toward the former President of the United States? It is no wonder why so many children wanted to emulate Bart.

In the early 1990s, everyone wanted to be like Bart. Still, the Bart Simpson T-shirts, which were banned in public schools across the United States, did not serve as a harbinger for disaster. Young school children did not run amok with slingshots. Prank calls may have become more popular in our society, but for the most part people did not have to change their phone numbers because of this phenomenon. And, perhaps most importantly, children still called their fathers "dad," as opposed to referring to them by their first names (as Bart did in early episodes).

So why didn't Bart's antics create serious troubles in contemporary society (as conservatives predicted they would)? The reason that Bart's bad behavior did not influence the behavior of young children is that *The Simpsons* was (and still is) aimed at a vastly different audience: adults. This certainly helps to explain why *The Simpsons* airs during prime-time (when adults can watch) as opposed to during the daytime (along with other children's shows). Adults saw the humor in Bart's antics, while young children, even if exposed to the show, didn't really understand most aspects of the series. Sure, children might have seen Bart make a prank call or two, but they would not have grasped the meaning behind most of the episodes. Thus, the influence of *The Simpsons* was—and is—greater on adults than on children. This point brings us back to my initial thesis: *The Simpsons* is more than just a cartoon. Cartoons are created for children; *The Simpsons* was intended for adults. What child would understand the political satire of Mayor Quimby or the stereotypical portrayal of police in Chief Wiggum? Children take *Simpson* characters for what they are, not for what they represent. Bart represents the American bad boy. He is a reflection of children in society and does not add fuel to the fire of misbehavior in American kids. Children made prank phone calls long before Bart did and shot rocks out of slingshots prior to the Dennis the Menace era. Thus, Bart was bad, but his mischievousness did not have much of a negative impact on American children. Although some children did watch *The Simpsons*, they probably were able to understand that Bart was a bad boy. To slightly alter my earlier contention that everyone wanted to be like Bart, children wanted to be like Bart—but only at specific times. Bart was cool when he misbehaved, but American children would quickly learn that performing Bart's antics would land them in serious trouble.

Bart, however, is rarely rewarded for his misdeeds. Consider the scene before each episode in which Bart writes on the chalkboard as punishment for his actions. Viewers are clearly able to see that there are consequences for behaving badly. In one particular episode, for example, Bart steals a video game from the local Try-N-Save store. When he is caught, he loses the trust of his entire family. Similarly, when Bart shoots and kills a bird (albeit accidentally), he temporarily loses the respect of his mother.

There have been numerous other times when Bart was punished for misbehaving. For example, Homer once decreed that Bart not be allowed to see *Itchy and Scratchy: The Movie*. The fact that Bart was punished for his misdeeds in this episode enables him to grow up as a successful individual later in life. (At the end of the episode, the writers take the viewing audience into the future, and we are able to see that because Bart was punished while he was young, he was able to grow up and become Chief Justice of the Supreme Court.)

Another example of Bart being punished for his misbehavior may be examined in the episode entitled "Radio Bart." In this episode, Bart is punished for duping the townspeople into believing that a boy (Timmy O'Toole) had fallen down a well. However, poetic justice is served when Bart himself falls down the well, and the townspeople, who had been so sympathetic to the imaginary Timmy O'Toole's dilemma, are reluctant to save Bart. Bart, of course, is eventually rescued, but the fear that he feels while stuck in the bottom of the well teaches him a valuable lesson: lying can get you into trouble.

The fact that Bart is punished for his actions reflects society's tendency to both educate Bart in the nuances of the status quo by outlining the "proper" way to behave and also to repress Bart's seemingly innate desire to break free of the said status quo. Bart rarely gets away with lying, cheating, and stealing, and his life as a self-described "petty thug" is often jeopardized by such punishments. During the first few seasons of *The Simpsons*, viewers were left wondering whether Bart would ever change and conform to contemporary standards for proper behavior as a result of receiving his inevitable punishments for acting improperly. But because of Bart's resiliency and inherent penchant for intransigence, he would continue to get into trouble week after week (or at least until he became more tame, but more on this later).

Is Bart's Bad Behavior His Own Fault?

In *The Simpsons* episode entitled "Girly Edition," Lisa defends Bart against virtually all of his critics. She certainly doesn't condone his antics, which in this particular episode, consists of deceiving people as Lisa's coanchor on the "Kidz Newz" broadcast. When Groundskeeper Willie hunted down Bart and was about to exact revenge on him for previous misdeeds (Bart filled his shack with creamed corn, effectively destroying it), Lisa rushed to the scene and proclaimed the following in defense of her bratty brother:

> **Lisa:** No, you can't hurt Bart! He's…well…he's your son!
> **Willie:** What?!
> **Lisa:** Well, not literally. But, in a way…isn't he everyone's son? For you see, that little hell-raiser is the spawn of every shrieking commercial, every brain-rotting soda pop, every teacher who cares less about young minds than about cashing their big, fat paychecks. No, Bart's

not to blame. You can't create a monster and then whine when he stomps on a few buildings! I'm Lisa Simpson.
[Willie sniffles, then drops the fender]
Willie: You're right. It's all Willie's fault! I've been a terrible father!

Lisa's analysis of the inherent causes of Bart's deviant behavior broaches an ongoing debate in contemporary society. After students in Columbine shot and killed fellow students and teachers, many people found it quite difficult to place blame entirely on the murderers themselves. Many wondered whether society at large was at least partially to blame for their actions. Were these teenagers influenced by violent movies and video games? Were they neglected by their families and teachers? Were they constantly criticized and ridiculed by classmates? Did society, as Lisa poignantly noted, "create these monsters"?

If Lisa is indeed correct, then we are left to consider whether or not we treat delinquents in the proper manner. Are we justified in "whining" when these "monsters stomp on a few buildings." In an age of harmful external influences, it is often difficult to decide how to justifiably attribute blame for one's actions. Is Bart the victim of society's ills? Or is society the victim of Bart's actions?

Willie's response to Lisa's comment, while humorous, serves also as a point of discussion. Certainly, Willie is not Bart's "father" in the biological sense, but in another sense, as Lisa contends, "isn't he everyone's son?" It can be argued that it is society's job to nurture Bart so as to prevent him from resorting to mischief.

Certainly, individuals are believed to possess at least a certain degree of free will, so Lisa's comment about Bart serves to pose more questions than it answers. The answers to all of these questions probably lie within a compromise between the two schools of thought: environmental theorists, who claim that Bart's actions are solely a result of the environment to which he belongs, and biological theorists, who claim that Bart's deviant tendencies are innate and inherited.

Why Bart's Not Like He Used to Be

In the earlier episodes of *The Simpsons*, the writers of the series introduced the American public to the bad boy antics of Bartholomew Simpson. The writers realized that bad was funny—for a while, anyway. After several seasons passed by, however, the writers made a fundamental change in the direction of the series: Homer became dumber, and subsequently funnier, while Bart's bad behavior was toned down a few notches. Homer eventually became the star of the series. The writers came to the correct conclusion that "dumb" is consistently funnier than "bad." In fact, if the writers had not made this significant change in the direction of the series, *The Simpsons* would probably not have enjoyed such a long, successful run. There are only so many prank calls that Bart could have made before *Simpsons* fans would have had enough of him.

Bart just isn't the same anymore. He's more soft-spoken and generally quieter. He's not as rude anymore, either. (In fact, in recent seasons Bart has most often referred to Homer as "Dad.") It seems society has had an impact on Bart. For example, the nationwide condemnation of the Columbine High School shootings gave "bad" a new name. Bart would never perform such an evil act and, if prompted, would probably realize that his petty rock slinging and parental disrespect pale in comparison with the actions of several other adolescents. In fact, Bart's actions may be deemed innocuous when compared with such acts of evil. Thus, Bart can no longer define what "bad" is. People in contemporary society have already outlined their definition of "bad," and somehow, Bart does not fit their definition. Bart is basically a good kid, and when he does do something wrong, he feels bad about it. In this way, he hasn't changed much at all. I've already theorized that

Bart has changed as a result of society, but what specifically has changed about Bart? Four words: he has toned down. Bart still has his occasional lapses: for example, he antagonized Homer with his creation of the "Angry Dad" Internet cartoon. Still, these instances are rarer than they were in previous seasons. Bart is by no means the ideal child, but his bad behavior is no longer the focus of the series. In fact, fewer episodes in recent seasons are centered on any aspect of Bart's character. He's still a member of the "fabulous five," i.e., the Simpson clan, but he has handed the spotlight to Homer. Perhaps that's why the series' three-hundredth episode ("Barting Over") was so interesting.

"Barting Over" focused on Bart's understandable anger at Homer. (Homer spent the money that Bart earned doing "Baby Stink Breath" commercials when he was a baby.) The episode focused on three main subjects: Bart, Homer, and skateboarding. Interestingly, this was one of the few episodes in which Bart became *really* angry at Homer. By contrast, in other episodes Bart performed actions that were against Homer's wishes and had to defend himself by denying responsibility. As Bart memorably noted in "Moaning Lisa": "I didn't do it. No one saw me do it. No one can prove anything." In the three-hundredth episode, however, Homer was on the defensive end. It was almost as though the roles of Homer and Bart had been *reversed*. Homer acted childishly: he initially attempted not to reveal to Bart how upset he was after Bart moved out of the house. Bart, on the other hand, acted independently: he moved out into his own loft. In these ways, the writers of *The Simpsons* demonstrated their unique ability to change the roles of some of the central figures on the series.

This episode is important to consider because it is one of the few episodes aired during the last several seasons that centered on Bart. Bart seemed more mature in this episode—until he became scared of sleeping alone in his new loft. It was then that we realized that Bart has not changed much at all: he's still a ten-year-old boy, a "bratty brother," and an incorrigible son. When Bart initially would not obey his parents and return home, however, something interesting happened: his family missed him. Lisa was stuck with the Indian burn in the shape of a heart that Bart had put on her arm. Homer was in tears (though he initially hid this from Bart), and Marge was struck with grief over Bart's sudden departure. If Maggie could speak, she probably would have called out for Bart as well. So if Bart is truly America's "bad boy," why isn't his family *happy* that he's gone? The answer is quite simple: Bart is not America's bad boy. He's just your everyday, run-of-the-mill ten-year-old. And his family loves him: Lisa's first word was "Bart." Marge has called Bart her "special little guy." Even Homer and Bart have, on at least a few occasions, said that they love each other.

And what does Bart think of all this? In a season thirteen episode, Bart explains his frustrations to Homer. Bart speaks about being the class clown and notes that it sickens him. This is one of the rare instances in which we are allowed entrance into the mind of Bart. Bart evidently wants to be perceived as a good child—at least in this episode. But his fate has been forever sealed: when there are T-shirts of Bart saying "I'm Bart Simpson, who the hell are you?" people tend to think about him in a certain way. He may have matured somewhat in recent seasons, but first impressions mean everything.

I've already discussed whether or not Bart is actually a bad seed, but the question remains of whether Bart is happy being *perceived* as America's bad boy. The answer to this question is two-fold: at times, Bart seems to enjoy the attention that he receives as a direct result of his bad behavior. On the other hand, Bart's frustration at being the "class clown" contradicts this point. When Bart does feel inclined to behave well, he often feels pressured to keep up his image. Because he is pressured to conform to a standard of badness, Bart does not seem to always enjoy being Bart. He is simply against the idea of conformity and, at times, does not like to be perceived in only a negative light. George Orwell ran into a similar problem in which he felt the need to keep up his image as a strong colonizer. He was put in a position in which he felt the need to show his strength by shooting an elephant in front of a large group of the colonized people. Orwell describes this situation in *Shooting an Elephant*:

"...To come all that way, rifle in hand, with two thousand people marching at my heels, and then to trail feebly away, having done nothing—no, that was impossible. The crowd would laugh at me. And my whole life, every white man's life in the East, was one long struggle not to be laughed at. But I did not want to shoot the elephant."

Similarly, Bart must keep up his image as "bad," once people expect him to misbehave. When he meets Reverend Lovejoy's daughter, Jessica, in the episode "Bart's Girlfriend," he initially feels the need to change his image and be perceived as "good" in order to win her approval. But when Jessica does not like the "good" side of Bart, he feels the need to openly declare his badness in order to impress her:

Jessica: You're bad, Bart Simpson!
Bart: No, I'm not.
Jessica: Yes you are. You're BAD...and I like it!
Bart: I'm bad to the bone, honey.

So it comes down to this: Bart enjoys being perceived as America's bad boy when it brings him glory. At other times, however, Bart wants to fit in, and desperately wants to be like his peers. It is almost as if Bart, over the years, has become tired of being "bad." Still, he is only ten years old and does have occasional lapses in character. So the next time Bart does something that authority figures would not approve of, do the boy one favor: Don't have a cow, man.

Chapter 4

Marge: Holding the Family Together

"I sense greatness in my family, too—it's not a greatness that others can see, but it's there. And if it's not, then we're at least average."
~ Marge Simpson, "There's No Disgrace Like Home"

In contemporary society, the mother generally takes much of the responsibility in taking care of the family. And in the Simpson household, just as an egg holds a cake together, Marge holds her family together.

Marge's crucial role as the unofficial caretaker of the Simpson family was made evident in the episode "Little Big Mom," in which Marge breaks her leg and must go to the hospital. In the episode, Marge asks Lisa to tend to the needs of Homer, Bart, and Maggie. Of course, Lisa runs into problems: Bart and Homer decide to play Marco Polo in the house and flood the entire kitchen. Additionally, neither Bart nor Homer were eager to do the chores Lisa attempted to assign to them. Marge is sorely missed by everyone in the family. Even though Homer and Bart had more "freedom" under Lisa's reign as caretaker, they undoubtedly would have welcomed Marge's guidance and orders.

In the episode, we learn that Bart and Homer cannot take proper care of themselves. For example, when Homer comes into the kitchen wearing only his underwear, Lisa questions him:

> **Lisa**: Dad! Where are your clothes?
> **Homer:** I don't know.
> **Lisa:** Don't tell me Mom dresses you.
> **Homer:** I guess. Or one of her friends.

Lisa is more intelligent than Marge, but because she is a young girl she lacks Marge's motherly instincts and experience. Marge's role is important because she ensures that everything runs smoothly in the household. The examples from this particular episode serve as evidence of her importance in the everyday affairs of the Simpson family.

The aforementioned episode is an important one to consider when defining the role of Marge. Her importance is only fully realized when she is gone. The situation outlined in this episode is similar to those that arise when a family member leaves home for an extended period of time in modern society. Like other contemporary mothers, Marge is taken for granted. She works assiduously to render specific services for each member of her family, but she is never truly appreciated until she leaves. It is when she leaves that the family (especially Lisa) begins to appreciate her value to the well being of the entire family.

In multiple episodes, men attempt to steal Marge away from Homer. In "Life on the Fast Lane," Marge's bowling instructor, Jacques, tries to woo Marge. Marge's date from the high school prom, Artie Ziff even offers Homer $1 million for the opportunity to spend one night with Marge ("Half Decent Proposal"). Even Homer's friend, Moe, has attempted to steal Marge away. Marge is certainly popular among the men in Springfield (especially in "Large Marge," the episode in which she accidentally gets surgical breast implants). Despite the temptations of leaving Homer to run off with other men, Marge sticks by her husband. She is a devoted wife and mother, and is wise enough to avoid flings and one-night stands with Springfield's bachelors, even when such opportunities directly present themselves. In Marge, we see a loyal, moral person who takes pride in taking care of her family— a family that, as we have seen, desperately needs her. Marge may seem "too good" to be part of her dysfunctional clan, but she stays with her family because she is needed and loved.

Without Marge, Homer simply would not be able to go on. In "Secrets of a Successful Marriage," Marge kicks Homer out of the house. Homer decorates a plant to resemble Marge but that just won't do. So Homer pleads with her to let him back by noting that he can provide Marge with "complete and utter dependence." He goes on to tell Marge that "I need you to take care of me, to put up with me, and most of all I need you to love me 'cause I love you."

Marge is clearly taken advantage of at certain times. For example, in the Shary Bobbins episode, Marge begins to lose her hair and visits Dr. Hibbert. While at the hospital, she receives a phone call from Bart and Lisa.

Bart: I want a glass of milk.
Lisa: Me, too.

Dr. Hibbert informs Marge that she is suffering from stress, and given the previous example, it is obvious that Marge is often taken advantage of. It is a wonder she keeps the Simpson family together, given their lack of independence.

Is Marge Happy with Her Life?

"Pride in homekeeping creates serenity and pleasure. I even experienced it standing around the microwave in the place where I was staying."

~ **Martha Stewart, meeting with her staff upon her release from prison**

"My life is pretty boring."
~ Marge Simpson, "Marge Gets a Job"

Marge certainly plays a critical role in her family, but since her character is supposedly representative of the contemporary housewife, it is important to discuss whether or not she enjoys caring for her family and household. A season sixteen episode entitled "She Used to Be My Girl" addresses this issue. In the episode, Chloe Talbut, Marge's rich, successful journalist friend from high school, drops by Springfield to cover a news story and meets up with Marge. Marge invites her for dinner, where she tells the family of all of her many exciting stories and adventures that she has had throughout her illustrious career. Chloe then inquires about Marge's life:

> **Chloe:** Marge, what's exciting in your life lately?
> **Marge:** Well, uh…oh, we finally found out why the dog was scooting around on his butt all day. Turns out he had an impacted anal gland. [Santa's Little Helper then scoots by on his butt]. The excitement never stops!

Chloe's life, it seems, is far superior to Marge's. Marge has little or no excitement in her life and becomes envious of Chloe:

> **Lisa:** Mom, Chloe just won the Peabody award!
> **Marge:** Well, I just made the bathroom floor smell like lemons. Where's the award for that?

On the surface, it seems as though Chloe simply has Marge beat: Homer enjoys the dish Chloe made for dinner, Chloe has won the admiration of Lisa, and Marge grudgingly admits that "even [Chloe's] serving bowl smells glamorous." Marge begins to regret not sticking with journalism (she worked with Chloe on the school newspaper in high school) and marrying Homer.

Homer tries to reassure Marge that she made the right decision:

> **Homer:** Oh, honey. [Chloe's] life can't compare to yours. You've got three kids, a TV tray from Expo 67, and you're married to King Sting.
> **Marge:** Yeah, I guess.
> **Homer:** Marge, listen to me. Chloe might have a flashy job, but you're the backbone of this family. You're like the electrical tape that holds the two halves of my car together.

Chock another one up on the ol' Homer brilliance meter. Homer's assertion that Marge is the "backbone of this family" is right on the money. Despite this fact, the question remains of whether Marge is happy with her role in the family. She's certainly a selfless person, but she undoubtedly deserves some happiness to be reciprocated back to her.

Later in the episode, Chloe takes Lisa on a field trip and brings her back to the Simpson house a little late. The following heated discussion (and shove-fest) ensues:

> **Marge:** How dare you show my daughter a life of fun and possibility? [pokes Chloe]
> **Chloe:** Hey, keep your dishwashing hands off the Armani!
> **Marge:** For your information, our electrical dishwasher is on the fritz. Not that you care about the ups and downs of my appliances! Do ya?!

In the above scene, Chloe is portrayed as a snob, while Marge seems to be looking for an excuse to get into a fight with Chloe. It is true that Marge has "dishwashing hands" and Chloe wears Armani suits, but the main difference between the lives of these two women is not highlighted until the end of the episode.

After a string of events leaves Lisa and Chloe stranded near an erupting volcano, Marge, risking her own life, defies Chief Wiggum's orders not to cross the police line and saves Lisa from certain death. Marge triumphantly declares that she possesses one thing that Chloe lacks: "Nothing is more powerful than a mother's love!" Indeed, the message in this episode becomes crystal clear: Chloe might have the more glamorous life (she's been married to Bill Clinton, for example), but Marge has the more fulfilling one. Raising and caring for a family brings Marge happiness in the sense that her family depends on her. (In one episode, for example, Homer declares that he can offer her what no other man can: complete and utter dependence.) Saving Lisa from the volcano was simply symbolic of Marge's "saving" her entire family from complete chaos. Marge is clearly happy with her role as caretaker of the family, despite its lack of glamour. But don't take my word for it:

> **Marge:** Looking at you kids, I know I made the right choice in life.
> **Lisa:** I'm sure you did. But still don't you ever wonder what might have happened if things had gone differently?
> [Marge then imagines herself as a reporter covering a hockey game at Lake Placid, and reports that the "Miracle on Ice" never happened. Marge's reaction to her own news: "No!!!"]

Marge Simpson will never experience any of the adventures or excitement that Chloe Talbut experiences on a daily basis. But more importantly, Marge would never be willing to give up what she has—a loving family, a loosely knit community of townspeople, or her blue hair dye—for anything in Chloe's life. Marge is *loved* by her family; Chloe is adored by millions of faceless television viewers. By the end of the episode, Marge realizes that it was wrong to try to compare her life with Chloe's: the two women lead separate lives, both replete with positives and negatives.

Chloe and Marge represent opposite sides of the roles that women play in contemporary society. Chloe is the outgoing adventuress, loyal and responsible only to herself. We see in Chloe a desire to succeed, to achieve personal glorification and respect. Marge, on the other hand, cares mostly about taking care of her family, and, as Homer noted in "One Fish, Two Fish...," achieves recognition through the home that she keeps and the "meals she prepares." Marge is a selfless woman—in many ways a flashback to the 1950s depiction of the American housewife. The tension between Marge and Chloe arises precisely because they come from two separate worlds, as they lead entirely different lifestyles.

Marge feels that she must defend her position that it is not only acceptable to a housewife, but that her role in society is worthy of special recognition. Chloe, on the other hand, is a classic example of the contemporary feminist—an energetic woman with a passion to win special awards and to serve as a functioning member of a society previously dominated by patriarchal inclinations and perspectives. Chloe believes that her contributions to society far outweigh Marge's. But because viewers have the opportunity to watch Marge at work every week, we realize that by disregarding the pressure to not be a housewife, Marge does indeed play a significant role in society: she holds her family together.

This is no simple task, mind you. Homer doesn't get dressed by himself. Bad boy Bart is hell-bent on causing destruction. Precocious little Lisa is always questioning everything, advocating some distant goal. And yet, through it all, Marge serves as the moral force that keeps the family members in check.

Without Marge, there simply would be no family. True, Marge is no longer the feminist that she was in high school (she supported the burning of bras), but she is the one leading a new fight: the right not to work outside of the home.

Marge is unquestionably the best thing to ever happen to the Simpsons. And perhaps being a member of the Simpson clan is the best thing to happen to Marge. I mean, does not her status as the wife of Homer Simpson make her the envy of every woman in Springfield?

Chapter
5

Lisa: True Simpson or Potential College Student?

"Dad, as intelligence goes up, happiness often goes down. In fact, I made a graph. I make a lot of graphs." ~ Lisa, "Homr"

"For now on, I will speak out against the evils in society—from dog-napping to cigarettes."
~ Lisa, "Lisa the Beauty Queen"

"Trust in yourself and you can achieve anything."
~ Lisa (via the Lisa the Lionheart talking doll), "Lisa vs. Malibu Stacy"

This chapter will explore the question of whether or not Lisa is truly a "Simpson." Does being named "Simpson" do justice for Lisa? Or is she too intelligent to be associated with such a name and all that it connotes—those attributes being dysfunction, commonality, and overall ignorance? At the young age of eight, precocious little Lisa Simpson is already the smartest person in her household. She is an analytical thinker, an activist, and a champion for human rights and dignity. In other words, little Lisa (gasp!) is an intellectual.

It has often been argued that intellectuals are alienated by the rest of society. We see this take place in Lisa's case even within her own family. Lisa is undoubtedly a good and righteous person, yet she is often cast aside as other members of her family bond with one another. Perhaps this is simply a result of Lisa being too intelligent for them. Lisa has, in fact, attempted to bond with the rest of the members of her family, only to realize that she cannot seem to connect with them the way most eight-year-olds connect with their families. But it's not that Lisa is weird. Indeed, she is, like all other intellectuals, a remarkable person with needs and desires, who longs for acceptance and commonality among both her elders and peers. But there is no denying that there is something very special—and unique—about the precocious Lisa Simpson that seems to prevent her from fitting in with the rest of the Simpson clan.

The Simpson family is comprised of five unique individuals. If we were to group the family members into separate spheres, we would almost certainly place Homer, Marge, Bart, and Maggie together, and place Lisa in her own separate (and special) group.

Why all the fuss over Lisa?

Lisa Simpson is a unique character who differs in many ways from the rest of her family. She is remarkably bright (a proud member of Mensa), a left-wing activist, and is rarely deterred from speaking her mind (she has appeared numerous times on Kent Brockman's *Smartline*). Lisa is extremely motivated to do well in life, which conflicts with Homer's principle that "trying is the first step towards failure." She is in a class of her own as she resides in a "town of lowbrows, nobrows, and ignorami." As Lisa notes:

> "[Springfield] has eight malls but no symphony. Thirty-two bars but no alternative theater. Thirteen stores that begin with 'Le Sex.'"

Lisa is obviously dissatisfied with the insipid nature of Springfield's residents and would love to experience "true" culture.

Lisa demonstrates her exuberance, as well as her keen ambition, in the episode entitled "Lisa vs. Malibu Stacy." In this episode, Lisa challenges the manufacturers of the Malibu Stacy doll (a Barbie-like doll) to portray women as intelligent and not mere sex objects. In an important statement, Lisa notes:

> "I've got a solution—you and I are going to make our own talking doll. She'll have the wisdom of Gertrude Stein and the wit of Cathy Guisewite, the tenacity of Nina Totenberg and the common sense of Elizabeth Cady Stanton. And to top it off, the down-to-earth good looks of Eleanor Roosevelt."

Lisa feels very strongly about women's rights. This marks a fundamental difference between Lisa and other women residing in Springfield. Case in point: a Springfield male executive (Wolf) whistles at a female employee (Harper) and audaciously exclaims:

> "Hey, Jiggles! Grab a pad and back that gorgeous butt in here."
> Harper coyly replies: "Oh, you, get away..." and giggles girlishly.

Lisa sees the need for change in her society and is willing to take on the responsibility of spearheading the creation of a new doll that promises to portray women in a more positive and meaningful manner.

If we are to truly examine Lisa's place in the Simpson family, it behooves us to explore the episode entitled "Lisa the Simpson." In this episode, Lisa fears that since she was born a Simpson, she will become dumber as she grows older. She expresses her fear by sarcastically asking, "Isn't there any way I can change my DNA, like sitting on the microwave?"

Lisa is well aware that she is too intelligent to be called a

Simpson. However, her Simpsonian roots come to surface, when, after solving a brainteaser in the same episode, she declares: "I got it! Woo-hoo! I mean, 'Splendid.'"

By saying Homer's classic "woo-hoo" catch phrase, Lisa displays a side of herself to which the audience is exposed on a less consistent basis. Lisa may not be content with being deemed a Simpson, but she is at times unable to escape her background.

In exploring the "Simpson side" of Lisa, it is vital to note her relationship with television. She enjoys watching the cartoon series entitled *The Happy Little Elves*, which centers on mindless characters singing and dancing. It would seem that the cartoon would be hardly entertaining for someone with Lisa's academic prowess.

Still, Lisa genuinely enjoys watching the cartoon. It is in this example that we begin to realize who Lisa Simpson truly is: an eight-year-old girl who is being raised in a community composed mostly of people with below-average intelligence (some notable exceptions include Mr. Burns, Dr. Hibbert, Apu, and Professor Frink). Springfield has been the town with the lowest voter turnout in the presidential election (as stated in "Two Bad Neighbors"). Lisa's family and community have influenced and molded some of her interests. For example, she has learned to love the violent cartoon *Itchy and Scratchy* as a result of spending so much time with Bart. These points portray Lisa as an "average" eight-year-old Simpson child. However, a wealth of wisdom lurks in her witty remarks and commentaries pertaining to Springfield. For instance, after landing a job on a children-run news program, she states:

"...and I'll be able to tackle all the hard-hitting children news the grown-up controlled media won't touch."

In another episode in which the teachers of Springfield Elementary School go on strike, Lisa is nervous about her lack of learning caused by the missed days of school. She frantically remarks:

"Relax? I can't relax. Nor can I yield, relent, or...only two synonyms? Oh my god! I'm losing my perspicacity!" (Say "D'oh" if you don't know the definition of perspicacity!) Lisa may be only eight years old, but she's smarter than a lot of her elders.

Obviously, the writers of *The Simpsons* have portrayed Lisa in two strikingly different, perhaps even contradictory, manners. On the one hand, Lisa is an eight-year-old little girl fighting to keep her head above water in a pool comprised of town idiots. On the other hand, she is a political advocate, a vegetarian, an avid reader of *Junior Skeptic* magazine, and, as mentioned earlier, a member of the academic institution Mensa. Whatever conclusion we may reach about Lisa, one fact is undeniable: she is a special character. And, if animation technology improves, and the Simpson family is reinvented into real-life, we may see Lisa roaming a college campus. She seems to be headed in this direction.

A Bit of Anti-Intellectualism

Much writing has been devoted to the way that the character of Lisa Simpson represents the anti-intellectual sentiment in contemporary society. Indeed, as noted in this essay, Lisa is often out of place in her everyday surroundings and finds solace only in associations for smart individuals, such as Mensa. I would like to focus on one quote in particular that quite accurately expresses Lisa's isolation from the rest of her society. In the season fifteen episode "Fraudcast News," Mr. Burns engages in the following conversation with Lisa in Burns's office:

> **Mr. Burns:** So, what do you think of today's popular music scene.
> **Lisa:** I think it distracts people from more important social issues.
> **Mr. Burns:** My god, are you always on!?

Burns's response is made even more powerful when we consider the fact that Burns himself is perhaps the man that is more out of touch with the contemporary world than anyone else in

Springfield. (In one episode, Burns was unable to make a telephone call or go food shopping. He also thinks that the majors just started allowing "foreigners" like Joe Dimaggio to play baseball.) In fact, the above exchange probably represents one of the few times that Burns has been able to single out someone else for being uncool and out of touch with reality. Lisa has already been isolated from the rest of society, but now it is the unhip, out-of-touch Burns who, in effect, tells her that she is a nerd.

So despite her attempts to fit in, Lisa, as well as many intellectuals, finds herself isolated from the "Simpsonian" society. But that doesn't mean Lisa is doomed to live a dull life: she could always decide to marry Milhouse, who "isn't a nerd," because as "the House" correctly noted, "nerds are smart."

She's An Intellectual Girl Living in a Non-Intellectual World

There are times, however, when Lisa gains respect for being an intellectual. In "Summer of 4 Ft. 2," for example, she meets a new group of friends and attempts to fit in, imitating their style and lingo ("like, ya know, whatever"). Although she attempts to hide her intellectual prowess, her friends learn that she is a nerd, but respect her for it. As one friend notes, "You taught us about cool things like nature and why we shouldn't drink sea water." Living as an intellectual in the non-intellectual world of Springfield thus has its advantages... "Like, ya know, whatever."

To Speak or Not to Speak: Maggie Simpson vs. Stewie Griffin

"Those who know don't talk. Those who talk don't know."
~ Tao Te Ching

"Ya know Maggie, the sooner kids talk, the sooner they talk back. I hope you never say a word."
~ Homer Simpson, "Lisa's First Word"

In contemporary society, it seems as though people who succeed in life are invariably the same people who speak their minds. Whether or not these people can contribute some worthy ideas to society is debatable. Still, more often than not, the mere expression of one's ideas leads to discussion of those ideas among one's peers. In order to explore these thoughts in greater detail, it behooves us to enter the world of the people who can have an impact on the future of the world. Perhaps another book may focus on the ideas of important national and international leaders. However, I am going to utilize a somewhat different approach in outlining this particular discourse: let's explore the realm of the *future* leaders of the world—that of cartoon babies!

Namely, let's understand the difference between the (quiet) world of babies such as Maggie Simpson and the (loud) world of Stewie Griffin (from *Family Guy*).

Maggie Simpson is an immensely important character for several reasons. Her character, for the most part, encompasses the virtue of true innocence. For example, Maggie was not sent to prison after accidentally shooting Mr. Burns ("Who Shot Mr. Burns?"). Her actions were certainly far from virtuous, but she was not punished because she did not possess malicious motives for firing the gun. Instead, Maggie is most often viewed as innocuous: her presence in the Springfield community is largely nondetrimental to the town as a whole. Since she is a baby, her actions can never truly be deemed reprehensible, as her very being is composed of a dearth of malevolence. Still, the soft-spoken Maggie (her only spoken word thus far has been "Daddy") is somewhat intelligent. For example, she saved Homer's life on at least two separate occasions: she fired guns at mobsters and saved Homer when he was drowning in the ocean. In addition, she also played Tchaikovsky's "Dance of the Sugar Plum Fairies" on her toy xylophone.

Maggie is content with her role as the often-forgotten third child. Maggie is a likeable baby—and this is not solely a result of her cuteness. For example, when Maggie encountered grizzly bears in an early episode of *The Simpsons*, she was able to win the love, adulation, and most importantly, respect of the fierce bears. Without speaking a single word, she was able to command the bears to bring her another pacifier along with many new toys, which the bears stole from other babies. Maggie Simpson's soft-spoken demeanor is only viable because she spends virtually all of her time sucking a pacifier. Still, Maggie, by means of her "pacifier sucking" can at times speak volumes without pronouncing a single word.

Maggie's only significant movement away from the virtue of true innocence lies in her relationship with Gerald, the baby with one eyebrow. When Maggie encounters Gerald, they momentarily stare menacingly into each other's eyes. Of course, the fact that Maggie has an enemy will help her adapt to the adult world.

Which brings us to the world of Stewie Griffin (the talking baby on *Family Guy*). Stewie, who was born holding a map of the world, is seldom hesitant to share his thoughts or add satirical comments in any given episode of *Family Guy*. His unfounded suspicion of the world around him demonstrates a fundamental difference between himself and Maggie Simpson. While Maggie accepts life, Stewie is constantly devising schemes to thwart (what he believes are) attempts by adults to limit his role in the world. Maggie refrains from involving herself in adult situations. While Stewie falls in love with a fellow toddler, namely Janet ("Dammit, Janet"), Maggie does not expose herself to situations in which heartbreak may result. By falling in love, talking back to his parents, and plotting to take over the world, Stewie distances himself from the ideal of true innocence that babies generally possess. Stewie is often more bitter than Maggie because he sets goals for himself that are virtually impossible to accomplish. His wise-cracks at the expense of others demonstrate maturity beyond his years: it is precisely this precocious mind-frame that leads to his state of unhappiness.

Stewie, furthermore, is not nearly as likable a baby as innocent Maggie. We live in a society that values and respects the ideal of innocence, and Stewie, who lacks this virtue, does not act like the babies we love. Stewie is in fact virtually unlovable. Maggie represents the ideal baby: a good-natured, innocent, pacifier-sucking baby. Stewie, on the other hand, reminds us of the corruption present in contemporary society. If a baby, a supposedly innocent and good creature, has the desire to wreak havoc on the world in his ongoing quest for world domination, we have much to question about the ways in which our young children are thinking.

The question of whether it is better for us to openly express ourselves or remain silent in given situations is open-ended and subject to intense debate. In examining the world of cartoon babies, we come to the conclusion that babies can have an influence on the world. As Maggie teaches us, it is often better to listen and learn from others than to voice our opinions about subjects in which we only possess superficial knowledge. In other words, edification can result if we simply sit back and quietly watch the world around us.

Chapter
7

Beyond the Fab Five: A Look at the Supporting Cast

The surplus of characters on *The Simpsons* has contributed to the longevity of the series. Many plots and storylines have centered on characters other than the Simpsons themselves, such as "I Love Lisa," which focuses on Ralph Wiggum's crush on Lisa. We learn more about secondary characters through episodes such as "I Love Lisa," and we come to appreciate the tremendous character development that the series has been able to produce. Each character has a defining role in the community (Moe the Bartender, Comic Book Guy, Gil the Salesman). These characters serve to attract viewers from every sphere: policemen will laugh at Chief Wiggum's antics, and salesmen will smile at Gil's numerous misfortunes.

The introduction of secondary characters also adds another dimension to *The Simpsons*; that being that Springfield is composed of different types of people. The abundance of characters on the series enables us to view Springfield as a realistic town. Just as we pop into our local hardware store perhaps once every couple of years, so too do the writers of *The Simpsons* give a small amount of airtime to some of the lesser-known secondary characters. Fans of the series are aware that these characters exist in Springfield, but they are often irrelevant to most aspects of the episodes. This chapter will explore the role played by some of the more important secondary characters on *The Simpsons*.

Michael Idato highlighted Al Jean's comments in his article entitled "Ready, Set, D'oh!":

"One thing that has changed, however, is the growth of the show's supporting cast. Originally, Castellaneta, Kavner, Cartwright, and Smith were hired to play the Simpson family, and the show didn't venture far beyond, respectively, Homer, Marge, Bart, and Lisa. Now the supporting cast numbers more than one hundred, and characters like Barney Gumble, Moe, Chief Wiggum, Waylon Smithers, and Ned Flanders have loyal followings among the fans."

"Definitely from the second year there was an increase [in] the size of the *Simpson* universe," says Al Jean. "We would explore who Patty and Selma might know, or how Burns related to Smithers. [One of the keys] to the longevity of the series is that there are about thirty or forty characters that people are really attached to, many of whom were there in the first year, and some of whom were even in the shorts, like Krusty or Grandpa. There is no question that it enables the show to stay fresh, having so many characters." These characters do indeed serve as the supporting cast of the series.

Let's take a look at a few select characters.

C. Montgomery Burns and the Pursuit of True Happiness

"One dollar for eternal happiness? I'd be happier with the dollar." ~ Mr. Burns

Homer: Ya know, Mr. Burns, you're the richest guy I know—way richer than Lenny.
Mr. Burns: Yes, but I'd trade it all for a little more.

Are billionaires truly happy? Sure, moguls such as Donald Trump possess a great deal of wealth, but is wealth always in direct correlation with happiness? To answer these questions, let us turn to an analysis of the actions and mindset of C. Montgomery Burns. Mr. Burns holds several distinctions in the city of Springfield. For instance, he is the city's oldest resident, the richest, and the most sinister, as well as the most ruthless capitalist. Still, the question of whether C. Montgomery Burns is happy is a difficult question to consider. On the one hand, he can afford any luxury he desires and is given much respect by his loyal confidant, Waylon Smithers. However, there are several instances in which Mr. Burns displays his desire to attain something more out of life. Indeed, there are several distinct times in which Burns exhibits true human emotion—emotions that cannot be satisfactorily abated through the utilization of his plentiful monies.

Mr. Burns's search for true love crops up in various episodes of *The Simpsons*. For example, Burns dreams about Marge Simpson flying through his window while he is neatly tucked under his blanket. At this moment, Burns is so entranced by Marge's beauty that suddenly he appears like the rest of us. He is victim to the insuperable conquering power of love. Burns's unrequited love for Marge demonstrates that money cannot buy true love—or even happiness.

In addition to Burns's desire to find true love, we also see the 104-year-old incessantly search for more money in attempts to increase his already prodigious worth. For example, he breaks into the Simpson household and steals the key to the Flying Hellfish treasure. Indeed, Burns demonstrates the characteristics of the ruthless capitalist, who will by no means stop in his quest for profits. However, one may consider why the fragile, ancient Burns would go to such lengths in order to obtain a strictly financial reward. Certainly, one may argue, Burns has all the money he needs and should have no legitimate reason for risking injury in an attempt to procure such superfluous funds.

Burns's insatiability in this case is psychological rather than physiological in nature. For example, at his Thanksgiving table in the episode "Bart vs. Thanksgiving," Burns is presented with a huge spread of different foods that Smithers has prepared for him. Burns compliments Smithers on the display, takes one small bite of turkey, and says something to the effect of, "Oh I couldn't possibly eat another bite." Burns may certainly not be considered a glutton, but he does not order Smithers to prepare a smaller meal next year. Despite the fact that Burns does not touch over 99 percent of the food displayed on the table, the viewer can detect a sense of happiness from Burns as he looks over the tremendous amount of food on the table. Burns is satisfied that the food is available to him, and this is where his insatiability ceases to exist.

Similarly, although he will never be able to spend all of his money, Burns would love to acquire as much money as he possibly can just so he can flaunt it about. Thus, his feud with Grampa over the Hellfish fortune is psychologically based. He does not require the money to build a "safety net," nor does he need any additional monies to finance any luxurious ventures. The only reason that Burns wants to obtain the money is so that he can attain (the impossible goal of) complete and total satiation.

Another important example of Burns's lack of complete happiness may be found through an analysis of his association with his bear, Bobo, in the season five episode entitled "Rosebud." Burns's love for his teddy bear is so strong that he is willing to pay a large sum of money to the Simpson family for its return to his hands. Burns teaches us that certain items may be deemed priceless and that money cannot serve as an adequate substitute for emotional attachment. Although the audience may find it comical that a rich individual holds an emotional attachment to a stuffed animal, we can also relate to the feelings over which Burns has no control. For example, those who have held onto a particular toy or memento for years have experienced similar emotions. C.

Montgomery Burns demonstrates that he is no different from the rest of us, despite his vast wealth. At times it seems as though the little things in life, the niceties, so to speak, are what make us truly happy.

Any thorough analysis of Mr. Burns's state of happiness must include a consideration of whether or not Burns is a perfectionist. Let us begin with an analysis of Burns's utilization of the word "excellent" on many occasions. When something goes exactly Burns's way, he taps his fingers together, and utters "excellent." He does so in an almost victorious fashion. His utterance of the word "excellent" demonstrates that Burns becomes content when something is absolutely perfect. Viewers can almost see the joy in stingy old Mr. Burns's eyes when something goes his way.

Perhaps perfectionism is a quality that is essential for a person to gain massive wealth. Mr. Burns will not settle for anything less than perfection in any endeavor. Perhaps this is why his "yes-men" accountants tell him that his stock options are great when they're all but bankrupt. They certainly do not want to report any news to Burns that fails to meet his standard of excellence. If Burns truly is a perfectionist (and the evidence tends to point in this very direction), then it is understandable why he is often unhappy. Life, even for those who are rich, is not always perfect, and perfectionists lack the capability to accept this critical slice of life.

Burns's cutthroat, selfish personality may also contribute to his discontent. He is not a "team player" by any definition of the phrase. For example, take the situation in "Team Homer," after the Pin Pals bowling team wins the championship:

> **Burns:** You mean, *I* won.
> **Apu:** But we were a team, sir.
> **Burns:** Oh, I'm afraid I've had one of my trademark changes of heart. You see, teamwork will only take you so far. Then, the truly evolved person makes that extra grab for personal glory. Now, I must discard my

teammates, much like the boxer must shed roll after roll of sweaty, useless, disgusting flab before he can win the title. Ta! [He leaves.]

Burns's lack of camaraderie with his teammates coupled with his inherently selfish nature alienates him from other members of society. Burns might attain momentary happiness, but in the long run he cannot achieve true happiness without the friendship of others.

Burns's realization of his infirmities also contributes to his lack of happiness. For example, in "The Springfield Files," in which Burns is mistaken for an alien, he states, "A lifetime of being in a nuclear power plant has left me with a healthy green glow—and has left me as impotent as the Nevada boxing commissioner." Thus, ultimately Burns's lack of happiness is rooted both psychologically and physiologically. He realizes that he is impotent and is mentally distraught by the concept. Since the actual cause of this stress is physiological, Burns has a legitimate reason to be distraught: he is inadequate as a man (sexually). While Burns is content that he is extremely wealthy, he is also upset that he cannot enjoy the pleasures (and perhaps duties, from a religious perspective) that most human beings carry out. Burns's lack of happiness is partially rooted in his incapacity to perform the same functions as other individuals. In reality, what Burns truly desires is to be like everyone else (in matters of love, sex, and performing everyday tasks). He despises these shortcomings and thus can never be truly happy.

Finally, further evidence of Burns's lack of true happiness comes from the fact that he occasionally engages in activities orchestrated to relate to the "common" man. Burns's participation in the following events serves to support this thesis: Burns comes over to the Simpson home to watch the big fight, joins the Pin Pals, and drinks beers with Homer at Isotopes games. In "Mountain of Madness," Burns talks with Homer, and effectively lowers himself to the common man, remarking, "Oh, yes, sitting—the great leveler. From the mightiest pharaoh to the lowliest peasant, who doesn't enjoy a good sit?"

Furthermore, it may be argued that Burns experiences his happiest moments in the episode entitled "Homer the Smithers," as Smithers is on vacation and Burns must drive a car, answer a telephone, and shop in a supermarket by himself. Burns tends to be happiest when he is not "himself." Not only does Mr. Burns's vast monies not buy him real world experience, his wealth enables him to hire the hapless full-time assistant Smithers, who performs all of Mr. Burns' everyday duties, rendering Burns incapable of fulfilling simple, everyday tasks that even a boob like Homer Simpson can himself undertake. Thus, he does indeed lack the ideal of true happiness. And if Mr. Burns ever realizes that he is truly unhappy, he may very well decide to blow off some steam by calling a lowly employee into his office, and, a la another famous billionaire, exclaim, "You're fired!"

Dr. Hibbert vs. Dr. Nick: The State of Healthcare

"Don't worry, Marge. America's health care system is second only to Japan, Canada, Sweden, Great Britain, well, all of Europe, but you can thank your lucky stars we don't live in Paraguay!" ~ Homer

Medical doctors are portrayed in strikingly different manners on *The Simpsons*. For example, the Simpson family generally relies heavily on their trusted family doctor, Dr. Julius Hibbert. Hibbert at times seems to be a serious, well-intentioned doctor. However, his numerous outbursts of laughter at inappropriate moments certainly serve to counter this point.

Dr. Nick, on the other hand, is a charlatan—a quack, a pretender of knowledge. Dr. Nick may not burst into fits of laughter, but he certainly does not take his job seriously. Between these two, we get a very interesting look at the current healthcare situation.

The Practice of Dr. Hibbert

Dr. Hibbert encompasses many of the qualities of the classic family doctor. For example, he is intelligent, kind (most of the time), and does not tolerate nonsense. Hibbert's businesslike approach is exemplified when he discusses his price for Homer's snoring surgery:

> **Dr. Hibbert:** This is what it costs. [Scribbles down a figure and hands it to Homer.]
> **Homer:** Hmm…here's my counter offer. [Writes something.]
> [Dr. Hibbert reads the note. It reads, "Do it for free."]
> **Dr. Hibbert:** [laughs as usual, but then becomes serious] Get out.

This example is important to consider because many doctors in contemporary society similarly work "only for the money." In this instance, both Hibbert's and Homer's comments were out of line. They should have negotiated further and found a middle ground. Unfortunately, this situation is not uncommon in contemporary society. There are many instances in which patients do not receive the proper medical treatment because they cannot afford the expenses. Thus, this example reflects certain medical practices (or lack thereof) in our society.

Since *The Simpsons* is a comedy, there are many instances in which Dr. Hibbert is utilized to produce humor. Most of these instances of humor do not take much away from the respectability of Dr. Hibbert as an established medical doctor. However, the following quotes and examples do serve to influence our perception of Dr. Hibbert in a negative way:

Dr. Hibbert, to Marge: I'm afraid your husband is dead. April Fools.

Grampa: How long do I have to live, Doc?
Dr. Hibbert: [laughs] I'm amazed you're alive now.

Dr. Hibbert attends to a shaking Carl, holding a Grandma Plopwell's pudding cup in "They Saved Lisa's Brain."

Dr. Hibbert: Do you suffer from diabetes?
Carl: No.
Dr. Hibbert: Well, you do now. [Hibbert breaks into his classic laughter.]

In these instances, Dr. Hibbert's sense of humor certainly translates into insensitivity. When we go to the doctor, however, we look for sensitivity from them. It is important for medical doctors in contemporary society to be people-friendly. People skills are incredibly important in the medical establishment. In the movie *Patch Adams*, for example, Dr. Patch Adams, played by Robin Williams, is extremely gentle and kind to patients in the hospital. He correctly remarks that medical books don't have the power to make patients feel happy. If people are treated well, he argues, their chances of recovery will improve. It is clear, however, that Dr. Hibbert's famous laugh does sometimes manifest itself as insensitivity.

Dr. Hibbert's laugh represents the lightheartedness (if not carefree) demeanor of many contemporary American medical doctors. For instance, I have heard some doctors attempt to convince patients to lose weight. A classic method: "You don't want to be a blimp," followed by a Dr. Hibbert-like chuckle. To be sure, many doctors do not display such a sense of humor. Still, the writers of *The Simpsons* have picked up on a small detail found in the personalities of some contemporary American doctors. As Dr. Hibbert himself once noted, his chuckle serves as a remedy for stress. Dr. Hibbert teaches all of us that a little laughter goes a long way in relieving stress.

The Malpractice of Dr. Nick Riviera

Dr. Nick, after seeing a picture of a pregnant woman: "That woman swallowed a baby."

You've been in a car accident. You want to—"ching-ching-ching"—cash in on your injury. Who do you call? Well, if you're a resident of Springfield, you'd probably first call Lionel Hutz. Then you'd call a doctor to receive a written description of your injuries. So do you call Dr. Hibbert or Dr. Nick?

Well, let's examine what the Simpson family did in a season two episode entitled "Bart Gets Hit by a Car." After Bart was hit by Mr. Burns's "luxury car of death," the family hires Lionel Hutz as their attorney. Hutz gives the family the following advice pertaining to doctors: "Doctors! Pffft! Doctors are idiots...you can ching-ching-ching cash in on this tragedy." Thus, Hutz brings the family to visit Dr. Nick, who proceeds to claim that Bart has many more injuries than he actually incurred.

Dr. Nick in this episode does not merely act irresponsibly, he acts recklessly. He and Hutz attempt to deceive the jury into believing Bart's injuries are worse then they actually are. But Burns's lawyers aren't fooled by the misstatements. When Burns's lawyers question Marge as to how she feels about Dr. Hibbert, Marge responds honestly:

> "He's been our family physician and trusted friend ever since I've been a mother."

When questioned as to what she thinks of Dr. Nick, she responds:

> "[Dr. Nick] seemed a lot more concerned about

wrapping Bart in bandages than about making him feel better; he mispronounced words...now that I think about it, I'm not sure he's even a doctor."

She is correct in her assertion that Dr. Nick is a quack. In fact, Dr. Nick is the definition of a quack. His lack of seriousness, unlike Dr. Hibbert's occasional lapses of levity, is completely unacceptable. Dr. Nick's motive for his recklessness isn't necessarily directly related to personal financial gain (although he did once remark, after performing work on Mr. Burns: "The most rewarding part was when he gave me my money"). Still, other than perhaps a few isolated incidents, Dr. Nick does not discuss financial matters. True, Dr. Nick may try to cut certain corners in attempts to save money, but his mishaps seem to be more directly related to his poor education than to his goal of achieving financial success. Recall that Dr. Nick attended "Hollywood Upstairs Medical College," the "Club Med School," and the "Mayo Clinic Correspondence School."

Dr. Nick's most important role is in episodes that center on potential medical disasters. In "King-Size Homer," for instance, Dr. Nick advises Homer on how to gain weight quickly: "You'll want to focus on the neglected food groups, such as the whipped group, the congealed group, and the choc-o-tastic."

In "Homer's Triple Bypass," Dr. Nick prepares Homer for potential disaster as a result of malpractice: Now, if something should go wrong, let's not get the law involved. One hand washes the other." The last words that Homer hears before going under the anesthesia were the following: "What the hell is that?" Not exactly the words one would most want to hear before being put to sleep in preparation for heart surgery.

In contemporary society, doctors must deal with the restrictions of managed care while also serving the interests of their patients. Dr. Hibbert is often shown to be interested in money—perhaps even more so than the incompetent Dr. Nick. Hibbert knows, however, that he is an able physician, while doctors like Nick are indeed quacks. Hibbert charges patients more money because he is competent, while Nick aims at attracting customers not by advertising his surgical success rate but instead by offering surgeries at super-cheap prices. Finding a competent doctor in the United States is not generally a difficult task. Finding a competent one that charges small fees for complicated surgical procedures, however, is quite rare.

A Small Dose of Dr. Steve: It's Chirotown

In the episode entitled "Pokey Mom," Homer incurs a back injury. He first sees Dr. Hibbert who tells him modern medicine has a lousy record of treating the back. "We spend too much time on the front." Dr. Hibbert recommends that Homer see a chiropractor (Dr. Steve). Homer then questions Dr. Hibbert's recommendation:

> **Dr. Hibbert:** I'm going to send you to my chiropractor.
> **Homer:** Hey, I thought real doctors hated chiropractors.
> **Dr. Hibbert:** Well, that is our official stance, but between you, me, and my golf clubs, they're miracle workers.

Homer then visits Dr. Steve and is given a minor adjustment. Homer notes that his back feels a little better. Dr. Steve then tells Homer that he'll have to, "see [him] three times a week for, uh...many, many years." This quote examines the perceived nature of chiropractors in contemporary society: they want to attract and *keep* customers. Later in the episode, Homer accidentally invents the "Spine-O-Cylinder," a garbage can that is indented in such a way that it magically cures back problems. As Homer starts to attract patients, chiropractors lose business. A few chiropractors break into Homer's garbage, and destroy the Spine-O-Cylinder.

Homer notes the irony of the situation in a conversation with Dr. Steve:

> **Dr. Steve:** Simpson! You're not a licensed chiropractor, and you're stealing patients from me and from Dr. Steffi.
>
> **Homer:** Boy, talk about irony. The AMA tries to drive you guys out of business, now you're doing the same to me. Think about the irony.
>
> **Steve:** [grabs Homer by the collar] You've been warned. Stop chiropracting.
>
> **Homer:** Not unless you *think about the irony.*

It is interesting to note Homer's brilliant commentary on medical doctors and chiropractors. What we realize is that the medical establishment is a business. If nobody ever became ill, medical doctors would lose most of their business. Similarly, if anyone ever develops a magical "Spine-O-Cylinder," chiropractors would have a difficult time attracting—and keeping—customers.

One Final Note

The Simpsons is unique in that it attacks and/or supports virtually every professional career in contemporary society. Medical malpractice is a serious issue in America, and *The Simpsons* serves an important role in discussing the issue in an open manner (via Dr. Nick). Still, we do believe that most doctors are qualified—even if many of those qualified have various character flaws (such as laughing at inappropriate times). Now give me a Dr. Hibbert chuckle…

The Simpsons and Other Television Sitcoms: Politics and the Nuclear Family

"Thank you Bill Cosby, you saved the Simpsons!"
~ Homer, "Saturdays of Thunder"

"Simpson, Homer Simpson, he's the greatest guy in his-tory. From the town of Springfield, he's about to hit a chestnut tree. D'oh!"
~ Homer, singing to the tune of *The Flintsones* theme song

When television viewers are asked to name the smartest television shows on the air, *The Simpsons* often tops their lists. *The Simpsons*, as we will continue to explore, is smart television. There is something that sets the series apart from the sitcoms of previous eras. For one thing, *The Simpsons*, although set in the framework of the context of a nuclear family's struggles and aspirations, is not a conventional show. *The Simpsons* is a show about a family, but the issues that this family faces reflect our reality—more so than, say, Lucy Ricardo's futile attempts to land a starring role in Ricky's show. Moreover, *The Simpsons* centers on a family that is, for all intents and purposes, reflective of a *real* family. *The Simpsons*, as we shall see, does not center its attention on an idealistic family, but rather exposes flaws in each family member and in society in general. This is in sharp contrast to the popular sitcoms of previous eras, such as *Leave it to Beaver*, where each family's slight imperfections—if any—are usually corrected by the end of a single episode. If Wally makes a mistake, he'll learn from it and never perform the same action again. But if Bart Simpson makes a prank phone call in an episode, I'd be willing to bet that he'll do that again at some point. This is a critical distinction, and one that serves to separate *The Simpsons* into a superior class of television sitcoms. That is not to say, of course, that *The Simpsons* is the only television show to have reached a higher plateau in terms of its messages, content, and reflection of reality. But I bet you'd be able to count the number of similarly high-level sitcoms on both hands.

Ed Bishop of *The Riverfront Times* pointedly notes that *The Simpsons* is a revolutionary show:

> "I know other shows on television are funny. But the appeal of *The Simpsons* goes beyond its humor. There's an angst, a kind of doom, in *The Simpsons* that's unlike anything else on television. The Simpsons are a family of losers and they know it. Homer and Marge will never get beyond their debts and the middle-class values they actually hate. Lisa will grow up and marry someone like her father, never opening up the poet inside her. Bart will likely die in a drag-racing accident. Yet, though there's angst and even self-pity in these characters, they are not defeated. Their awareness of their limitations and their struggle against them are a rare combination for television sitcoms....On *The*

Simpsons, it's the world that's dysfunctional. In other words, unlike the narrative neatness on even the best TV shows, these cartoon characters have a reality about them. A kind of joy exists in that."

How does *The Simpsons* match up against other television sitcoms? Every sitcom has its own agenda at hand, and thus it is interesting to examine the fundamental similarities and differences between *The Simpsons* and other television sitcoms of the twentieth century.

The Role of the TV Husband

Several immediate similarities can be found between the role of the husband in many television sitcoms. For example, Homer Simpson often goes to Moe's Tavern to get out and away from his family. As Homer once remarked, "To Marge, and all the blissful years I've spent hiding from her in this bar." Similarly, Dan Connor's (from *Roseanne*) favorite beverage is beer. Additionally, Fred Flintstone and Ralph Cramden share similarities with Homer, as they often went bowling at night and were both members of a club. (Homer has attempted to join the Stonecutters. Homer also enjoys bowling: in one episode he bowled a perfect three hundred game.)

The adult male figure in many sitcoms has the following characteristics: fat, lazy, enjoys beer, and is generally a good guy. For example, Fred Flintstone and Ralph Cramden, despite their sharp tempers, are well-intentioned individuals. Ralph, on *The Honeymooners*, wants nothing more than to earn more money so that he and his wife can live a more luxurious lifestyle. Each of the aforementioned figures (Fred Flintstone, Ralph Cramden, Homer Simpson, and Dan Conner) love their wives, but at times feel constrained by the borders of their homes. Thus, the adult male figure in these sitcoms feels the need to join a club outside of his home.

The general consensus among the aforementioned male figures pertaining to the membership in clubs is a reflection of adult male figures in contemporary society. For example, many married adult men join bowling leagues, social clubs, play poker (just as Dan Conner plays poker), or drink beer. Each sitcom portrays marriage as rewarding, but challenging at times. The social clubs and poker games enable the adult male figure to free himself, for a short duration, from the frequent struggles and challenges that inevitably come with married life. None of the figures mentioned above gets a divorce from their female counterpart. Perhaps the reason for this is that they set aside time for themselves, and when they return home, they can more easily concentrate on overcoming the challenges (and reaping the benefits) of married life. Their social outlets (bowling, poker) eliminate some of the stresses of married life. Perhaps the balance of work and pleasure is the key to sustaining a successful marriage.

The Role of the TV Wife

"If I wasn't a housewife, I think I'd be a homemaker, or maybe a domestic engineer." ~ Marge Simpson

The role of the conventional television wife is also important to consider. It may be argued that Marge Simpson's character is an amalgamation of previous TV wives from June Cleaver, Alice Cramden, Wilma Flintstone, and Edith Bunker to the likes of more recent TV wives such as Peg Bundy. The role of the TV wife in sitcoms that aired before 1980 was to take care of her children and to support her husband. As society has progressed, and many married women now work, so too has TV reflected these changes. For example, Marge once attempted to begin a career as a real estate agent. However, for the most part, Marge is a stay-at-home wife. She has been known to have liberal views pertaining to the role of women in society: in high school, she spoke up for women's rights

("The Way We Was"). Still, Marge's character is not revolutionary; she is largely conventional.

Marge was certainly not the first TV wife to attempt to land a career. Lucy Ricardo, in *I Love Lucy*, constantly strived to be cast in Ricky's shows at the Tropicana club. In one episode, she also landed a job as a chocolate wrapper. And who could forget the famous "Vitameatavegamin" commercial she attempted to star in? Lucy was more revolutionary than Marge because she was one of the first—if not the first TV wife—to actually work outside of the home. As members of society have become more open-minded in their views pertaining to the role of women, TV wives began to work outside of the home. Marge's character combines the perceived complacency of June Cleaver with the motivation of revolutionaries such as Lucy.

Marge doesn't lack power in the Simpson household nor does she possess a lot of power. Although this statement may seem to contradict itself, let me explain what I mean. Let's examine *Roseanne*. Roseanne Conner had power. She was the queen in the Conner household, and she knew it. Conversely, Wilma Flintstone did not possess much power in the household. Her role was more traditional: cook, clean, take care of her family. Although Roseanne also cooked, cleaned, and took care of her family, she felt that, outside of those boundaries, she had the power to make important decisions. For example, she decided to purchase a restaurant (which served loose meat sandwiches) with her sister Jackie. It's difficult to envision Wilma opening up a restaurant. Now here's why the issue of power in the household is not relevant in our discussion of *The Simpsons*. Marge can do anything she wants—Homer won't stop her. Still, her approach is more laid back: she is content being a housewife, and although she occasionally pursues other interests (painting, real estate), she is happy with the way things are. Thus, she is the paradigm of the modern housewife in contemporary society. She doesn't *have* to be a housewife—she *wants* to be a housewife. And she teaches us that there is nothing wrong with that; perhaps it is admirable. She places her family above all else and has fun while doing so. Marge once noted that she prepares several meals before she serves dinner in order to practice. She knows that her job is important, and she is content with her role as the contemporary TV housewife.

Bill Cosby vs. The Simpsons

The Simpsons' portrayal of Bill Cosby (not actually voiced by Bill Cosby):

> "[Kids today] listen to the rap music that causes the brain damage, with their bippen' and a boppin' and they're trippin' and a hoppin,' so they don't know what the jazz is all about. You see, jazz is like Jello pudding—no wait, it's more like Kodak film—no wait, it's more like the common cold: it will never go away."
> **Bill Cosby:** Now my good man, what do you like to play?
> **Kid:** Pokémon!
> **Bill Cosby:** Pokémon!? Pokémon with the poke and the mon and the thing where the guy comes out of the thing, and he makes a fraaagh fr fra aagh aagh aagh!
> **Homer:** He he—kids say the darndest things!

What was Fox thinking when they decided to air *The Simpsons* on Thursday nights at 8 p.m. opposite *The Cosby Show*? *The Cosby Show* had it all—talented and likeable characters, interesting storylines, and, perhaps most importantly, a large audience. Still, Fox's decision to air a prime-time cartoon during the same time slot as *The Cosby Show* obviously paid off big time.

The Simpsons has had a longer run than *The Cosby Show*. One likely cause of this is the fact that real actors are required to produce nonanimated sitcoms. When publications such as *TIME* and *TV Guide* started to compare *The Cosby Show* with *The Simpsons*, they only added fuel to the fire. *The Simpsons* eventually moved to its current time slot: Sundays at 8 p.m. The series is Fox's third highest-rated show, while *The Cosby Show* is frequently aired on Nick-at-Nite. It's unfair to say that *The Simpsons* beat *The Cosby Show*, but the prime-time cartoon certainly made a name for itself by successfully competing against such a popular series.

Prime-Time Parenting

It would be exceedingly difficult to argue that Bill Cosby was portrayed as a subpar father on *The Cosby Show*. In most instances, he tries to resolve issues with his children in the proper manner, teaches morals to his children, and acts as the ideal father in many situations. Dr. Huxtable won the respect of his children because he took the aforementioned measures. His children certainly would not dare call him by his first name, Cliff.

Conversely, both Lisa and Bart have referred to their father as Homer, although they do also at times call him Dad. (Lisa, in fact, generally refers to her father as "Dad," but has, at times, called him "Homer.") Parental respect is an important issue in contemporary society, and the writers of both *The Simpsons* and *The Cosby Show* were well aware of this truth. Still, their approaches to the issue at hand were strikingly different.

The writers of *The Simpsons* decided to address the issue of respect for one's parents in a unique but interesting manner. In sharp contrast to critics' comments that *The Simpsons* fosters a lack of respect, it may be argued that *The Simpsons* may actually encourage respect for parents.

Here's why: the influence of the series pertaining to the matter of respect depends on the audience at hand. Of course, if young children are watching the series, they may try to imitate the actions of Bart. However, *The Simpsons* is intended for a more mature audience (it is the highest rated sitcom on Sunday nights for males between the ages of eighteen to forty-nine). For older audiences, the lack of respect displayed by Bart in the earlier years of the series' run is simply comedy.

Many of Homer's parenting techniques, which are examined in Chapter 1 of this volume, are certainly not praiseworthy. However, *The Simpsons* portrays the average American family correctly: not every father is a great father. *The Cosby Show* creates the illusion that families always run into problems that can be quickly resolved. In addition, *The Cosby Show* creates the sense that children always behave in manners that are quickly correctable with the proper utilization of parenting techniques. *The Simpsons*, on the other hand, addresses the issue of behavior by showing that parents often cannot control their children. Thus, *The Cosby Show* provides the American audience with what they *desire*; *The Simpsons*, conversely, provides the public with what *is*.

Section
Three

The Simpsons and
Contemporary Life:
The Issues

Chapter
9

Ay Carumba! Simpsonian
News and Views

*Homer, on voting: "I voted for Prell to go back to the old
glass bottle. Then I became deeply cynical."*

*"See these? American donuts. Glazed, powdered, and rasp-
berry-filled. Now, how's that for freedom of choice?"* ~ **Homer**

*"I'd expect that from a French poodle, but not from an
American dog."* ~ **Marge**

"You're a real life Martha Stewart—I mean without the evil."
~ **Becky, "It's a Mad, Mad, Mad, Mad Marge"**

As I read last week's edition of *TIME*, I noticed a commonality between most of the news issues discussed. Of
course, the news itself isn't interconnected in terms of
content, but many of the national and international stories have
been discussed on television. I'm not talking about news reported on network or cable news programs—I'm talking about news
that has been reported on *The Simpsons*.

Diehard fans of *The Simpsons* are well aware that the program
is not an average cartoon. *The Simpsons* has explored every realm
of society, including religion, politics, the arts, sports, alcohol,
law, and current events. For example, in the political sphere, *The*

Simpsons' writers have portrayed Mayor Quimby, whose voice is strikingly similar to those of the Kennedy family, as a womanizer and a corrupt politician. Other characters are portrayed in a stereotypical sense as well (a fat, lazy Comic Book Guy, an uptight Principal Skinner, a nerdy Martin Prince, and a drugged-up bus driver, namely Otto, just to cite a few examples).

By means of an analysis of any episode of *The Simpsons*, the aforementioned is overtly obvious. However, *The Simpsons* is also skilled at reporting (and satirizing) current events in the news. For example, several years after the Gulf War was over, the animators drew a soldier on the battlefield that was about to kill Saddam—only to fail in her attempt as a result of Krusty the Clown's antics. In the realm of politics, Sideshow Bob, who has been convicted of attempted murder several times, once remarked "society needs a cold-blooded Republican." Similarly, a Republican news channel on *The Simpsons* once reported that 92 percent of Democrats are gay. While these views involve political jokes, the ideas expressed on *The Simpsons* seem to even out over the years (although some have argued that *The Simpsons* is indeed more left-wing). *The Simpsons* pokes fun at both Republicans (fans will recall Rich Texan's "yee-haw" after chopping down trees) and extreme left-wing liberals (recall Jesse Grass's plea for Lisa to sit in a tree so that they wouldn't chop it down).

Any thorough examination of Simpsonian politics must include a consideration of the episode in which Homer beats up former President George Bush. Bush was portrayed as a stingy classical conservative, who did not enjoy Bart Simpson's Dennis the Menace-like antics. While *The Simpsons* incorporates politics into the series, the Bush administration incorporated *The Simpsons* into their politics! As George Bush once remarked, "We want American families to be a lot more like the *Waltons* and less like the *Simpsons*." The Simpsonian rebuttal (by Bart):

"We're just like the Waltons—we're praying for an end to the Depression, too." The reason that *The Simpsons* will probably become the longest running series in television history is due in large part to the fact that the writers are not afraid to comment on, and often attack, politics and individual politicians. Bush may very well have deserved Homer's bashing...

Politics also played a fundamental role in "Mr. Lisa Goes to Washington." In this episode, Lisa, who is a finalist in an essay contest, travels to Washington D.C., only to find political corruption—specifically in Congressman Bob Arnold's chicanery. She becomes angry, but when she reports the corruption to higher officials, their response is frantic, and serves as a Simpsonian classic: "A little girl is losing faith in democracy." The officials then bust the corrupt congressman, and democracy resumes its proper function.

There is no news media program that can support and promote democracy the way *The Simpsons* does on a weekly basis. To further examine this point, let us reflect on the following lines from Lisa's original essay: "When America was born on the hot July day in 1776, the trees in Springfield Forest were tiny saplings trembling towards the sun, and as they were nourished by Mother Earth, so too did our fledgling nation find strength in the simple ideals of equality and justice. Who would have thought such mighty oaks or such a powerful nation could grow out of something so fragile, so pure?" Once Lisa witnesses firsthand the corruption of Bob Arnold, however, she revises her essay and harshly criticizes the American political system. Tron, the contest winner, is gracious in victory and thanks Lisa for her contribution to the contest: "I'd like to thank...Lisa Simpson, whose inflammatory remarks reminded us that the price of freedom is eternal vigilance." In a few words, Tron expressed the way we feel about our beloved nation—and what we must do to protect the liberties of our people. Hmm...kind of difficult to remember that *The Simpsons* is just a cartoon, right?

The Simpsons is often at the forefront of controversy. For example, after the airing of the Brazil episode in season thirteen, the Brazilian government threatened to sue Fox unless they received an official apology from Fox. (Fox did apologize.) The episode did indeed poke fun at Brazil—Homer was kidnapped by an unlicensed taxi driver, Brazilian children were portrayed as thieves, and Brazilian children's television was depicted as containing graphic sexual elements. Despite the criticism that the episode received, the American virtue of free speech enables the episode to continue to be aired over and over again on Fox. Since *The Simpsons* is a cartoon, it does possess a sense of innocence that other TV programs do not. As producer-writer David Mirkin noted, "If people saw [Simpsons humor] in live-action, they'd be much more offended, but a cartoon makes it cute. People don't realize how dark *The Simpsons* is because it's a brightly colored, happy-looking cartoon. That's how we get away with it." As Jay Leno put it, "Brazil is threatening to sue *The Simpsons* over last week's episode. *The Simpsons* could not be reached for comment BECAUSE THEY ARE CARTOONS!" *The Simpsons* has also reported a great deal of news throughout their fifteen seasons. To list a few events:

Michael Jackson dangling his baby, the downfall of dot.com companies, and, as the butt of one memorable joke, O.J. Simpson.

> **Homer:** This is the biggest frame-up since O.J. Wait a minute. Blood in the Bronco. The cuts on his hands. Those Jay Leno monologues. Oh my God, he did it!

As long as there is news to report, *The Simpsons* will be there for satirical comment. So the next time you watch *The Simpsons*, try to pay particular attention to the intricate details that focus on news and politics. (There's a reason why former President Bush was seen sitting at an execution service—and why former President Clinton was seen dancing with Marge). As I finish this section, I can assure you that Simpsonian-flavored politics have a lot to offer the American public. While you may not agree with a particular view expressed on *The Simpsons*, do the writers of the series one simple favor: Don't have a cow, man.

So with that in mind, let us now turn to an analysis of some of the most important issues that *The Simpsons* has addressed.

The Simpsons and Globalization

Lisa, after Selma decides to give up trying to find a baby to adopt:
Don't give up, Aunt Selma. China has thousands of baby girls who need adoption.

Homer: Great—another job lost to a foreigner. ~ "Goo Goo Gai Pan"

Homer: Ah, the miracle mile, where value wears a neon sombrero and there's not a single church or library to offend the eye.

In a season sixteen episode entitled, "On a Clear Day I Can't See My Sister," Homer walks into the local Spawl-Mart, a large store created as an overtly obvious parody of Wal-Mart—despite the sign at the front of the store reading "Not a Parody of Wal-Mart." Homer, in a statement symbolic of the insatiable American consumer, notes his satisfaction with Sprawl-Mart:

> "Oh, I just love it here. So many things and so many things of each thing."

Sprawl-Mart is a great place for consumers—lots of products, good prices, and, as Homer soon learns, friendly greeters. But at what cost to America—and the world—are stores like Sprawl-Mart able to create such a buying environment?

This chapter explores the benefits and disadvantages of McWorld, the "Walmartization" of America, and globalization in the new world order. *The Simpsons* has addressed all of these topics in interesting and unique ways, and it is valuable to take a close look at the way the writers address these important issues. We'll also examine the unique position of *The Simpsons* itself in this new global order. Because *The Simpsons* crosses borders, it will be interesting to see how the show infiltrates American culture into other cultures across the world. And it will be even more interesting to see how and why foreigners react as they do to *The Simpsons*.

The Walmartization of America

In "On a Clear Day I Can't See My Sister," Homer is offered a job as a Sprawl-Mart greeter. Homer views this as a seemingly unimportant job—until he sees that customers are helpless without the aid of a greeter: one woman cries, another simultaneously drops change on the floor, and a man repeatedly bumps into a wall. Seeing the importance of such a position, Homer inquires further about the job:

> **Homer:** Is there a chance for advancement?
> **Manager:** No.
> **Homer:** Woo-hoo! No pressure!

This certainly sounds like a great job for Homer—except that he has a family to feed. (Wal-Mart has undergone intense criticism for both not paying high wages and not offering ample advancement opportunities.) The message here is clear: just because a store is owned by a large multinational corporation does not necessarily imply that the employees will be treated well—in terms of salary, at least. Sprawl-Mart even went to the extent of forging a fake Mexican ID for Homer. Scandals in such chains are not unprecedented—a recent suit filed by a group of female employees at Wal-Mart charge that the chain discriminates in terms of pay and advancement for women. The case, *Dukes et al vs. Wal-Mart Corporation,* cited the following of evidence of its claims of sex discrimination against women:

Women and Wal-Mart
On average, women working for Wal-Mart Stores Inc. in 2001 earned less than men in various job categories, according to a statistician's analysis of company data supplied to the court.

Gender Breakdown:
35 percent of hourly employees were men and 65 percent were women while about 33 percent of management employees were women.

Average Earnings:
Full-time employees working at least forty-five weeks:
Women earned about $1,100 less than men
Salary employees:
Women earned about $14,500 less than men

Wal-Mart has also been under fire for allegedly paying low wages to a large number of both male and female employees. Wal-Mart, known for its low prices, has been hit hard in terms of negative publicity with negative slogans from various protest groups. One that sums up the issues particularly well: "Wal-Mart, Always Low Prices, But Who Pays?" Indeed, consumers at both Wal-Mart and Sprawl-Mart pay low prices for brand-name goods, but as evidenced from the above, much of this seems to come at a price for both local merchants and employees. As the sign outside Sprawl-Mart read, "If you worked here, you'd be poor by now." (The sign had previously read "Don't watch *60 Minutes* this week.")

Back in Sprawl-Mart later that same day, as Homer gets ready to go home after a day's work, the manager locks all of the employees inside of the store, explaining that he wants them to work "all night" to do the work he assigned them to complete. He adds insult to injury by then swallowing the bathroom key. Homer tries to escape but learns that a compliance V-chip was placed in the back of all of the employees' necks. Homer manages to pull the chip out of his neck and encourages the other employees to do the same. The following conversation ensues:

> **Employee:** Homer, we took our chips out years ago.
> **Homer:** Really? Then why do you still work here?
> **Employee:** We've learned to accept the things we cannot change—and steal everything that isn't nailed down. [All of the employees, including Homer, loot the store.]

The key line of this exchange—and perhaps of the entire episode—was the employee's assertion that he's learned to accept what he cannot change. The inevitability of the situation apparently helps to keep employees in their place. What options do they have? If employees were to open up their own small businesses, they would surely be put out of business by the insurmountable competition that Wal-Mart would provide. Just because Sprawl-Mart greeters are friendly does not mean that they are truly happy.

Our examination of this critical episode leads us to our discussion of the influence of globalization, or the universalizing of sameness throughout the global world. Corporations like Wal-Mart confer many advantages to the global public, but these come at an expense. Not surprisingly, there is some resistance to the intrusion of corporate culture by nations, communities, and protest groups. Corporate culture instills upon peoples the sameness, or uniformity of values. Those seeking to retain ties to traditional culture cite their many qualms with the undemocratic intrusion of large corporations into towns just like Springfield all across the world. Creating a balance between the creation of a global empire and retaining traditional identities is at the crux of this ongoing debate. The debate may be characterized into two opposing camps: McWorld and Jihad.

Jihad vs. McWorld

In 1995, American political theorist Benjamin Barber published a seminal book entitled *Jihad vs. McWorld*. The theory behind Barber's work is that the world is currently torn between two competing political agendas and that there is an ongoing battle between the two as they jockey for position in the global arena. He explains that Jihad, or holy war, is, by its very nature, undemocratic. Jihad is a "retribalization" of cultures, he continues, where "war and bloodshed" reign, and "culture is pitted against culture, people against people, tribe against tribe" in an effort to ward off any notion of interdependence in the political sphere. The second political tendency, McWorld, or global uniformity and integration, is also fundamentally undemocratic, since people living in a particular culture do not choose whether they want to be incorporated in a new integrated world order (Japanese people, for example did not necessarily *choose* to have McDonald's restaurants in their country). Barber vehemently argues that the result of the battle between McWorld's "centripetal black hole" and Jihad's "centrifugal whirlwind" is "unlikely to be democratic."

McWorld is essentially what the Jihadists are fighting to prevent. McWorld can be defined as the "globalization of politics," and requires integration and global uniformity of culture.

McWorld advocates the creation of a "commercially homogenous global network" that is tied together by four market-driven imperatives: technology, communications, commerce, and ecology. It helps to think of McWorld as the "McDonaldization" of culture, where peoples across borders are exposed to, tempted by, and succumb to the offerings of large multinational corporations that set up shop virtually everywhere. In contemporary society, it is not uncommon to find McDonald's or Wal-Mart, both hallmarks of American corporate culture, in distant lands like China and France. In this way, McWorld can be understood as the "universalizing [of] markets," where national borders hold less inherent value than the merging of identities in the name of a larger global face. In McWorld, we experience globalization at its pinnacle.

So of these two forces, which is the best for society? *The Simpsons* takes an interesting look at each side.

The Simpsons and American Corporate Culture

Springfield, the hometown of the Simpson family, is generally depicted as a microcosm of America. Corporate culture undeniably predominates here: in "Treehouse of Horror VII," for example, corporate logos like *Zip Boys*, *Mr. Peanut*, and *Lard-O-Lad* come to life; in "She of Little Faith," the First Church of Springfield, in need of money, sells out to corporations in return for advertising revenue; in "Simpson Tide," Bart goes to get his ear pierced and is told by the employee that he "better hurry up [because] this place [along with every other store in the mall] is becoming a Starbucks in five minutes"; in "Homer and Apu," a large supermarket, the Monstro Mart ("Where Shopping is a Baffling Ordeal"), seems to supplant the smaller, though still multinational, Kwik-E-Mart chain, by offering consumers better prices and more product choices.

In the latter example, Apu initially has his qualms about the

Monstro Mart's grandeur and supposed "lack of love," but his criticisms are soon laid to rest:

> **Marge:** Ooh, that's a great price for twelve pounds of nutmeg.
> **Apu:** Oh, great selection and rock-bottom prices. But where is the love?
> **Man:** [over loudspeaker] Attention, Monstro Mart shoppers: just a reminder that we love each and every one of you.
> **Everyone:** Aw.
> **Apu:** [impressed] Hmph.

We see from this example that large business enterprises (in Springfield, at least) may not be so evil or heartless after all. Large corporations generally build bigger and better stores, create more jobs, and offer goods at reduced costs to the public. What, therefore, is all of the controversy over corporations like Wal-Mart and McDonald's springing up all over the place? Is the question all about the amount of "love" the store provides consumers? Are large corporations healthy for America? But the questions stretch across borders, too:

If you travel to Italy, would you rather eat authentic Italian food or go for the "Tour of Italy" special at the Olive Garden?

According to Barber, you soon may not have too much of a choice.

In *The Simpsons* episode entitled "30 Minutes Over Tokyo," the Simpson family visits Japan. Homer reads an advertisement about a Western-themed area called "Americatown." A place like Americatown is surely intended to achieve two fundamental objectives: 1) serve as a hotbed for tourists from Western countries wishing to feel more at home, and 2) introduce elements of American culture into traditional Japanese society. When Lisa suggests going to an "authentic Japanese noodle house," though, she is rebuked by Marge who is interested in seeing how aspects of American culinary culture mesh with Japanese society, noting that she'd "like to see the Japanese take on the club sandwich! I bet it's smaller and more efficient."

Marge's comment, aside from its scathing social commentary pertaining to products produced by Japanese manufacturers, relates to our discussion of McWorld in the sense that certain products will be produced differently in different geographic locations. Just as Hollanders dip their French fries in mayonnaise, Marge expects that Japanese subs will be different from American club sandwiches. Any notion of uniformity among cultures is disrupted before the family steps foot into Americatown.

Upon arriving at Americatown, the family immediately notices all of the ways in which American culture is depicted. American popular culture and political logos and themes dominate the area. The influence of American culture on traditional Japanese society here is clear and pervasive. Popular culture and political icons like Marilyn Monroe, E.T., Abraham Lincoln, Elvis, Uncle Sam, and the Kool-Aid Man appear on signs and as robots. Yep, this is America, all right. As American as the apple pie and baseball games at your local corner coffee shop. The tables at the restaurants are all shaped like U.S. states, and the family sits at one shaped like Massachusetts.

Wearing a T-shirt with the words *UCLA*, *Yankee*, and *Cola*, the waiter, who is Japanese, arrives and greets the family in anything but a traditional Japanese manner:

> **Waiter:** Howdy gangstas! I'm average American Joe Salaryman waiter.
> **Bart:** These prices suck! Ten thousand yen for coleslaw?
> **Lisa:** Don't you serve anything that's even remotely Japanese?
> **Waiter:** Don't ask me; I don't know anything! I'm

product of American education system. I also build
poor-quality cars and inferior-style electronics.
Homer: [cackles] Oh, they got our number!

Yes, Homer, Americatown has your number. But does
Americatown represent what is special and/or unique about
Japan? Absolutely not. More than anything else, Americatown is
a business model based loosely on the world's most successful
business model: the United States. Sure, some American car
manufacturers may produce "poor quality cars," but the
American economy remains the most dominant in the new world
order. "Americanizing," therefore, from this waiter's perspective,
probably is not such a terrible thing. At the same time, the opponents of McWorld (the Jihadists) would be troubled by the very
prospect of Americatown. The existence of Japanese cultural
identity here is simply gone. The cause? The almighty dollar.
What we learn from Americatown is that in order to create a new
world order based on globalization, cultural and tribal identities
must become less visible—or in the case of the permanent residents of Americatown, nonexistent.

But that does not necessarily mean that American tourists are
content with visiting places like Americatown. Lisa wanted to do
something authentically Japanese:

Marge: Maybe we should just head back to the hotel.
Lisa: But you promised me we'd do something
Japanese!

Tourists do not visit distant lands simply to experience their
own culture. As a result of the influence of McWorld, however,
the Simpson family's experience is far from unique.

Observations similar to those in "30 Minutes Over Tokyo"
can be found in the season sixteen episode entitled, "Goo Goo
Gai Pan." In many ways, the show lends support for Barber's

thesis about the West's "cultural imperialism," as we see a "Krusty's Fried Chicken" and "America's Choice Apple Pie"— both located in China (the apple pie was being exported to the United States). For better or worse, Springfield's (and America's) influence is evidently felt by the rest of the world.

This influence can be seen in real life. Wal-Mart has had a successful entrance into the Chinese economy by focusing on consumer culture and the way that businesses are run. In a June 27, 2005, article printed in *TIME* magazine entitled "Wal-Mart Nation," Joe Hatfield, the head of Wal-Mart's retail operations in China is quoted as saying that "The culture of Wal-Mart is stronger in China than anywhere else in the world." What has made Wal-Mart such a major force in China has to do with the Wal-Mart culture that Americans (including Homer Simpson) are quite familiar with: gigantic "supercenter" stores boasting thousands of items at "everyday, low prices." Wal-Mart represents a major shift in the culture of the Chinese economy. Many Chinese employees view the Wal-Mart culture as a "liberating" experience because of the open channels of communication between employers and employees. Wal-Mart's entrance into China certainly has endured its fair share of criticism—from those concerned about cheap labor to small business owners trying to compete with the retail giant. These concerns notwithstanding, Wal-Mart's leap into China is an example of McWorld in action. For better or worse, the Wal-Mart culture has pervaded the style of consumerism in China—from buying and selling goods to employer-employee relationships to the actual size of the large supercenters.

Resistance to McWorld

The Simpsons does not always reflect the power for McWorld, though. Take, for example, the following conversation between Chief Wiggum and Lou, a Springfield police officer:

> **Lou:** You know, I went to the McDonald's in
> Shelbyville on Friday night—
> **Wiggum:** [interrupting] The McWhat?
> **Lou:** Uh, the McDonald's. I, I never heard of it either,
> but they have over two thousand locations in this state
> alone.
> **Eddie:** Must've sprung up overnight.

In this scene, we can clearly see that Springfield is depicted as a separate entity, not a clear and accurate representation of America. The Springfield police are, for some reason or another, oblivious to the name "McDonald's," and are surprised to learn of its immense business operations in their own very state.

If this were set in, say, Switzerland, this scene would not appear so strange: American corporations go overseas with a "bang" and expand as far across borders as their large budgets allow. But, now that the cops have heard of *McDonald's*, shouldn't they want to jump on the bandwagon and try a *Big Mac*? Well, maybe not:

> **Lou:** You know the funniest thing though; it's the lit-
> tle differences.
> **Wiggum:** Example.
> **Lou:** Well, at McDonald's you can buy a Krusty
> Burger with cheese, right? But they don't call it a
> Krusty Burger with cheese.
> **Wiggum:** Get out! Well, what do they call it?
> **Lou:** A Quarter Pounder with cheese.
> **Wiggum:** Quarter Pounder with cheese? Well, I can
> picture the cheese, but, uh, do they have Krusty par-
> tially gelatinated nondairy gum-based beverages?
> **Lou:** Mm-hm. They call 'em, "shakes."
> **Eddie:** Huh, "shakes." You don't know what you're
> gettin.'

So here's the classic situation: a multinational corporation enters your country. It brings with it new jobs, ideas, and, of course, the Quarter Pounder with Cheese. But something intangible seems to be lost in the arrival of this new empire. No, it's not the loss of the pure, wholesome goodness of "Krusty partially gelatinated nondairy gum-based beverages." Instead, it's the scary idea that your beloved local hamburger joint can be replaced by a strange, new corporation.

And that's not to say that this corporation is any less friendly than the local hardware store owner or hometown waiter: Wal-Mart greeters and Home Depot customer service agents can be pretty darn friendly. The idea that big businesses replete with an abundance of cash can take away everything you've grown accustomed to—be it the local bookstore supplanted by Barnes and Noble or the family pet store replaced by Petco—is a frightening concept. The new environments, while not necessarily negative, seem peculiar and out of place.

People don't like change. People like what they know and are often hesitant to try the unfamiliar, better though it may be. Barber is therefore correct that the globalization of culture is undemocratic because people do not generally willingly choose to part with their Krusty Burger with cheese in exchange for a Quarter Pounder with Cheese. It is the corporation that decides to set up shop, and because of the corporation's intense marketing campaign and publicity efforts, it will eventually (and inevitably) supplant the business of the local hamburger joint. As evidenced by Joseph E. Stiglitz in *Globalization and its Discontents*, "soft drink manufacturers around the world have been overwhelmed by the entrance of Coca-Cola and Pepsi into their home markets." Corporate advertising quickly makes people forget about their old, familiar environments. There is only so much marketing people can take before they bog down and try the Filet-O-Fish.

The aforementioned scene from *The Simpsons* is actually a parody of a classic conversation between Jules and Vincent in the film *Pulp Fiction*. In the conversation in this film, however, the two gangsters expand on the ideas already addressed, and present a new dimension to the current debate on the impact of McWorld and globalization. The following is an excerpt from the middle of their conversation. (Keep in mind that Vincent recently returned from his trip to Europe.):

> **Vincent:** You know what they put on French fries in Holland instead of ketchup?
> **Jules:** What?
> **Vincent:** Mayonnaise.

Jules and Vincent are both clearly turned off by the idea of using mayonnaise on French fries. Furthermore, they are both disturbed by the fact that a "Quarter Pounder with Cheese" goes by a different name in Paris. These revelations speak volumes about the *limits* of the power of corporations in spreading one nation's ideals, customs, and preferences across borders. Europeans may have no real say in the decisions of multinational corporations to establish business in their continent, but they clearly are not willing to give up certain traditions unique to their own particular culture. McDonald's may present itself as a universal entity, but certain traditions and practices that it takes for granted to hold true across borders—the belief that *everyone* prefers to dip their fries in ketchup, for example—seem to fall short of expectations. By dipping their fries in mayonnaise, Hollanders, in a small but significant manner exhibit some resistance to the seemingly indomitable force of the uniformity of McWorld. Cultures often clash because of subtle differences, and it can be quite difficult to expect *all* aspects of a dominant cultural brand to adhere to a concrete standard of uniformity across borders.

In a July 2005 article in *TIME* magazine entitled, "Disney's Great Leap to China," writers Michael Schuman and Jeffrey Ressner chronicle the Walt Disney Company's entrance into

China. Disney recently decided to build a theme park in Hong Kong, but, as the reporters note, the new park has a "surprisingly un-Midwestern twist." The theme park caters to various aspects of Chinese culture, including traditional Chinese landscapes; murals depicting the animated Chinese girls; Mulan; menus consisting of Dim Sum, seafood fried rice, sushi, mango pudding, and Indian curries; and, perhaps most strikingly, Mickey Mouse wearing traditional Chinese garb. Disney's attempt to enter the Chinese market requires all of these measures. "Disney has learned," notes Dennis McAlpine of McAlpine Associates, "that they can't impose the American will—or Disney's version of it—on another continent." Disney's entrance into China serves as a classic example of a nation's resistance to the globalization of McWorld. It would be much easier for Disney to simply design the Hong Kong park in the exact mold as their theme parks in the United States. But, as Disney CEO-elect Robert Iger notes, "a variety of aspects [of the Hong Kong park] are respectful of local culture." For Disney to be accepted in China, it has no other choice but to do so. Just as Hollanders want mayonnaise with their French fries, so too do Chinese consumers want to see Mickey Mouse wearing a red-and-gold traditional Chinese suit. The Chinese consumer can protect his culture from outside influences by showing resistance to the Disney-Western-American culture. It's not that Disney isn't welcome in China; instead, Disney's chances at success hinge entirely on the reception by people whose native culture is Chinese. The Walt Disney Company, not the consumers, must adjust to the culture.

Disney has learned that it must appeal to the cultures of the areas where it sets up shop. In Euro Disney, which is based near Paris, many Europeans were turned off because restaurants located in the theme park refused to serve wine—a significant part of French culture. The animated children's movie, *Mulan*, did poorly in China because many felt that the story was too "westernized" and did not appeal to local interest. Disney claims that it has found a better balance, and one of the park's architects, John Sorenson, notes that "We've come at it with an American sensibility, but we still appeal to local tastes." If it is indeed true that Disney has "bent over backward to make Hong Kong Disneyland blend in with the surroundings," as McAlpine notes, then the company's chances at success increase tremendously.

On the McWorld side, Kevin Wong, a Chinese tourist economist, notes that the Chinese consumer is not appalled by the prospect of Westernization. He argues that the Chinese will "want to come to Disney because it *is* American. The foreignness is part of the appeal." While Chief Wiggum may disagree with Wong's assessment of the situation, many consumers around the world are indeed infatuated with Western culture and want to be part of it—or at the very least, experience it. For all of Disney's attempts to blend in with traditional Chinese culture, consumers must realize that Disney is essentially a "slice of Americana." It will be interesting to see whether Disney's attempts to bring Mickey Mouse to China will pay off. Either way, there will always be some Chinese consumers in favor of resisting the influx of the House of Mouse, and other Chinese consumers that embrace the Disney-American culture.

The Coexistence of American Principles and Traditional Cultural Identities

So in the ongoing battle between McWorld and Jihad, where does the solution lie? Perhaps somewhere in the middle. Apu Nahasapeemapetilon understands this better than anyone else. Eclipsed by a new world order in which America is often seen as an overbearing, domineering influence—the term "cultural imperialist" is often used by critics in their analyses of America's pervasive influence throughout the world—America is often characterized as a new empire built on passing judgments on others in order to achieve moral and cultural superiority. These criticisms are inevitably tagged to any superpower and, I believe, are at times overstated, although at least partially accurate.

But let's examine the case of one famous Kwik-E-Mart operator who loves America for the right reasons and is not so quick to criticize the greatest and most benevolent democracy the world has ever seen. Apu, like all Americans, is "free to say, to think, and to charge" whatever he wants. America might exert its influence in places like Americatown and flex its muscle in the global scene, but when it comes to the domestic scene, tribal identities can often be (at least partially) maintained within our own market-driven economy. This is actually quite fascinating, considering the immense pressure that corporations place on other nations to conform to a new global order, where American ideals and culture dominate. Here at home though, citizens of all cultural identities help to shape this very culture which we export.

Apu's cultural identity, while not wholly respected by everyone in Springfield, is, at a minimum, generally tolerated by the rest of the community. Sure, Homer may make fun of Apu's religion and even dishonor the Hindu god Ganesh. In "Much Apu about Nothing," the residents of Springfield vote to deport Springfield's entire immigrant population. But if the residents could have chosen which immigrants to deport, Apu would be one of the ones that they certainly would have allowed to stay. (As it turns out, Apu takes and passes his citizenship test and is thus not forced to leave the country.) As Homer tells him, "I got so swept up in the scapegoating and fun of Proposition 24, I never stopped to think it might affect someone I cared about. You know what, Apu? I am really, really gonna miss you." It turns out that Apu is an integral part of the Springfield community and, had he left, would have been missed by many. Before Apu passes his citizenship test, he dons a cowboy hat, purchases phony identification cards, wears a Mets jersey, and suddenly loses his accent—all in an attempt to blend in with American culture. Apu expresses his discomfort with his new way of life: "I cannot deny my roots and I cannot keep up this charade. I only did it because I love this land…"

But before the creation of Proposition 24, Apu never felt pressure to change his garb or voice. His identity had never previously bothered the residents of Springfield. From this, we realize that traditional cultural identities *can*, therefore, coexist alongside American principles in Springfield. America is a great place precisely because of our acceptance of peoples from diverse cultures. And, unlike the voters who said "Yes" to Proposition 24, most of us are smart enough to realize that immigrants help to make this country great.

One of the main lessons that we can take from *The Simpsons* is that it is both dangerous and wrong to impose a particular way of life on others. Apu knows this better than anyone else. In "Lisa the Vegetarian," he tells Lisa that "I learned long ago, Lisa, to tolerate others rather than forcing my beliefs on them. You know you can influence people without badgering them always." This lesson is addressed in a number of different episodes. In "Missionary: Impossible," Homer becomes a missionary and sets up casinos—a representative element of American culture—on the natives' land. The result is disastrous, with the people becoming intoxicated and outwardly displaying their rage and sorrow. In another episode, a woman pleads that she just wants to raise her children as good "secular humanists" and doesn't want the views of the religious right to influence the lives of the members of her family. Respect for diverse religious and cultural identities make America a special and unique place, and the writers of *The Simpsons* have brilliantly used satire to express this very point. We learn from Apu that the coexistence of traditional cultural identities alongside American principles of government and culture is not only a viable option but the preferable one.

Western Cultural Hegemony: An Overstated Case?

Bart: I'll be going now. I'm sure you want to get back to your ten-year-old American reruns.

Australian representative: Don't tell us who shot JR!
~ Deleted scene from the original script of "Bart vs. Australia"

Economic and political theorists continue to debate the extent to which the world has become—and is becoming—globalized. The use of "soft power" by a nation can often lead to the creation of a dominant cultural hegemony. Soft power, as Joseph S. Nye, Jr., notes, "refers to the idea that a nation's cultural appeal, coupled with its pursuit of high ideals (moral suasion), can bend other nations toward its aim of influence without the use of military, diplomatic, or commercial coercion. Whether or not soft power accounts for some or most of the globalization of the world is debatable: do foreigners drink Coca-Cola simply because of the luminance of Western culture's appeal? Or is this a direct result of commercial coercion? These questions notwithstanding, is it even fair to say that the world is indeed inevitably heading towards McWorld?

Not everyone agrees that the world, as Thomas Friedman puts it, has become "flattened" by the utilization of soft power by the world's dominant industrialized nations. While markets, as Friedman correctly asserts, have indeed become largely globalized—with this trend toward McWorld seemingly inevitable—other data suggest that cultural identities have not been completely diminished by the purportedly dominant Western brand of popular culture. Take the case of Amitabh Bachchan. Don't know who that is? Well, according to a worldwide 1999 BBC poll, Bachchan, an Indian film actor, is the most famous movie star in the world. Furthermore, a *Reason* magazine editor notes that "as of 2001, more than 70 percent of the most popular television shows in sixty different countries were locally produced." In terms of the argument that recent advances in communication technologies are fostering a dilution of cultures, John Gray points out that "by enabling practitioners of different cultures who are geographically scattered to interact through new communications media, globalization acts to express and to deepen cultural differences."

Furthermore, it is widely understood that not every aspect of a society is a viable candidate for globalization. In "Bart vs. Australia," for example, Bart is not allowed to bring his bullfrog to Australia because the Australian continent is not suited for such animals. Westerners cannot easily bring their home-grown pets into Australia. At the end of the episode, the point is made even clearer:

> **Homer:** Hey, look, those frogs are eating all their crops! [The family laughs.]
> **Lisa:** Well that's what happens when you introduce foreign species into an ecosystem that cannot handle them. [A koala bear is then shown to have latched onto the Simpsons' plane back to the United States.]

It is evident, therefore, that not everything—at least certain environmental aspects of a culture—is a readily viable candidate for globalization without significant modifications to a society's environment.

So while Western culture can often be correctly identified as the world's dominant culture, such a blanket statement must be qualified. What is undeniable, however, is that the many peoples of the world, by and large, are quite familiar with Homer Simpson.

The Simpsons: Global Empire

In 2004, a *TIME* magazine poll revealed that 20 percent of all foreigners polled would willingly boycott American-made products. Widely held perceptions of American arrogance in terms of its cultural and economic dominance, coupled with a general lack of support for U.S. military operations in Iraq, contribute to these feelings of hostility toward the United States. Still, foreigners don't hate everything about the United States. Don't forget: America is the place where *The Simpsons* was born (even though the series is animated at South Korea's AKOM Production Company). And for that the world has been eternally grateful. Most people around the world would certainly have qualms with boycotting *The Simpsons*.

But what is it about *The Simpsons* that gives it its global appeal? True, the satirical knocks at American institutions and ideals may serve to give critics of America some legitimacy. But the more pressing reason for the global dominance of *The Simpsons* is that the series provides viewers with a glimpse into the hearts and minds of a not-so-unique nuclear family. Sure, the Simpsons are American, but the show would not lose its satirical bite if we were to imagine that they were German, French, Italian, or—as I'm sure Humberto Velez, the former voice-over actor for Homero Simpson would agree—Spanish. There seems to be something globally appealing about seeing a family explore life with a crisp critical lens.

The global appeal of *The Simpsons*, does, however, provide us with a foundation for discussing the forces of McWorld and Jihad. *The Wall Street Journal*, for example, recently reported that *The Simpsons* has entered several Middle Eastern nations, as the show has been picked up by the Arab satellite TV network, MBC. But despite *The Simpsons'* universal appeal, certain elements of the series had to be tweaked in order to be successful in these nations. The show was retitled "Al Shamshoon," with Omar Shamshoon replacing the name Homer Simpson. To fit in with Arabic culture, MBC decided that Omar should not drink beer (the consumption of which violates Islamic law) and instead should drink soda. Omar does not eat donuts, and instead enjoys the traditional Arab cookies, khak. Omar also gives up bacon. So we see that although the influence of McWorld has indeed brought *The Simpsons* to the forefront of the Arabic telecinemac experience, resistance to Western cultural influences can be seen in the unwillingness of Omar Shamshoon to consume beer and donuts and engage in other aspects of Western culture. While the basic global appeal of *The Simpsons* is indeed universal—all international adaptations of the show do center on the fundamental idea of a family living in a community replete with a myriad of different institutions—the scripts in general have had to be made more acceptable and adaptable to international audiences.

Speaking to fans in other countries, however, has given me the sense that the main essence and global appeal of *The Simpsons* has not really been lost simply because of a few changes and adaptations to scripts. I was fortunate enough to have recently given interviews about *The Simpsons* with radio stations in Canada and Ireland. The interviewers were extremely happy—even giddy—to talk about their favorite television show. But what was more interesting was the emphasis of their questions. The Irish broadcaster inquired about episodes such as "The Crepes of Wrath," in which Bart travels to France, and "Bart vs. Australia," in which the Simpson family travels to Australia (a true haven for diehard *Simpsons* fans!), along with other internationally-based episodes. I had never ranked episodes like "The Crepes of Wrath" toward the top of my favorite or most important *Simpsons* episodes lists. But because the broadcasters viewed the series from an international perspective, their emphasis was quite different than my own. The Canadian broadcasters mentioned the frequent references to Canada—"Why should I leave America to visit America Jr.?"—the playing of the Canadian national anthem, and the infamous criticisms of the Canadian health care system and Olympic basketball team. These knocks at Canada, however, did not seem to bother the broadcasters one bit. They were thrilled that aspects of their culture were mentioned on *The Simpsons*.

I also had the opportunity to personally meet with Ika Johannesson, a reporter for the world-renowned Swedish popular culture television program, *Kobra*. We had arranged to meet at a book signing at Jim Hanley's Universe in New York City that I held in August 2004. Upon arriving at the store, Ms. Johannesson was overwhelmed by the sheer quantity of Simpsons-related merchandise that the store had for sale. She was fascinated by the extent that *The Simpsons* had existed as its own industry in the United States. Upon purchasing a singing and dancing Mr. Burns figure, Ms. Johannesson noted that while *The Simpsons* was extremely popular in Sweden, the merchandise was generally limited. Purchasing the Mr. Burns doll, then, had to have been the ultimate souvenir for this diehard fan. *The Simpsons* are as symbolic a notion of American pop culture as anything else. The doll would, to be sure, be the envy of her family and friends back home.

Fans from across the world operate thousands of Simpsons websites, none more comprehensive or informative than *The Simpsons* Archive (www.snpp.com) Run by webmaster Jouni Paakinnen, who hails from Finland, the archive links together fans from across the world, from New Zealand to Australia to Israel to Latin America. The one thousand-member *Simpsons-L* list also serves to strengthen this cyber community of diehard *Simpsons* fans. In my conversations via email with Jouni Paakinnen, I was able to get a true sense of the energy and enthusiasm that he has for the show. The Internet has served an important role in contemporary society—if for no other purpose than bringing smart and enthusiastic Simpsons fans together to discuss groundbreaking episodes.

The adaptability of *The Simpsons* to diverse homelands in the global arena has helped to engender the notion that *The Simpsons* itself is representative of everything that globalization is all about. McWorld has indeed brought *The Simpsons* to the forefront of the international stage, but Jihad has served to limit the absolute influence of Western cultural traditions presented in the series to other areas of the world. All in all, *The Simpsons* is such a widely successful international television show because of its unique ability to adapt and appeal to different cultures, while still achieving its goal of presenting clear messages about the world in general that resonate with a global audience.

Television, the Typographic Mind, and Selling the Three-Eyed Fish

"In a culture dominated by print, public discourse tends to be characterized by a coherent, orderly arrangement of facts and ideas." ~ **Neil Postman,** *Amusing Ourselves to Death*

This chapter will explore the influence of the print and televisual mediums on the information that we receive— and also on the way that we *think* about the world. The advent of the relatively new medium of television has altered the messages that we receive as consumers of news and information. We will explore the influence of television on the contemporary political climate, while analyzing the ways in which *The Simpsons* (which obviously uses the television medium to present its own messages) has identified this phenomenon and explored its effects on the viewing public. *The Simpsons* shows us that television's ability to present ideas in new ways has profoundly affected the ways in which we perceive the world.

The Typographic Mind

In "She Used to Be My Girl," Chloe Talbut, Marge's successful journalist friend, criticizes the news media for its gullibility, its tendency to report news that is unimportant, and its lack of professionalism in reporting the news. Kent Brockman, embarrassed on the air, tries desperately to defend his Channel 6 against these criticisms and responds as follows:

"Channel 6 News Rocks! A car chase every night or the weather girl wears a tube top! And if she doesn't, you win a pizza!"

Brockman's comments about his own news channel are, unfortunately, not confined to Springfield. In contemporary society, morning news programs across the country often air footage of fires where no one is injured, and car chases simply because the footage is exciting to watch. The news, as we often see, does not always report true news.

Neil Postman, an ardent critic of the television medium, argues that newspapers provide a much more concrete basis for learning about events across the globe. In *Amusing Ourselves to Death*, Postman explores a time in which the printed word became the dominant medium for the exchange of information, and argues that in such an age, reporting like Kent Brockman's was unseen.

Typographic America refers to the era in which the printed word monopolized the media industry (this covers the period from the expansion of the use of the printing press up until the late nineteenth century). Widespread reading served an integral role in creating an atmosphere of rational thought in early America. High literacy rates spurred the development of the typographic mind as Americans began to believe that the reading process encourages rationality. Rationality began to play an important role in politics as voters read pamphlets and listened to debates between candidates running for political office. Postman attributes the prodigious impact of print media to two major factors: high literacy rates (in New England, 89–95 percent of men could read or write; 65 percent of women were literate) and the fact that printed matter was virtually *all* that was available. Since print was the only medium through which information could be exchanged on a widespread basis, the news media was able to create a sense of national consciousness in the psyche of the American public. For example, the *Federalist Papers* were read almost as widely in the South as the North. The Typographic Age witnessed the birth of a unifying information source that need not (yet) worry about outside competition.

Postman also argues that print fosters the rational use of the mind. Furthermore, he states, "It is no accident that the Age of Reason was coexistent with the growth of a print culture." Indeed, the printed word enables the public to analyze issues and form opinions through the utilization of the rational mind. The print media fostered political debate between candidates running for office. For example, the public was quite interested in listening to the Lincoln-Douglas debates, despite the fact that the debates were lengthy. Each candidate utilized proper grammar and complex sentence structure in attempts to persuade the public to vote for him. The structure of these debates was possible only because the printed word encouraged the American public to identify themselves with the English language. If Americans had been unfamiliar with the English language in printed form, they could not have understood the debates. As Postman states, "They [Lincoln and Douglas] consistently drew upon more complex rhetorical sources—sarcasm, irony, paradox, elaborated metaphors, fine distinctions, and the exposure of contradiction, none of which would have advanced their respected causes unless the audience was fully aware of the means being employed." Evidently, both Lincoln and Douglas respected the intelligence of the American audience.

Television and Politics

In the modern world, this is not often the case. In *The Simpsons* episode "Two Cars in Every Garage and Two Eyes on Every Fish," Mr. Burns, who is running for governor, blatantly dismisses any notion of intelligence existing within the voting community. The incumbent governor of Springfield, Mary Bailey, seems to use the strategy of Lincoln and Douglas. She notes the following to reporters:

"My worthy opponent seems to think that the voters of this state are gullible fools. I, however, prefer to rely on their intelligence and good judgment." What is most interesting, however, are the sarcastic reactions of the reporters to Bailey's strategy:

Reporter #1: Interesting strategy.
Reporter #2: Good luck.

It is not only Burns who believes that voters are dumb and gullible. The reporters—and perhaps society at large—*expect* politicians to claim to cater to the needs of voters. Running an honest campaign that is respectful of voters' intelligence and judgment is, evidently, not how things run in Springfield.

Another important aspect of the Typographic Age was the public's keen focus on ideas as opposed to physical appearance. The printed word allowed the public to consider what they had read and form logical conclusions based upon the ideas stressed by the print medium. For example, newspapers discussed the ideas of various political candidates so as to inform the public of the major issues at hand at election time. Readers were able to formulate concepts based on what they had read in the papers. Since print monopolized the media industry, the ideas discussed in newspapers served to influence politics tremendously.

However, as America moved out of the Typographic Age and into the "visual" age, *pictures* began to exert a tremendous influence on the minds of the public. The advent of television was arguably the most important media development since the invention of the printing press. Television provides a unique visual framework for analyzing various aspects of the news.

The utilization of television as a medium greatly affected political campaigns. For example, it is commonly accepted that John F. Kennedy won the presidential debates due in great part to the fact that the television audience perceived him as good-looking. The physical appearance of candidates began to serve an important role in the political process. Debates previously broadcast on radio would now be broadcast on television, where the public could see how the candidates looked. In "Two Cars," Mr. Burns' campaign strategists were well aware of the importance of the physical appearance of their candidate: they photographed Burns in various settings—including on top of a battle tank a la Michael Dukakis—and even hired a personal trainer to get Burns into shape. Before the advent of television, Americans were *readers* and *listeners*, but they were never before *viewers* of the news. Instead, Americans had depended on the semantics of the written word to convey meaning. While television provides news in a visual context, the print media requires readers to interpret the news, and form mental images of the actions, people, and events reported in the stories covered.

Television is also the home of major advertisements for political campaigns. While politicians in the Typographic Age often respected the intelligence of the American public—as they provided the public with lucid arguments pertaining to vital issues—contemporary politicians utilize the television media to broadcast thirty-second advertisements in which more "candidate bashing" is expressed than actual ideas. For example, close to the recent New York gubernatorial election, New Yorkers were more likely to hear Pataki slander his opponent on short commercials than actually state his views on specific policies. True, there are occasional televised debates between candidates for high political offices, but most political engagement that is broadcast on television is less informative (and thus less useful) than information published by the print media. Unfortunately, as newspaper readership declines, and television viewing continues to dominate the media, many voters are not properly informed about vital political issues.

Television's prodigious influence in contemporary society has been examined on a number of episodes of *The Simpsons*. In one episode, for example, Homer was adamant about a particular stance on an issue, but was told that "television" had advocated the opposite point of view. In the midst of being hopelessly confused, Homer remarked, "TV said *that?*" and shook his head in utter confusion, effectively acknowledging that he could not compete with the perceived intelligence of television. This satirical line truly demonstrates the impact of television as a conveyor of information to the American public. While Homer will believe anything he hears on television, the message subtly hints that intellectual members of American democracy should not be easily influenced by everything that they hear on television. However, the viewing of attractive newscasters and the use of persuasive tones of voice often do have an impact on the minds of many intelligent members of American society.

This lesson was reinforced in the episode "Girly Edition." In the episode, Bart and Lisa coanchor the *Kidz News* television news program. Bart's sentimental segment titled "Bart's People," relies on inciting people's emotions. Lisa correctly refers to Bart's stories as "drivel"—partly because no real news is actually reported and partly because many of the stories themselves are semifabricated concoctions if not outright lies. Television viewers should be aware of the fact that news programs rely heavily on ratings, and sometimes use gimmicky tactics in order to attract viewers. Ideally, viewers should possess some knowledge of the news before watching television. The alternative is to allow television to fill people's blank slates with stories that may be derived and produced by gimmicky tricks. *The Simpsons* has actually shown some examples of these gimmicks: newscasters posing an absurd and misleading question, only to answer their own question with the response viewers knew before watching the show. My example: "Can blue mattresses cause cancer? Find out at 11." Viewers then must wait until the end of the newscast to hear a reinforcement of their previously held belief: "Of course not."

Media Distortion and "Homer: Badman"

The idea that we should not be completely influenced by what we hear on television was more deeply examined in *The Simpsons* episode entitled "Homer: Badman." In the episode, Homer is falsely accused of sexual harassment, and, in an attempt to sway public opinion to his side, decides to appear on television to tell his version of the story. He appears on *A Current Affair*-type news program called *Rock Bottom* and gives a recorded on-camera interview. The producer of the show, however, edits Homer's words to make him appear to be a sexual pervert. Not surprisingly, the segment, when aired, influences viewers to believe that Homer was guilty. But more interestingly, Homer, after watching the program air, begins to also believe that he was guilty, lamenting, "Maybe TV is right. TV is always right." Homer is so entranced by television that he even believes in his own guilt, while clearly possessing the knowledge that he is indeed innocent of the charges.

Later in the episode, Lisa provides the voice of reason, noting that "[the media] doesn't care about the truth. All they care about is entertainment." But Lisa fails to convince Homer. At the close of the episode, the following exchange takes place:

> **Homer:** [watching *Rock Bottom*, which accuses Groundskeeper Willie, the man who proved Homer's innocence, of being a criminal] Listen to the music, he's evil!
>
> **Marge:** Hasn't this experience taught you that you can't believe everything you hear?

> **Homer:** Marge, my dear, I haven't learned a thing!
> [He then kisses the television set.]

Obviously, Homer possesses very strong convictions about television's power to serve as an all-knowing source of information. By watching Homer's unhealthy—and perhaps dangerous—devotion to television, we learn that we should enable other mediums to also serve as sources of information in order to get a clearer and more accurate picture of the world.

Despite the advent of different news mediums, the printed word continues to have a strong impact on what news stories are reported to the public. For example, on Sunday mornings, reporters on the television channel NY 1 buy several papers and actually read selections from the papers during their newscast! Since most of the news reported to the public is thoroughly researched by journalists and newspaper reporters, newspapers continue to serve as the cornerstone of information and news.

In contemporary society, the public does not take a monolithic approach to understanding and interpreting politics in the news. We are fortunate enough to be living in the Information Age and thus have many opportunities to gather news from various sources. The public has the ability to compare and contrast news from several sources, and then, after reviewing information from all of the sources, formulate informed opinions pertaining to various ideas discussed in the media. While television and the Internet seem to be the wave of the future in terms of news coverage, the public must realize the important contributions of the printed media—both in the Typographic Age as well as in contemporary society.

The Simpsons and the Television Medium

The Simpsons is unique in the sense that it was one of the first television programs to show family members watching television. As noted by David Grote, "one could watch years of families at home in sitcoms and never see them do the one thing that almost every family does at home—watch television." The Simpson family, like most families in contemporary society, love to watch television. But they do on occasion make jabs at their favorite medium.

In "I Married Marge," for example, Lisa engages in the following conversation with Homer:

Lisa: It's not our fault our generation has short attention spans, Dad. We watch an appalling amount of TV.

Homer: Don't you EVER talk that way about television.

Here, Homer and Lisa discuss one of the perceived negative impacts of television on its audience: the reduction of the collective attention span of the American public. In "Homer's Barbershop Quartet," Bart similarly discusses the aforementioned perceived negative impact of television:

> **Bart:** Dad, when did you record an album?
> **Homer:** I'm surprised you don't remember, son. It was only eight years ago.
> **Bart:** Dad, thanks to television, I can't remember what happened eight minutes ago.
> [Everyone laughs uproariously except Bart]
> No, really, I can't! It's a serious problem.
> [Everyone laughs again, and Bart finally relents and laughs too]
> What are we all laughing about?
> **Homer:** [joyously] Who cares? Anyways . . .

Still, this does not necessarily mean, as Lisa notes, that television has shortened our attention spans. In fact, as Steven Johnson argues, television (along with other popular media such as video games and films) has strengthened certain human cognitive abilities. Modern television audiences, Johnson notes, crave television shows like *24*, where viewers must engage in remembering complex relationships between the characters as well as multiple plot lines all within a single episode. For viewers to truly grasp the plot lines and content of soap operas and complex shows like *24*, they must possess relatively large attention spans. Homer's defense of television, therefore is not without warrant.

In an age where television airs questionable content and supposedly reduces attention spans, the generation raised on such programming has seen an increase in IQ scores and overall intelligence. In rare instances like these, *The Simpsons* produces messages that are questionable: certainly television is not all that bad. But then again, the writers of *The Simpsons* are almost certainly well aware of that.

Selling the Three-Eyed Fish: Modern Shifts in Political Discourse

"In America, the fundamental metaphor for political discourse is the television commercial."
~ Neil Postman, *Reach Out and Elect Someone*

"Vote Quimby. If you were running for mayor, he'd vote for you."
~ Campaign slogan used on Mayor Quimby's reelection campaign commercial

The political television commercial is the symbol of political discourse in the twenty-first century. The pervasiveness of the television medium enables political commercials to reach a large number of potential voters. For example, Neil Postman notes that, "an American who has reached the age of forty will have seen well over one million commercials in his or her lifetime and has close to another million to go before the first Social Security check arrives." Since politicians are well aware of the fact that Americans are constantly inundated with commercials, they continue to flood the airwaves with commercials in support of their political campaigns. In an age dominated by visual media, candidates often utilize the insuperable power of television to achieve their personal political goals. The purpose of political commercials is to *sell* a particular candidate. The role of the politician is to make his audience *believe* he is qualified. In fact, more emphasis is placed on whether a politician appears to be qualified than whether or not he does indeed possess the necessary skills for office. As Postman notes, "what the [political] advertiser needs to know is not what is right about the product, but what is wrong about the buyer." Instead of stressing political issues, campaign advertisers attempt to find *weaknesses* in the general voting public to secure votes.

Furthermore, Postman correctly states that on television, "the politician does not so much offer the audience an image of himself, as offer himself as an image of the audience." Mr. Burns is well aware of the importance of this idea. As noted, the episode "Two Cars in Every Garage and Three Eyes on Every Fish," focuses on the evil Mr. Burns and his decision to run for governor. Burns's political campaign staff warns him that early polls dictate that "98 percent of the voters rate you as despicable or worse." Voters—at least initially—knew the *real* Mr. Burns: a cold, heartless, greedy, selfish, mogul. The real Mr. Burns is so cold that he has trouble smiling. But after a good deal of media image tweaking, Burns's staff is able to convince almost a majority of voters that Burns is "imperial and Godlike."

But Burns needs to take his campaign to the next level. His advisors suggest that he have a televised sit-down dinner with one of his employees and his family. The employee, befittingly, turns out to be Homer, and Burns understands the power of the message that such a dinner will send, noting that "Every Joe Meatball and Sally Housecoat in this Godforsaken state will see me hunkering down for chow with Eddie Punchclock. The media will have a field day." Though more appropriately classified as a contrived media photo opportunity than an actual political commercial in the technical sense, the goal of Burns's campaign strategy team is the same: trick the voters into believing that Burns relates well to the average man. Burns desperately wants to identify with the voting public—without doing so, he will have no chance of winning the election. In fact, the dinner turns out to be a complete disaster, with Burns spitting out a piece of the three-eyed fish mutated by his own power plant and served by Marge for dinner. Luckily for the residents of Springfield, Burns fails to win the election. Mr. Burns shows us that politicians have come to realize that they can only sell themselves to potential voters if they appear to possess similar desires as those of the voters. Thus, a good political commercial offers the voting public a portrayal of a candidate as simply an *extension* of the average American voter.

Tricks of the Trade: Corrupt Quimbys and Other Political Gimmicks

Postman argues that the development of the political television commercial was an inevitable extension of the television medium. The very nature of a visual medium such as television provides viewers with images that in turn engender a strong emotional response. Indeed, political commercials adhere to the adage that a picture says a thousand words. For example, political commercials often show the opposing candidate in a gray-colored visual framework, while the "good" candidate is shown in full color (often smiling). Postman's remark that "drama is…preferred over exposition" is certainly true in the televised political sphere. Sixty-second political commercials almost invariably portray one candidate as the "good guy who works hard for the people" and his opponent as "the evil, corrupt politician." Political advertisers and strategists are well in tune with the fact that Americans enjoy competition. In addition, they are aware that human nature dictates that we often choose our "heroes" based on their good deeds and determine our enemies by means of an analysis of their misdeeds.

Some political commercials that are shorter in length (those that are less than sixty seconds each) often do not have the time to portray one candidate as "good" and the other candidate as "evil." Instead, many political commercials tend to solely portray the opposing candidate as evil and corrupt. Evidently, political television commercials foster the idea of voting for one candidate by default. In other words, the goal of many marketers is often to knock out one candidate without even considering the ideas of the candidate they are attempting to sell to the voting public.

The issue of dissuading voters from voting for a particular candidate was examined (and satirized) on "Sideshow Bob Roberts." In the episode, a political commercial pertaining to the upcoming mayoral election was broadcast on the television in the Simpsons' family home. Sideshow Bob's political commercial went as follows:

"Mayor Quimby supports revolving-door prisons. Mayor Quimby even released Sideshow Bob—a man twice convicted of attempted murder. Can you trust a man like Mayor Quimby? Vote Sideshow Bob for mayor."

The commercial is ironic because Bob argues that Quimby presents a danger to society simply because he allowed Bob out of prison! The marketers had the audacity to admit Bob's serious crimes in order to make Quimby appear even worse.

One fundamental change in political discourse is politicians' perception of the American public. For example, during the Lincoln-Douglas debates, political discourse was based on the belief that the audience was intelligent enough to understand and interpret cogent arguments. Conversely, modern political commercials present an idea to the public in simple terms so as to not confuse or bore the audience. Mr. Burns, in tandem with this modern trend, views the television audience as even dumber and participates in outlandishly contrived political commercials and media events aimed at the American voting public. Postman notes that "today, short and simple messages are preferable to long and complex ones." Indeed, the television medium is unique in that most of its messages are segmented and do not require much rational thought on the part of the viewer.

Disinformation

Postman also introduces the concept of *disinformation*. Disinformation, which in essence provides potential voters with misleading information, differs from *misinformation*, in which information is by all means false. The danger of disinformation as expressed in political television commercials centers on the sad fact that many viewers believe they are receiving concrete, truthful information when they are actually receiving misleading information directly provided by campaign marketers. The *illusion* of possessing knowledge is perhaps the most dangerous component of the political television commercial. As Postman later notes, "TV does not ban books, it simply displaces them." Since television commercials create the illusion that they provide knowledge, people often feel they need not turn any further than television as the source for all their political knowledge. Furthermore, disinformation provides an undeniable threat to democracy: in theory, it is better *not* to vote unless a voter has all the facts straight. Disinformation is perhaps the greatest contributing factor to the establishment of the political television commercial as the most dominant force in modern political discourse. For example, if Americans were simply uninformed, they would have the power to exercise either one of two options: they could either seek more information about campaigns via books or the Internet, or they could not vote altogether. However, since political commercials covertly provide the voting public with disinformation, many, if not most voters are not properly informed as they enter the voting booths.

I'd like to highlight two particularly egregious examples of political disinformation satirized on episodes of *The Simpsons*. In the season three episode entitled "Mr. Lisa Goes to Washington," a photo opportunity featuring corrupt Congressman Bob Arnold and Lisa Simpson is printed in newspapers and effectively wins the hearts of Springfieldians who are unaware, at this point, of Arnold's corrupt actions. (Moe the bartender's reaction to the photo: "Aw, isn't that nice. Now there's a politician who cares.") Photo opportunities serve as a classic form of what I consider a "media distraction." I use this term because photo opportunities are staged in order to portray a politician in a positive light. This helps to gain the trust and loyalty of some voters, who, hood-winked by the appearance of a political photo opportunity, fail to search deeper to find the personality of the politician behind the photo op. And don't think for a moment that Bob Arnold doesn't know the value of a good photo op.

The second example is from the "Two Cars" episode, in which Burns uses the political television commercial to assuage the fears of voters who believe that the power plant is unsafe. In a ridiculously biased and contrived display of political propagan-da, Burns's commercial is set in the 1800s, where Charles Darwin tells viewers that Blinky, the three-eyed fish mutated by the toxic waste from the power plant, is a kind of "super fish" since it pos-sesses three eyes to see. The commercial works well, and the scene cuts to Barney Gumble, who excitedly exclaims, "Wow! Super fish!," and Abraham Simpson, who notes that "Burns is just what this state needs: Young blood!" Barney, Abe, and other vot-ers choose to look no further than their television sets for answers to serious questions. If it is commonly believed that "television never lies," then voters are in for a whirlwind of trouble.

The Effects of the Contemporary Political Television Commercial

In dissecting various components of the political television commercial, it is also vital to note the means by which television presents political commercials. One serious consequence of the political television commercial is that Americans have lost their innate ability to *reflect* on new information. Television, by its very nature, is a fast-paced, segmented, loud medium that does not foster rational thought. Instead, dozens of segmented images flash by the screen in a matter of seconds. Once political marketers reach and alter our inner psychological framework, we have little choice but to follow the emotions engendered by political commercials. Furthermore, even if we do choose to search for more information about candidates, our inner psyche has already been permanently tampered with by the commercials. For example, if a televised political commercial announces that Bush favors tax cuts for the wealthy, we would certainly remember, if not believe, that idea even if we found additional outside sources denouncing the claim.

Another consequence of the rise of political television commercials centers on the fact that many Americans believe politics can be properly discussed on television. In reality, thirty-second commercials are targeted at an audience of potential voters who generally believe much of what they hear on television. Consider the "average" man, namely Homer Simpson, and his adherence to television. If television presents itself as an omnipotent, all-knowing power, all other forms of political discourse—such as debate and print media—are deemed irrelevant. Once again, we can clearly see the adverse effects that a single, dominant medium can have on the American public. The core principle of democracy requires that discourse be developed in different mediums and contexts. Thus, the fact that the political television commercial has become such a dominant force in the media industry threatens our cherished perception of democracy.

If we combine each of the aforementioned aspects of political television commercials, we come to the realization that the commercials are a hindrance to democracy. For example, political commercials tend to undermine the democratic principle of *informed consent*. While voters may believe that they are informed about a particular candidate's election platform, they are actually "disinformed" as a direct result of the disinformation pervasively dispersed in political commercials. Democracy requires voters to possess a tight grasp on campaign issues once they reach the voting booths. However, political commercials tend to concentrate on persuading voters not to vote for a particular candidate—as opposed to openly discussing the issues at hand. If voters often do not give their informed consent pertaining to election platforms at the voting booths, the future of democracy must be placed in question.

The mass media plays a major role in shaping both what people know and the ways in which they think about the world. Television viewers are essentially *consumers* of the news, and because of a recent trend of media consolidation, we have less choice for our collective palates.

Media Consolidation and "Fraudcast News"

In the season fifteen episode "Fraudcast News," Mr. Burns sets out to purchase all of the media outlets in town in order to control the media and use this as a means of enhancing his image. It's not that Burns disagrees with the public's assessment of him—he just doesn't like it: "Well, I'm going to change this town's accurate impression of me," he notes. After quickly dismissing Smithers's suggestion that Burns improve his image by performing "various good deeds," Burns begins amassing a vast media empire, once again insulting the intelligence of the public by referring to them as "hateful morons." Once Burns officially gains ownership of all of the media outlets (with the exception of Lisa's "Red Dress Press"), Smithers helps Burns ameliorate his image by literally tweaking Burns's picture to make his visage appear friendlier. (This picture is juxtaposed with the contrived newspaper headline "Beloved Hero Cheats Death," which refers to Burns's near fatal experience at the beginning of the episode when Geyser Mountain crumbled directly on top of him). In another scene, Burns even uses the characters in the popular children's cartoon series *Itchy and Scratchy* to provide support for nuclear power and the Republican party.

Lisa's paper, the "Red Dress Press," as noted, is the only paper that refuses to be bought by the Burns media empire. Still, her morale is lowered by Burns's complete dominance of the media scene, sadly noting that "one little paper can't make a difference in this world." But, as Homer observes, Lisa's penchant for free thought and independent thinking encourages other residents to publish their own papers. In an episode that parodies the contemporary trend toward consolidation of the media industry, where large media companies purchase small independent presses in order to simultaneously gain both market share and influence, the end result of this episode—the creation of a large number of small, independent presses—would seem to be the perfect rebuttal to the trend of a smaller number of media companies attempting to exert a great deal of influence throughout the world. The episode, however, does not close on precisely this note. The writers decide to take a step back from harshly criticizing the contemporary consolidation of the media, and we see the residents of Springfield publishing their own newspapers replete with inane headlines such as Lenny's "The Truth about Carl: He's Great!" Homer observes the following:

> "See, Lisa, instead of one big shot controlling all of the media, now there's a thousand freaks Xeroxing their worthless opinions."

Upon hearing this, viewers are left to consider whether small independent presses are actually as important as they may at first seem: I certainly would not want to waste my time reading Barney Gumble's uninformed opinions on the war in Iraq. Perhaps, therefore, media consolidation isn't so bad after all:

when Time Warner (which owns CNN) merged with AOL, Internet users were actually exposed to news culled by a number of different sources (CNN, *TIME* magazine), despite the fact that this news was branded under the distinction "AOL News." *The Simpsons* would never go so far as to support the trend of media consolidation, but it does show us that for all the immense disadvantages that media consolidation brings about (biased news feeds, excessive mogul influence), it can also save us the time and energy of finding meaningful news without wasting time reading Captain McCallister's views on abortion. In an ideal world, we would have the time to sift through everyone's views and make educated decisions about pertinent matters. But in a world where time is so key, media consolidation does in fact help us to gain a somewhat educated (though perhaps biased) view of the world without having to sift through thousands of different small newspapers.

But *The Simpsons* is *The Simpsons*, of course, so the episode closes with some self-referential humor aimed squarely at NewsCorp CEO Rupert Murdoch, the owner of the Fox network and *The Simpsons*:

> **Burns:** Well, I guess you can't control all the media. Unless of course you're Rupert Murdoch.
> **Smithers:** [who, along with Burns, looks directly at the television screen] I couldn't agree more.

Here again, we see that media consolidation is—overall—an unfortunate (if not inevitable) trend in contemporary society. Burns and Smithers feel the need to "suck up" to Rupert Murdoch because they are fully aware of the fact that if they were not cartoon characters, but instead real-life sitcom actors, he would be the ones paying their salaries. And thus if they want to keep their jobs, they better play nice.

Always a Television Family

As we've seen in this chapter, *The Simpsons* has explored many of the shifts in political discourse during the Age of Television. And it has been in a unique position to do so. Analyzing the medium while producing and sending its messages through the very medium which it critiques, positions *The Simpsons* to provide a unique perspective on modern shifts in political discourse—from political television commercials to media consolidation to the effects of television viewership in general. As the Age of Television continues to dominate, we can only imagine what *The Simpsons* will have to say next.

The Simpsons and American Exceptionalism

"I do not want to end up with an American style of politics with us all going out there beating our chest about our faith." ~ British Prime Minister Tony Blair

This chapter will explore the concept of American exceptionalism and its manifestations in contemporary society. *The Simpsons*, along with other television shows such as *Perfect Strangers*, *Gilligan's Island*, and *Family Guy* have addressed the issue of exceptionalism. By analyzing the roots of this concept in the Classical Greek tradition and highlighting the ways in which the issue is portrayed in the mass media, we can analyze the ways in which exceptionalism pervades facets of contemporary society.

The Concept of American Exceptionalism

American Exceptionalism is the idea that America is a special nation that is uniquely positioned to exert great influence throughout the world. Exceptionalism is tied directly to the idea that America has a special mission to promote its ideals abroad. Proponents of such a view argue that Americans are a chosen people whose mission it is to hold up the torch of democracy for the world to see. Also related to the concept of exceptionalism is the idea that a particular group of people can be deemed superior to other groups of people. This partially serves to explain why the American mission to spread democracy is often viewed by critics of American foreign policy as an example of arrogance and hypocrisy.

The idea of "Exceptionalism," or that one people is superior to all others, has its roots at least as far back as ancient Greece. In Homer's *Odyssey*, for example, the voyager Odysseus comes across several groups of people who he deems inferior, including the Lotus Eaters and the one-eyed Cyclopes. He reasons that since these outsiders have roots in traditions dissimilar to the superior Greek tradition. Odysseus notes the following upon encountering the Cyclopes:

"We sailed hence, always in much distress, till we came to the land of the lawless and inhuman Cyclopes. Now the Cyclopes neither plant nor plough, but trust in providence, and live on such wheat, barley, and grapes as grow wild without any kind of tillage, and their wild grapes yield them wine as the sun and the rain may grow them. They have no laws nor assemblies of the people, but live in caves on the tops of high mountains; each is lord and master in his family, and they take no account of their neighbors…

"For the Cyclopes have no ships, nor yet shipwrights who could make ships for them; they cannot therefore go from city to city, or sail over the sea to one another's country as people who have ships can do; if they had had these they would have colonized the island, for it is a very good one, and would yield everything in due season."

By deeming the Cyclopes "lawless" and "inhuman," Odysseus expresses his belief that his culture is superior to that of the Cyclopes. In citing the evidence for a lack of ships among the Cyclopes, Odysseus implies that the Greek practice of using ships for various purposes was a fundamental component of any legitimate civilization.

Greek exceptionalism was not limited to Homer's works, however. In Thucydides' *History of the Peloponnesian War*, Pericles delivers a funeral oration in which he praises Athens and asserts that the city-state serves as a role model for others to follow. Athens, according to Pericles, served as the ultimate standard to which other city-states should be compared. Pericles notes the following, for example, in regards to the Athenian form of government: "Our form of government does not enter into rivalry with the institutions of others. Our government does not copy our neighbors but is an example to them."

The idea of Exceptionalism, however, is not as pervasive a concept as it may seem given the above evidence. In *The Histories*, the ancient Greek writer Herodotus travels to Egypt and writes appreciatively of Egyptian customs. He asserts that certain traditions and customs are even better than Greek customs. Herodotus, in praising the customs and traditions of another people, was the exception to the generally accepted notion that "my culture is better than your culture." Still, it is interesting to note that such exceptions do indeed exist. While there is certainly a precedent for the creation of American Exceptionalism, the development of such a notion should not be regarded as an inevitable consequence of the immense power that the United States possesses. By analyzing specific episodes of *The Simpsons*, and the words of Homer Simpson, we can gain insight into both the concept of Exceptionalism and the way that the rest of the world views America.

Homer Simpson: Exceptional American
"You [Homer] are the greatest hero in American history."
~ Lionel Hutz

Homer Simpson is, in certain ways, the quintessential American male. He represents the elements of American culture that merit both praise and criticism. It's understandable, then, that we, as Americans, can relate to Homer. His actions and mindset incorporate the elements of our collective culture that make us truly American. Homer is not CNN, nor is he the FOX News channel. He's not Al Franken, nor is he Rush Limbaugh. Perhaps these observations serve to partially explain why non-Americans look toward Homer for keen, unfettered insight into all aspects of American culture.

But still, there is something about Homer that could potentially perturb peoples of other cultures worldwide. Despite Homer's honesty about what it means to be an all-American male, he tends to criticize peoples of other cultures. For example, upon learning that he would be taking his family to Canada for a brief stay, he famously remarked, "Why should I leave America to visit America Jr.?"

This is but one example of Homer's political incorrectness that makes him so accessible and beloved by Americans. Whether we would like to admit it or not, the collective American psyche is embedded with a covert sense of superiority. We prefer to keep this superiority complex tucked down beneath a false exterior by constantly uttering phrases and statements that reflect a misleading sense of political correctness. Homer undoubtedly places his country on a pedestal when comparing his homeland to that of others. Whether he is poking fun at the English Royal Guard, checking the direction in which the toilet water flows in Australia (the hotel, as we shall discuss further toward the end of this chapter, reversed the flow to make it go the "*correct* American way"— Homer's response: a teary-eyed partial rendition of "My Country 'Tis of Thee"), telling Apu that when "they were handing out religions you must have been out taking a whiz," asking an Italian woman why she wouldn't learn his language (he had, of course, learned to eat their food), or demanding that those that dissent with his opinions to "go back to Russia," Homer shows us that he consistently values his culture over that of others.

All of the above examples of Homer's political incorrectness on *The Simpsons* provide insight into the way that the rest of the world views America. Homer's comments about other peoples, cultures, and religions translate into a broad sense of arrogance towards others. And because everything else about Homer's character is designed to supposedly encompass the ideas and desires of the "average" American, his views pertaining to other cultures are often taken to be representative of how most Americans view the rest of the world. It is no secret that the rest of the world views America as arrogant for the reasons cited above, but few domestically-produced television shows have chosen to highlight this fact.

American Exceptionalism and "Homer's Enemy"

So Homer views America as exceptional. And why shouldn't he? As pointedly noted by Frank Grimes in the season eight episode "Homer's Enemy," Homer enjoys a life that he could lead in no other country. The lessons learned about Homer in this episode teach us valuable lessons about what is both right and wrong about America and how the rest of the world views it.

In *On Paradise Drive: How We Live Now (And Always Have) in the Future Tense*, David Brooks presents us with a dichotomy that exists between two competing types of people in contemporary American society: the blonds and the brunettes. Emphasizing that this distinction is not based in any way upon hair color (there are smart, reflective blond-haired persons, vapid brunettes, and vice versa, of course), Brooks notes that the vapid person—the blond—never becomes aware of his shortcomings because he is promoted and treated like royalty by his peers and superiors. In many cases, for whatever reason, the blond person is the "One Who Is Chosen." He is essentially the "zero-gravity hero." "Vapidity," Brooks asserts, "is the one character flaw that comes with its own missile defense system." "It has never occurred [to this person] that he is not the richest, the fullest, the deepest emblem of human accomplishment and worthiness. His con-science, like everything else about him, is clean." This frustrates the brunette, who works hard for what he has, lives a life of reflection, and is more qualified than the blond at all worthy tasks. The blond person breezes through life and uses his missile defense system to brush off any of the naysayers (the brunettes) who claim that he does not deserve the life that he enjoys. "This phenomenon," Brooks notes, "represents a gaping flaw in the structure of the universe." And, of course, in Springfield.

Okay, now take a guess—is Homer Simpson the blond bimbo who coasts through life or is he the smart, reflective brunette who believes that the examined life is the only kind worth living? Enter Frank Grimes—professional brunette, a man who works hard for the little that he has and is frustrated with the fact that nobody else seems to realize that Homer is the ultimate bimbo.

Homer Simpson is a fat, bald, lazy, dumb, crude individual who is able to successfully support a family, own a beautiful home, have a job in which he is "dangerously unqualified" to hold, and, in this particular episode, eat lobster for dinner. Frank Grimes, on the other hand, is a single, hardworking American intellectual, and, if you think about it, of a rare breed. In the episode, Grimes enters the Simpson home only to be stunned by the extravagant lifestyles that Homer and his family lead: Bart happens to have purchased a factory at an auction house (for $1), and Marge is cooking lobster for dinner. All of this, of course, on top of the fact that the Simpsons live in a beautiful home ("a palace," according to Grimes). Homer goes on to show pictures of himself in outer space and with the Smashing Pumpkins, a photo of Homer meeting President Gerald Ford, and his Grammy award. Grimes is perturbed by the fact that Homer gets by so easy in life, while he has to struggle to survive (he notes that he lives in a single-room apartment "above a bowling alley and below another bowling alley"). Grimes sums up his frustrations and jealousies, while criticizing Homer for his laziness:

> **Grimes:** I'm saying you're what's wrong with America, Simpson. You coast through life, you do as little as possible, and you leech off of decent, hardworking people like me. Heh, if you lived in any other country in the world, you'd have starved to death long ago.
> **Bart:** He's got you there, dad.
> **Grimes:** You're a fraud. A total fraud. [he leaves]

Grimes unabashedly points out that Homer deserves none of what he has in this life. It's pretty difficult to argue with most of "Grimey's" accusations. He correctly argues that Homer represents a lot of what is inherently wrong with America. Now, Frank Grimes is indeed an American, but his constant struggles through life coupled with his incredible work ethic mirror the lives of only a small segment of people in American society. On a grander scale, Grimes represents all of those people—both foreigners and those supposedly hurt by perceived social injustices of the United States—that are not as fortunate as all of the Homer Simpsons out there in mainstream, middle-class America. "Homer's Enemy" shows us that Homer is a really lucky guy.

It also shows us, however, that there are other people in the world who cannot afford to live the lifestyle of Homer Simpson. As some cultural critics point out, it is the tendency of Americans to ignore the fact that we lead such wealthy lifestyles that helps to engender the misguided notion that Americans are selfish and inconsiderate of others. If Homer had listened to Marge's words of wisdom (she explained that Grimes was frustrated with Homer because Homer had been given a better hand at life) then perhaps he would have been more sympathetic to the needs of those less fortunate than himself. Homer, being Homer, misinterprets Marge's words, of course, and decides that Grimes' real problem is that he is a "crazy nut." But here is where Homer gets it wrong. Homer, rather than Grimes, is the inconsiderate one: Grimes shows Homer that he lives a life of luxury, and Homer fails to consider that there are billions of people living in the world that are less well-off than him. Homer may not realize it, but he does indeed view himself as exceptional. His upbringing has ingrained in him the belief that, as a middle-class citizen of America, he has certain expectations and entitlements that other people do not have.

This is not Homer's fault of course; he was born in a country of surplus, raised in a middle-class family, met the woman of his dreams while enrolled in high school, holds a relatively high-paying job for a position in which he is deemed unqualified and, through all of this, never had to truly struggle just to get by. Meeting Frank Grimes should have been an enlightening experience for Homer, had he considered any of the above. But, alas, Homer is so inconsiderate of Grimes that he falls asleep during Grimes' funeral at the end of the episode.

"Homer's Enemy" is an immensely important episode in the series' run because it shows us that for all of *The Simpsons'* criticisms of foreign nations and cultures, sharp criticism of American culture itself is not off limits. Indeed, *The Simpsons* has built its reputation on critiquing elements of American society. But this episode breaks a previously insuperable threshold in the sense that Grimes criticizes American life in *general*. This is quite different, from say, critiquing singular aspects of American culture, such as America's obsession with celebrities or our fascination with consumer goods. The power of Grimes' statement that Homer represents everything that is wrong with America comes from the inherent broadness of the assertion. Grimes is not simply critiquing a part of what it means to be a contemporary American; rather, the generality of his statement forces us to briefly review *everything* we know about Homer, and, in turn, to consider the possibility that everything about the average American makes America a less-than-perfect place. Whether it is Homer's lack of a work ethic, his laziness, his girth, his stupidity, his insensitivity, or his brashness, we are left to ponder all of the ways that Homer could potentially ameliorate virtually every aspect of his character. Because Homer, as noted, is intended to represent the average American, viewers are left to consider that they, too, may be part of "what is wrong with America."

As Americans, Grimes' words, when taken to heart, are extremely difficult to swallow. Certainly, his frustration with his own life leads him to overstate his case that people like Homer are the sole cause of his misery. It may be correctly noted that Homer represents not what we *are*, but what we wish *not* to become. All of this may help Americans to soften the blow of Grimes' words. But ardent critics of America will continue to view Homer as a more-or-less realistic depiction of the quintessential American male, rather than what Homer Simpson truly is: a fictional character comprised to intentionally display all of the flaws that we as Americans work so hard to prevent from being attributed to ourselves. By criticizing everything that Homer Simpson represents, Grimes, in this light, serves as the spokesperson for all of those who hate America.

In the end, the ultimate reason why foreigners love Homer Simpson (as previously noted, he was rated as the "greatest American of all-time" in a 2003 BBC poll) is that he is readily willing to critique aspects of the culture in which he is a part—despite holding onto his belief that America is an exceptional place. But he does so honestly—just as he critiques other cultures in such a manner. Sure, he'll get into trouble for either being too enthnocentric at times or too critical of foreign cultures at others (Brazil threatened to sue over one episode), but in the end Homer is honest about what it means to be an American, and conversely, how he—and other Americans for that matter—define what it means to be a non-American.

So it comes down to this: everyone can love Homer Simpson for a plethora of reasons. Dictators can find solace in Homer's (comical) assertion that "democracy doesn't work," while Americans can see in Homer a realistic (though satirized) notion of American culture at work. For Americans, Homer allows us to be honest with ourselves. He shows us that it is possible to be both ethnocentric (again, this is not necessarily a negative thing) and highly critical of some our most cherished values. Being a true American requires us to think about who and what we are as a collective people and to also think about what it means to be a non-American. Homer's brain, in this instance, allows us to think about these things a little more closely.

Other *Simpsons* episodes have similarly addressed the concept of American Exceptionalism. One technique utilized by the writers to explore this topic has been to place the Simpson family in international settings. The episode in which the Simpson family visits Australia serves as a prime example of this.

"Bart vs. Australia"

In the controversial season six *Simpsons* episode entitled "Bart vs. Australia," the Simpson family visits Australia and is told that the toilet in their hotel room had been installed to combat homesickness for their American guests. The water in the toilets, the Simpsons are told, had been adjusted to spin the "correct" American way. The assumption here, of course, is that the toilet water in America spins the *right* way, and that the water in the Southern Hemisphere, spins the *wrong* way. Forget any notion of "different but equal." No, here America is portrayed as *exceptional*—a land where everything we do, have, or think is better than anything else taking place elsewhere. Because the water spins a certain way in America, it is assumed that this must be the proper way for it to spin.

Another key example of American Exceptionalism occurs in the same episode when Homer criticizes the practice of corporal punishment in Australia. When an Australian judge decrees that Bart's punishment is to be kicked with a boot, Homer quickly denounces the practice of corporal punishment:

When will you Australians learn? In America, we stopped using corporal punishment, and things have never been better! The streets are safe. Old people strut confidently through the darkest alleys. And the weak and nerdy are admired for their computer-programming abilities. So, like us, let your children run wild and free because, as the old saying goes, "Let your children run wild and free."

One can easily argue that Homer's words are intended as a satire on America, and that perhaps we should treat criminals in a different manner. But I would like to address this quote in a different manner. Homer's insistence that America's practices in terms of dealing with criminals are superior to Australia's provides a second example of American Exceptionalism seen in this episode. Homer harshly criticizes the practice of booting in Australia: "What kind of a sick country would kick someone with a giant boot?" According to Homer, America's practices are better because America itself is supposedly culturally superior to Australia.

The dialogue's focus on punishment is interesting to consider in terms of what the scene also says about exceptionalism. It is interesting to point out that in this scene, we see foreigners attempting to impose their own laws on Americans, despite Homer's objections to Australian methods of punishments. On the one hand, we see Homer attempting to impose the American viewpoint in Australia; on the other side of the debate, we see the Australian court attempting to enforce their brand of punishment on Bart. Both parties view their own ideas as exceptional, and both fail to make real attempts at coming to a compromise that would satisfy each culture.

Debates in terms of jurisdictional distinctions for punishment occur in contemporary society as well. The International Criminal Court was established in 2002 for the purpose of creating binding international law and punishments for prosecuting those accused to have committed "genocide, war crimes, and crimes against humanity." Fearful of prosecution of Nationals who have allegedly committed "war crimes," the United States has undertaken measures intended to exempt certain individuals from what it charges is unwarranted prosecution. Because of the conflicting cultures and modes of punishment between the international community and the United States, such actions on the part of the United States were necessary to give it the power to continue some of its activities and engagements throughout the world. The International Criminal Court has stirred so much controversy for precisely the same reason that Bart's punishment aggravated Homer: different cultures have differing standards and modes of punishment for crimes.

Other examples of American Exceptionalism can also be found within "Bart vs. Australia." At one point, the Simpson family is told that "during the 1980s, the U.S. experienced a short-lived infatuation with Australian culture," and that this "down-under fad fizzled." It is assumed that the fad fizzled, of course, because Americans supposedly realized that Western culture is so superior to that of Australia that we have no need to incorporate their culture into ours.

Not Just The Simpsons

Examples of American Exceptionalism parodied in elements of popular culture are not limited to *The Simpsons*. In the children's movie *Finding Nemo*, for example, a frustrated shark engages in the following discussion with a fish:

> **Shark:** Humans, they think they own everything.
> **Fish:** Probably Americans.

Blaming humans for their troubles wasn't specific enough for these oceanic creatures, so they decide to single out Americans as the cause of their problems. As evidenced by the above, discourses on the concept of American Exceptionalism often can be found in some unexpected places.

Paul Cantor, for example, makes the prudent point that the television sitcom *Gilligan's Island* promotes the notion of American superiority. This can be seen, he notes, in the castaways' reaction to and treatment of island natives and foreigners who had found their way onto the island. Cantor also notes that the castaways establish a democratic way of life on the island, while striking down any notion of an inherent right to rule by the Skipper (military might), the Professor (wisdom), or the Millionaire (wealth), thereby reinforcing the superiority of the American form of governance over those used by authoritarian governments or totalitarian dictatorships. In addition to the ideas expressed in *Gilligan's Island*, the concept of American Exceptionalism is visible in the sitcom *Perfect Strangers*.

The ABC sitcom *Perfect Strangers* was one of the funniest shows on television at the time it was aired during the TGIF lineup on Friday nights from 1986–1993. The premise of the show was the interaction between two extremely distant cousins, Balki Bartokomous, who hailed from the fictional island-nation Mypos, and Larry Appleton who was raised in Wisconsin and lived in Chicago. Balki moves into Larry's apartment, and the cousins become best friends and go on a number of fun and crazy adventures together. Aside from being enormously hysterical and well-written, the show's appeal was based on the cultural interaction between two people hailing from entirely different worlds. *Perfect Strangers* is a sitcom that examined how persons of different cultures interact and relate to one another.

In many episodes, the show's premises centered on Balki's curiosity about American customs and his desire to become Americanized. Larry taught Balki a lot about America, providing guidance about everything from the stock market to purchasing a used car. In an episode that aired during the fourth season, Larry attempts to teach Balki how to bowl. At the bowling alley, the cousins engage in the following conversation:

> **Balki:** [upon watching Larry roll the ball down the lane] Cousin, you know what? This is just like "Knock-knock roll-a-rock"!
> **Larry:** [quizzically and slightly mockingly] "Knock-knock roll-a-rock"?
> **Balki:** Exactly! It's the Myposian game the whole family can play!
> Later in the conversation, Larry is condescending and tells Balki the following:
> "I'm sure 'knock-knock roll-a-rock' is a real challenge in Mypos, but in America, where we've already gone through the Industrial Revolution, sports are a bit more sophisticated."

Larry declares that American bowling is superior to the Myposian game of "knock-knock roll-a-rock," despite never actually being exposed to the game. This particular theme is a central aspect of the show: America is portrayed as superior in every way to the "backward" island of Mypos, where sheep herding is the chief occupation. (Balki even refers to himself as a simple sheep-herder from Mypos.) It is true that Larry ends up learning certain customs and traditions from Balki that he does enjoy: the "Dance of Joy" is enjoyed by both of the cousins. The underlying point that the show makes, however, is that America is a complex and sophisticated place while other lands are undoubtedly inferior.

This classic example of American Exceptionalism, however, is qualified by another perennial theme of the show: Larry's character flaws. Despite the fact that Larry knows more about America than Balki, his greed and poor judgment often gets Larry into trouble. Balki, who is depicted as simple but morally flawless is actually the one that guides Larry in the right direction most of the time. The fact that Larry teaches Balki about America and our "better" customs and traditions is underscored each time that Balki teaches Larry how to be a better human being. Balki might be a simple Mypiot boy, but he is the exceptional human being, not Larry. We learn that Americans practice more deceit than Myposians, as Larry's depiction as a lying, conniving person controlled by greedy ambition serves to cast American culture as less morally sound than Myposian culture. Balki tries to adjust to America, but he is so moral and just that he simply does not fit in here. In this latter sense, *Perfect Strangers* can be seen as reaffirming Herodotus' idea that aspects of foreign cultures can be superior to those of one's own. Larry learns a lot of lessons from the simple Mypiot boy and becomes a better person in the process of befriending Balki.

Because the writers of *Perfect Strangers* decided to have Balki hail from the fictional island Mypos, they were able to constantly poke fun at Myposian customs and traditions. The writers were thus able to portray Mypos as a backward island without offending any particular culture. I argue, here, however, that American Exceptionalism was nonetheless displayed here: In terms of ethnocentrism, Myposian culture can serve as a stand-in for the generic foreign culture when compared with American culture.

Dozens of additional examples of the concept of Exceptionalism can be found throughout the *Perfect Strangers* television series. In one particular episode, for example, Balki attempts to teach Larry something about love in Myposian culture:

> **Balki:** On Mypos, the size of a man's love is determined by the size of the goat he gives his beloved. Big goat equals lots of love. Little goat equals "that's all she wrote."
> **Larry's sarcastic response:** Fascinating culture.

As we can see, Larry often fails to give due respect to his cousin's culture.

In a season three episode, Balki and Larry engage in the following conversation towards the end of the episode:

> **Balki:** I was just trying to follow my Myposian proverb.
> **Larry:** Well, Balki, nobody enjoys a good Myposian proverb more than I do [he is interrupted by the laugh track], but life is a little more complicated in America. You may have to adjust your proverbs.
> **Balki:** Well, I guess I could use some fine-tuning. You know, on Mypos, when you say you have to talk "right now," it's not so much of a problem because there is nothing else to do.

So Larry essentially convinces Balki that American life is more "complicated" and that respected Myposian proverbs don't really have a place in Chicago. Is Larry actually asserting that the "complicated" American life is better than life in Mypos? This point is further outlined in another episode, in which Larry condescendingly asks Balki, "Don't they have anything else on Mypos other than sheep?" And in another episode, Larry is even more blunt, telling a woman that "You'll have to excuse [Balki]. He comes from a very small island with a defective gene pool." The universal sitcom laugh track follows Larry's one-liner, but the point that he makes here is a quite serious one. Because Mypos is a "simple" island, and because its people (Balki is a case in point) are unfamiliar with American customs, Larry sarcastically intones that there must be something inherently wrong with the backward Myposian people. The line is funny, of course, since Mypos is not a real island, but if we use Mypos as a stand in for another nation, we find Larry's harsh charges not only unfunny but also considerably more dangerous.

Being Abroad and "The Crepes of Wrath"

The Simpsons also explored the concept of Exceptionalism during its first season. In "The Crepes of Wrath," the Simpson family participates in the student foreign exchange program, sending Bart to France to live with two Frenchmen, in exchange for allowing an Albanian boy, Adil Hoxha, to come to live with the rest of the family in Springfield. Upon Adil's arrival at Springfield Elementary, Principal Skinner feels that it is appropriate to formally introduce Adil to the rest of the students. He tells the students the following:

> "You may find his accent peculiar. Certain aspects of his culture may seem absurd, perhaps even offensive. But I urge you to give little Adil the benefit of the doubt. In this way, and only in this way, can we hope to better our backward neighbors throughout the world."

Certainly, one can argue, as Cantor notes, that the quote does provide at least some evidence that Skinner is interested in learning more about different cultures. Still, what gives this quote its main thrust is the word "backward." Once again, viewers are exposed to another classic example of American Exceptionalism. Sure, Skinner deserves some credit for at least acknowledging that other cultures exist and play some role in the world (as discussed previously, this is obviously more than we can say for Bart and Homer). But by referring to Albanians as "backward neighbors," Skinner proclaims that America is superior—intellectually, culturally, and technologically—to Albania. Skinner is an educator, so he does understand the value of learning more about the world around him. But here he is also portrayed as ethnocentric, denouncing other cultures when compared from an American cultural perspective.

In another scene from this episode, Lisa tells Homer about Albania's unit of currency and the colors that comprise the nation's national flag. Homer laughs out loud, denouncing both the Albanian flag and unit of currency. He also strongly suggests that America is superior: "give me the old stars and stripes," he intones.

By far, the most interesting discourse presented in this episode comes at the Simpson family dinner table. Lisa and Adil engage in the following heated debate about their respective countries:

> **Adil:** How can you defend a country where five percent of the people control 95 percent of the wealth?
> **Lisa:** I'm defending a country whose people can think and act and worship any way they want!

The conversation represents the strong ideological conflicts existing between the two countries—put more broadly, between capitalism and communism. What is even more interesting, however, is Homer's attempt to quell the dispute: "Please, please, kids, stop fighting. Maybe Lisa's right about America being the land of opportunity and maybe Adil has a point about the machinery of capitalism being oiled with the blood of the workers." In classic Simpsonian fashion, Homer finds flaws in both ideologies, siding entirely with neither and subverting *everything*. The message here is that no man-made ideology is perfect, and that every system we create is inherently flawed—though perhaps some more flawed than others.

What Bart Has to Say

Bart Simpson's failure to recognize that countries in the Southern Hemisphere even *exist* was made apparent in an episode of *The Simpsons*. While debating the direction of the spin of water in the United States in "Bart vs. Australia," Bart engages in the following conversation with Lisa:

> **Lisa:** Bart, water will only go the other way in the Southern hemisphere.
> **Bart:** What the hell is the "Southern hemisphere"?
> **Lisa:** [sighs] Haven't you ever looked at your globe? [said globe is still wrapped for Bart's birthday from Abe]
> **Lisa:** [pointing] See, the Southern hemisphere is made up of everything below the equa—[stops, sees Bart looking blankly]—this line.
> **Bart:** Hmm. [spins globe] So down there in, say, Argentina, or…[reads logo] Rand McNally, all their water runs backwards?
> **Lisa:** Uh huh. In fact, in Rand McNally, they wear hats on their feet and hamburgers eat people.
> **Bart:** Cool!

Several key points come to mind when analyzing the above discussion. Firstly, Bart is used here to represent the idea that Americans are ethnocentric. The idea here is not simply that Bart is too dumb to realize that the Northern Hemisphere doesn't constitute the entire earth. Instead, the message is more disturbing: Bart's ignorance with regard to the world around him is intended to demonstrate that Americans are so ingrained with ideas of Western civilization that they tend to disregard the fact that other vibrant cultures exist in the world.

The extent to which this is true, of course, is highly debatable: The United States is an amalgamation of peoples from diverse cultures, and the American identity itself relies on the contributions of peoples hailing from every country in the world. Still, there is something striking about Bart's willingness to believe that people in the Southern hemisphere "wear hats on their feet" and that "hamburgers eat people." To Bart, America represents everything that is normal and distant lands may be as weird as weird gets. This idea leads into the discussion of the "Us" vs. "Them" dichotomy, where Bart views Americans as the "Self" and outsiders as the "Other." Anthropologists argue that ethnocentrism is an inevitable—and not necessarily negative—effect of the development of states. Still, Bart's incredulity with regard to the existence of a Southern hemisphere satirically denotes one of the negative effects of becoming so ingrained in one's own culture that you fail to realize that others even exist.

A prime example of American Exceptionalism may be discovered through an examination of another quote from Bart Simpson. The quote serves to provide clear evidence for Bart's consciousness of his perceived superiority. In the episode "Little Big Mom," Bart asks:

Why would God punish a kid? I mean, an American kid?

For one reason or another, Bart feels that American children are God's favorites. The question posed by Bart Simpson is quite similar to the questions that we asked immediately after September 11th. We had previously seen thousands of children murdered in other nations, yet we suddenly became frightened, questioned our religion, and, for the first time, began to interpret fear as reality once terrorism struck at home. September 11th engendered a new sense of awareness in the hearts and minds of Americans. America may be a rich and powerful country, but it too was shown to be vulnerable to pernicious forces. September 11th, to an extent, humbled Americans and made us more fully aware only of our own vulnerabilities. In doing so, however, we also came to feel a closer connection to other peoples threatened by unthinkable terrorist attacks. Because of our new global "war on terrorism," we feel a closer bond to other nations that are taking on the fight against terrorism as well. September 11th showed us that even Americans could be harmed by terrorist criminals. By forming bonds with other nations afflicted with terrorist threats, we are acknowledging the fact that any nation can be struck by terrorism, and asserting that we will stand side by side in the fight to rid the world of terrorists.

Dissolving the Concept of American Exceptionalism

While much of the concept of American Exceptionalism is based on religious principles—such as the idea that we are a "chosen people"—an important quote from the *Babylonian Talmud* serves to dismiss the merits of the concept. The *Talmud* explicitly states, "Whoever saves a single life…is as if he or she saves the entire world." This religious idea discredits Exceptionalism in the sense that the single life referred to in the quote does not explicitly denote a single American life. According to the *Talmud*, each life is significant, regardless of whether or not the life belongs to that of a chosen person. The *Talmud* supports an egalitarian viewpoint of people of different cultures.

The Simpsons examined the idea of the equality of life between people of all cultures in the episode entitled "Dude, Where's My Ranch?" In the episode, Lisa and Homer approach a sign located on the dude ranch where they are staying. Lisa reads the sign aloud:

> On this spot fifty-six Indians lost their lives and four brave Americans lost their hats.
> **Homer:** Those brave souls. [referring *only* to the Americans]

Much to Lisa's chagrin, Homer views the loss of *American hats* as being more heartwrenching than the loss of lives of non-Americans. We sympathize with Lisa and are frustrated by Homer's words. By satirizing the ways in which a notion of superiority can manifest itself, *The Simpsons* helps to make the point that no culture is truly superior over another. Some of the flaws of American Exceptionalism can be seen when *The Simpsons* looks at the flaws of our society, such as poverty.

The Simpsons and Poverty

"Well, I hope you learned your lesson, Lisa: never help any-one." ~ Homer Simpson

"This is America—justice should favor the rich." ~ Mr. Burns

The Simpsons has explored the issue of poverty in a number of unique and subtle ways. The series has, at times, also examined the topic incidentally while simultaneously discussing other issues. In "Bart's Inner Child," for example, Homer is seen reading a book entitled *Owning Your Okayness*. The title and content of this book are in sharp contrast to the flurry of popular self-help books in contemporary society. Despite Americans' unrelenting and defining desire to improve themselves—financially, spiritually, and cosmetically—the title of Homer's book serves as a reasonable reflection of our contentedness with how our nation treats others less fortunate than ourselves. Critics of American foreign policy argue that when it comes to helping the less fortunate survive, the United States tends to "own its okayness" in the sense that American politicians often contribute little more than the bare minimum in terms of helping others.

Such a sentiment was expressed during President George W. Bush's election platform, in which he declared that Africa was not a main priority of his foreign policy agenda. Critics also heavily criticized Bush for initially pledging to donate only a small sum to the Tsunami relief fund, raising the pledge only when pressured to do so. The United States, critics note, donate only 0.1 percent of the nation's total GDP to foreign aid, the lowest percentage of any contributing industrialized nation. (Supporters of such a decision correctly note that the United States contributes more in real dollars than any other nation).

Critics of the American character in general often argue that Americans are selfish and ignore the basic needs of those less fortunate. Many Africans, they note, subsist on less than $1 a day and lack what we perceive as the bare necessities of life. I believe that such critics are partially correct in their assertion that people's basic needs are often ignored but are misguided in their harsh criticism of the American character. Americans, for example, showed an unprecedented outpouring of support for the victims of the 2004 Tsunami disaster, donating everything from money to books to clothing. This fact at least partially vindicates Americans from the claim that they are selfish.

Another obstacle to giving charity does, however, stand in the way: human beings in general, and Americans in particular, are cursed with a psychological phenomenon I like to call "individual helplessness." This, in essence, is the belief that "one man cannot change the world." When an individual hears about some horrific disaster that requires the use of resources in excess of what he or she is able to reasonably contribute, he often concludes that the problem is too complex to be solved and decides to contribute nothing at all. The reasoning behind the Tsunami donations and mega-charity events like the Jerry Lewis MDA telethon is different, however: Americans literally see or hear about other Americans donating money and thus feel that their contribution can contribute to an overall resolution of a major problem. Collectively, Americans feel as though they can solve such problems. Without widespread support from fellow Americans, however, they know that such problems can never be solved.

Such a sentiment was ironically expressed by Homer in "E-I-E-I—Annoyed Grunt." In this episode, Homer has the opportunity to destroy the world's sole remaining tomacco plant (a combination of tomato and tobacco), thus freeing the world of the plant's evil and potential for disaster. Lisa insists that Homer destroy the plant that he holds in his very hands:

Lisa: You're about to launch a terrible evil on the

world. You've got to destroy this plant.

Homer: I know, honey, but what can I do as an individual? I wouldn't know where to begin.

Lisa: Just burn that plant right now and end this madness.

Homer: I wish I could make a difference, Lisa, but I'm just one man.

Lisa: [growls]

Homer: I agree, but how?

Homer's assertion that he wishes he could make a difference, but that he, as an individual, is not in a position to do so, is a reflection of the principle of "individual helplessness." Imagine for a moment that one hundred tomacco plants existed and that one hundred individuals had possession of the tomacco plants. If each person were to decide to forego potential profit and agreed to destroy his or her own plant, then the dangers that the plant posed would be completely eliminated. But if most of the individuals decided not to destroy the plant, the potential for evil would not be eliminated—or even conspicuously lessened—by the few others destroying their plants. Therefore, it is reasonable to predict that, given a situation in which no individual could know what the other ninety-nine individuals decided to do with the plant and that the desire for profit is assumed to have an influence on people's decision making, at least some of the plants would not be destroyed, and the threat that the plants pose would continue to exist.

This is one argument for the reason that poverty persists in the world: if everyone decided to donate, say, 10 percent of their personal income to charitable causes, the lives of one billion poverty-stricken people would be improved. But since some people will inevitably decide not to give charity, then the problems of the world tend to fall on the shoulders of fewer people. These people, in turn, understandably become overwhelmed, and, perceiving their charitable efforts as inevitably futile, all those but the most tenacious and passionate fail to donate an amount equivalent to what they would have had everyone followed the general standard of a 10 percent donation. Furthermore, those less passionate about the task at hand may question the fairness of sacrificing their own monies when others fail to do so. An individual may want to change the world but almost always lacks the resources and perhaps resolve to make a noticeable impact by himself or herself. Just as destroying one tomacco plant when others continue to exist will not eliminate the threat, neither will donating one's time and money significantly help when others fail to do the same.

I'd like to highlight one other cause of poverty in the world: self-distraction. Poverty and other atrocities are not exactly what we would prefer to spend our time dwelling on. It is more fun to watch a movie than to watch a *Feed the Children* infomercial. Sadly, we often distract ourselves from the real problems in the world and focus on the more mundane aspects of existence. A *Simpsons* episode entitled "*The Simpsons* Spinoff Showcase" highlights this unfortunate phenomenon perfectly. The Simpson family prepares for their "big musical number"—"I Want Candy"— in the following scene:

> **Marge:** Inflation, trade deficits, horrible war atrocities...how are we supposed to do our big musical number with so many problems in the world?
> **Homer:** Well, I know one thing in this world that's still pure and good.
> **Marge:** Christian love?
> **Homer:** No. Candy! [climbs on table] Sweet, sweet, candy!
> [The orchestra strikes up the "I Want Candy" tune.]
> **Homer:** [singing] I want candy!
> **Marge:** But don't you want to end world famine?
> **Bart:** [hops out of the booth] I want candy!

> **Marge:** Or save the endangered Alaskan salmon?
> **Lisa:** I want candy!
> **Marge:** Well if you won't think of society's ills...
> **H + B + L:** [singing] I want candy!
> **Marge:** At least, think of our dentist bills.

Marge, the requisite voice of Simpsonian moral virtue, notes her concerns about the problems afflicting the world. Here, though, the rest of the family seems to care more about candy than ending world famine or saving the endangered Alaskan salmon. But I would argue that such a superficial notion of what is important in the world is *not* representative of how the American public feels about global problems. Americans would care about ending world famine—*if* they took the time to truly contemplate its implications (massive death, hungry children, etc....) Just as we enjoy watching a movie more than watching an infomercial with images of dying children, so too does the Simpson family prefer to sing an upbeat song than concern themselves with all of "society's ills." Distracting ourselves to the problems of the world is an unfortunate tendency; it is, however, part of our nature as human beings.

Therefore, lessons gleaned from *The Simpsons* pertaining to the issues of exceptionalism and poverty serve as lessons in humility and help us to perceive the world on a broader scale. Thankfully, we're light years ahead of Bart and Homer in terms of our awareness of the existence of other vibrant cultures in the world. Still, as *The Simpsons* has shown us, we can enrich our own lives by learning more about other peoples and cultures.

Chapter
13

Industrialization and the Worker: Homer Simpson as the Industrialized Employee

Bart: I'm through with working. Working is for chumps.
Homer: Son, I'm proud of you. I was twice your age before I figured that out.

"I want to share something with you—the three sentences that will get you through life. Number one: 'Cover for me.' Number two: 'Oh, good idea, boss.' Number three: 'It was like that when I got here.'" ~ **Homer Simpson**

Okay, so we all know that Homer Simpson is lazy. But he's not a bum. Homer is the long-time safety inspector at the Springfield Nuclear Power Plant. He is by no means a model employee, but he has held onto his job for a number of years. Throughout the duration of the series, Homer has also held a plethora of other jobs—from bodyguard to boxer to food critic. It might sound a bit strange at first glance, but I would contend that Homer, at times, seems to be motivated to succeed—especially at the jobs that he enjoys the most. In one episode, he starts a Internet business after learning that "they have the Internet on computers now." In another, he becomes the founder and chief of Springshield, a new security force in Springfield. Perhaps the most telling example of Homer's motivation to succeed was examined when he set out to establish himself as a famous inventor a la Thomas Edison. These specific instances demonstrate that Homer possesses some sort of entrepreneurial spirit.

At times like these, we can accurately view Homer as an individual who is searching to become more than the "average" man. He might be dumb, but Homer deserves credit for at least attempting to be creative. The question we may ask is to what degree his job at the nuclear power plant either broadens or stifles his creative spirit.

As will be argued in this chapter, Homer Simpson represents a relatively new type of employee—the industrialized employee—one distinct from the craftsman and the entrepreneur, and one who works for others and takes little or no pride in his work. Homer is certainly not brilliant, but he does feel a sense of pride after he designs his own inventions. This sense of pride is lost in Homer, however, when he punches in for work at the Springfield Nuclear Power Plant. And because of a lack of work ethic, his productivity suffers as well. Believe it or not, Homer Simpson does not put the full range of his talents to best use. And, because of the nature of their jobs, neither do many industrialized employees in contemporary society.

The Industrial Revolution and Alienation from Work

The Industrial Revolution has had a prodigious impact on the worker's way of life. Throughout the course of history, work has played an important role in society. However, the importance of work changed significantly as a direct result of industrialization. A new type of worker was introduced into society, namely, the industrialized employee. In addition, the manner by which work was to be done shifted as a result of new technologies. The characteristics of the factory system have had profound negative effects on the psyche of the worker. Since the origin of mankind, work has held special significance in society. A fundamental reason for performing work has been to sustain a living. Work has often served as a means of acquiring wealth. For example, John Locke states that "the measure of property nature has [been] well set by the extent of men's labor." In this important statement, Locke introduces the Labor Theory of Value, which claims that labor gives people property, and property creates wealth. Thus, it is possible to deduce that labor invariably makes wealth. Since men are driven by self-interest, they often work very hard in order to obtain great wealth.

Understanding the ideals of capitalism is a vital component in a discussion about the impact of alienation in the industrialized workplace. In the *Wealth of Nations*, Adam Smith lays down the fundamental components of capitalism. Capitalists strive to earn profits, as profit determines wealth. Capitalists are often ruthless in their methods of obtaining profits. For example, as a result of the industrialization of America, workers were often exploited so as to procure profits for the capitalist. Thus, the concept of greed is a fundamental aspect of capitalism.

The greediness of corporate executives, such as those in the Enron scandal, as well as factory owners, has had devastating effects on the industrial worker. The Industrial Revolution altered the industrialized worker's perception of work. Indeed, work continues to serve the purpose of sustaining a living, but industrialized workers feel a sense of *alienation* from their work. Alienation results from workers having no ownership of the means of production or ownership of the processes of production.

For example, employees on a factory line do not produce the entire finished product and thus do not feel pride in the completed work. In addition, employees do not reap the fruits of their labor, as they are often paid wages or salaries and thus do not take pride in the finished work.

C. Wright Mills describes a former state of work in which the craftsman produced his own goods, was self-employed, and thus took pride in his work. In fact, Mills cites that from the perspective of the craftsmen, work and play were one and the same. In contrast to this model, the industrialized employee, as a direct result of industrialization, does not feel the same degree of closeness to his work. Rather, he works for the sake of making a living and does not take a special pride in the product that the factory produces. The finished product is not a reflection of the individual employee's work; rather the product reflects the collective work of multiple employees. The individual employee is not involved in each aspect of producing the finished product and thus feels separated, or alienated, from his work. Homer Simpson explains what happens when an employee does not like his job: "If adults don't like their jobs, they don't go on strike. They just go in every day and do it really half-assed. That's the American way."

The roots of alienation in the workplace may be examined through an analysis of the historical context of the Industrial Revolution. The Industrial Revolution has created a battle within the workplace. The employer, a capitalist whose goal is to produce a profit, often exploits workers to achieve the corporation's financial goals. For example, historian Norman Ware cites:

> "[Workers in Newburyport] are compelled to do all of one-third more work, and in some cases double. Whereas in 1840 the weekly time wages were from 75 cents to $2 per week and board, in 1846 they ran from 55 cents to $1.50, making a 25 percent reduction in spite of the fact that they were doing 33 percent more work."

Although the standard of living increased during this period, the average wage of the worker declined. The Industrial Revolution embittered the economic conflict between the employer and employee. In years to come, employers would attempt to use any means necessary to produce a profit.

In the early stages of industrialization, the conditions under which the employee worked were horrific. Employees often worked twelve-hour days. Many workers lost hands or fingers from using machinery that they were not properly trained to operate. Child labor was also predominant in the early stages of industrialization. Employees worked for very low wages, as the government did not set a minimum wage. Employers demonstrated their ruthlessness, as their ultimate goal was to produce a profit. Shortly after factory worker H. Dubreuil immigrated to America, he observed the conditions in a machine factory:

> "A wooden structure, cluttered and dusty; machines dating back more than forty years; an uneven and hard earth floor deep in powdered rust that covered your shoes after five minutes of walking; lathe men drowsing over the castings in their machines. I asked myself whether I was in America."

Conditions such as these caused workers to despise work and inevitably become alienated from their duties. In the late 1870s, workers collectively expressed their disgust with horrid working conditions and reduction of wages by forming unions. The unions were created in an effort to protect the rights of workers in the workplace. Workers were not satisfied with the conditions under which they worked. As historian Sidney Pollard states, "...the acclimatization of new workers to factory discipline is a task different in kind, at once more subtle and violent, from that of maintaining discipline among a proletarian population of long standing." Carleton H. Parker supported this view by theorizing that the labor movement grew mainly out of the difficulty of workers in adjusting to factory life. The unions understood that employers did not place a high value on the lives of their workers.

Since the introduction of unions into industrialized society, workers have seen several significant changes in the workplace. For example, unions have been successful in lobbying for a minimum wage. Still, present work conditions do not serve to mentally engage workers in their work. Despite the fact that unions have fought for the rights of workers and have helped instill a code of ethics in the workplace, many workers are still discontent with their work. For example, factory worker H. Dubreuil states that employers "are doing everything possible to disgust the worker with labor." While work conditions may have improved over time, workers are still discontent because of their sense of "alienation" from their work.

Another core cause of alienation in the psyche of the industrialized worker lies in the fact that many workers do not utilize their skills to the fullest extent possible. For example, a worker on a factory line may have a creative mind, but his thoughts are restricted by the insipid, mundane work of the factory system. Jean Jacques Rousseau stated that men should combine their skills in an effort to ameliorate society and improve upon what the individual man can accomplish alone. While the factory system allows workers to combine some degree of their skills, it restricts many of their innate skills. As Frederick Taylor (the "father of scientific management") once stated to an employee, "You are not supposed to think! There are other people paid for thinking around here." Obviously, the workplace is not functioning at its full potential since its individual workers are not fulfilling their own personal potential. The restrictions on creativity set by the modern workplace are detrimental to the worker, who will sadly never experience his abilities at maximum potential.

Alienation has had a profound effect on the work ethic of the modern industrialized employee. If we take into context the psyche of the craftsman, we can better understand why the modern employee lacks a work ethic. Craftsmen, as well as other small entrepreneurs, worked for themselves. The more products they made, the more profit they would obtain. The quality of the work was also important to the craftsman: the better his product was, the higher price he would be able to charge for the item. However, since the industrialized employee is often not directly affected by the quality of his work, he has little reason to work hard. Indeed, the craftsman must perform his work satisfactorily, as he will be unable to earn a living if he does not do so. However, the industrialized worker performs his work perfunctorily, often with an overt apathy that invariably stems from his boredom.

The former ideal of the work ethic has been replaced by the modern leisure ethic. Mills states, "This replacement has involved a sharp, almost absolute split between work and leisure." In modern industrialized society (1900–present), leisure serves as a break from the gravity of a job. Employees have lost a sense of freedom in the sense that they no longer freely design what they are to produce. Since employees do not enjoy their work, they have found another means of pleasure—that of leisure. This has shaped the entire realm of global culture. For example, Leo Lowenthal meticulously observed that "the idols of work" have declined, while the "idols of leisure" have risen. The industrialized worker seems to hold more respect for the professional baseball player than the wealthy factory owner. Leisure, which came about as a means of providing pleasure to the employee, has actually replaced the respectability of work. As Homer once noted, "Movies are the only escape from the drudgery of work . . ." Work is done for the sole purpose of earning a living; pleasure is no longer a notable aspect of work.

The concept of alienation has also brought the worker closer to traditionalist ideals. For example, although the United States remains capitalistic, the effects of industrialization have, with much efficiency, destroyed the principle of a work ethic. Thus,

American workers often adhere to traditionalist ideals. For example, a traditionalist, as described by Max Weber, would sacrifice money for time. Traditionalists value time with family and friends over profit. As American factory workers opt not to work double-overtime, they are effectively adhering to traditionalist principles. The American employee would rather spend time with his family than perform "meaningless" work because he favors leisure over work. However, the driving force that leads employees to work is that of the acquisition of money. Traditionalists are those individuals who work to live but do not live to work. Capitalists are those individuals who live to work, and their efforts often produce large profits. The American employee seems to be caught in the middle of these conflicting economic theories. Since the employee despises work so much, he sometimes cannot bear to work overtime. Thus, as a direct result of industrialization, workers often drift away from capitalist concepts and adhere to traditionalist principles.

One long-term effect of industrialization on the life of the industrialized worker has been his diminished role as an individual. For example, a worker on a factory line may be easily replaced and thus does not carry a high value with respect to the employer's financial objectives. Because he is easily replaced, his employer does not give him respect, and his value to the corporation is nominal. The functions performed by low-level employees do not require much skill, and factories have experimented with new techniques to reduce expenses. Factory worker H. Dubreuil observes that "great efforts are made to diminish the importance of manual labor." Industrialization continues to diminish the importance of the individual worker, as new technological innovations execute the work formerly performed by workers.

Interestingly, our favorite cartoon character, Homer Simpson, reflects the attitude and work ethic of contemporary employees. His position as an employee under the greedy Mr.

Burns reflects the shift from craftsman to industrialized employ-ee. Let us examine Homer's role as the contemporary worker in greater depth.

Homer Simpson: The Industrialized Employee

"I'm no longer the money-driven workaholic I once was."
~ Homer

In "And Maggie Makes Three," Mr. Burns puts up a "demo-tivational" plaque in Homer's office. The plaque, which sits directly in front of Homer's line of sight at his desk, reads "You're here forever" and is intended to punish Homer for previously quitting his job. But Homer has other plans. In order to combat the gravity of those three words, he covers some of the letters on the plaque with pictures of his daughter, Maggie. With some of the letters covered, the plaque now reads "Do it for her." These four words speak volumes about the purpose of work in contem-porary society. While many Americans do not like their jobs, they must keep their jobs in order to provide financial support for the ones that they love. Homer is not excited about work for a num-ber of reasons: he feels extremely alienated by his boss, intensely frustrated by his lack of knowledge of his job duties, bored because of his lazy nature, and aloof and "demotivated" because he is paid a base salary and does not reap the actual fruits of his own labor. Homer may lack a work ethic, but this is caused in part by how he is treated at his job.

The industrialized employee is exemplified by Homer Simpson. Homer, the inane safety inspector of the Springfield Nuclear Power Plant, feels psychologically alienated from his work. He is employed by the rich capitalist Mr. Burns, who can-not seem to remember Homer's name, even though Homer has been employed in the power plant for many years. (More on this later. Burns also has been known to refer to his workers as "faceless employees.") Homer is often seen sleeping at his post, as he is intelligent enough to realize that he will be paid regardless of whether the work he does is satisfactory. In fact, since Homer became safety inspector of the power plant, meltdowns have tripled! While the industrialized employee does need to perform at a certain standard so as to not be fired, he may not take pride in his work. Homer Simpson is a man who does not enjoy his work, has no interest in the economy, and is eager to spend his time at home watching television with his family. While his character may be fictitious, the industrialized employee similarly enjoys spending time with his family rather than spending time at work.

Homer Simpson, a traditionalist by nature, works to live, but does not by any means live to work. One manufacturer's journal sums up the attitudes of the industrialized worker: "Don't expect work to begin before 9 a.m. or to continue after 3 p.m." Just as Homer Simpson does not "live to work," neither does the real-life industrialized worker.

In *The Simpsons* episode entitled "Last Exit to Springfield," Homer Simpson leads an employee union fight against cutting the company's health insurance plan. Mr. Burns, his employer, watches him on a television screen. Burns is angered by this employee's rebellious nature in this particular episode. Burns has the following exchange with his confidant, Waylon Smithers:

> **Burns:** Who is that firebrand, Smithers?
> **Smithers:** That's Homer Simpson.
> **Burns:** Simpson, eh? New man?
> **Smithers:** [brief chuckle] He thwarted your campaign for governor, you ran over his son, he saved the plant from meltdown, his wife painted you in the nude…
> **Burns:** Doesn't ring a bell.

The above quote outlines the dynamics of the employer-employee relationship in contemporary society. Rich capitalists such as Mr. Burns often care more about making money than about forming relationships with their employees. Mills correctly argues that employees feel alienated from their work because they are largely ignored by their employers. Employees are perceived as potential surplus-producers but not as human beings. When Burns does talk to Homer, he treats him with profound disrespect, as evidenced in the following exchange in which Homer insists that Marge bring a sufficient amount of gelatin dessert to Burns's party ("There's No Disgrace Like Home"):

> **Homer:** Are you sure that's enough? You know how the boss loves your delicious gelatin desserts!
> **Marge:** Oh Homer, Mr. Burns just said he liked it...once.
> **Homer:** Marge, that's the only time he's ever spoke to me without using the word...bonehead.

Homer might indeed be a "bonehead" but being repeatedly called as such by his boss certainly does not serve to improve his morale. If Burns treated Homer better, Homer might work harder. If treated properly, would Homer Simpson work harder and actually be considered a model employee? Hey, you never know...Homer's severe alienation from his work was specifically addressed during season six in the seminal episode "Who Shot Mr. Burns? Part I." Homer was so angry at Burns for not knowing his name that he became a prime suspect in the shooting of Burns. (He didn't shoot him, but he certainly wanted to do so!) Homer sadly noted his dissatisfaction with his job at the dinner table: "Oh, I hate my job. I mean, what's the point when your boss doesn't even remember your name?" It's not that Burns is senile: in the past, after all, he has been shown to recall the names of everyone else in the Simpson family, as well as the names of a

186 THE WORLD ACCORDING TO THE SIMPSONS

couple of his other employees. The idea here is that Homer is nothing more to Burns than a faceless "surplus-producer." Homer may be dumb, but he knows when he is not appreciated. And he doesn't like it one bit.

Homer's reflection of the contemporary industrialized employee is not limited to his actual time spent in the office. Homer is portrayed as a man who cares more about going home after a day's work than understanding the dynamics of the marketplace. In "Homer's Enemy," Homer exclaims, "Don't ask me how the economy works!" This line correctly sums up the feelings of the industrialized employee, who accepts his paycheck, spends his money, and does not involve himself in the workings of the economy in any other manner. This viewpoint is contrary to that of the entrepreneur who was forced to be knowledgeable about the workings of the economy so as to support himself. The industrialized employee does not need to be involved in the inner workings of the economy because his salary does not depend on his knowledge of any aspect of life outside of his work. The Industrial Revolution has created the disgruntled industrialized employee. The factory system, which has alienated workers from their work, was created for the sole purpose of maximizing profits. The capitalist employer views the worker as a pawn in the prodigious factory system and thus cares little about the employee's needs and desires. While the role of the worker may very well change in the future (e.g., due to the effects of automation and other new technologies), the constant function of the worker is to help the employer achieve his specific financial goals. In the process, the worker will earn a small sum of money. Still, given the opportunity, the industrialized employee would rather win the money by means of a lottery drawing than by performing his duties at work. And, as Homer has said, "If you really want something in life, you have to work for it. Now quiet, they're about to announce the lottery numbers."

The Simpsons and Celebrity Culture

ABC's *The View* recently revealed that more eighteen to twenty-four-year-olds voted in the 2004 *American Idol* competition than in the 2000 presidential election. This is a disturbing statistic, indeed. But eighteen to twenty-four-year-olds cannot accept all of the blame.

The Influence of the Mass Media

People have always been interested in the lives of other people—especially famous people. Americans' obsession with celebrities, however, expanded with the publication of *TIME* magazine in 1923. Henry Luce, the cofounder of *TIME*, placed an emphasis on the people behind the issues discussed in the publication. As noted in Wikipedia, "Many people still criticize [*TIME*] as [being] too light for serious news and…[for focusing energy on] its heavy coverage of celebrities [including politicians], the entertainment industry, and pop culture." *TIME*'s writers were encouraged to describe aspects of the daily lives of important people—such as politicians and war generals. *TIME*'s stories, for example, often open with a description of what the president had eaten for breakfast. (*Sports Illustrated*, another *TIME* publication, has followed in stride: it was recently revealed that basketball phenom Lebron James starts his day with "a big bowl of Fruity Pebbles.") There was, of course, a more pressing imperative behind Luce's decision to have his writers focus on the private, miniscule, and virtually insignificant portions of the lives of the people discussed in the stories. Luce believed that if the reporters were able to demonstrate knowledge of minor details in the private lives of the people discussed, readers would develop an inherent trust in the words of the reporters. For example, if a reporter notes that the president invariably sleeps on the right side of the bed, eats a bowl of Crispix with exactly half a cup of milk each morning, and drinks three quarters of a cup of Mango Blend herbal tea, the reader will believe that the reporter is replete with insight into the inner-workings of the man in power. Luce theorized that readers would then accept the writers' words as fact when it came to discussions of politics and pertinent issues in contemporary society.

Luce's own Republican views were certainly expressed in *TIME*, but were often introduced in the aforementioned mode. The idea was to create a sense of trust between the reader and reporter and in this way infiltrate the reader's mind with Luce's blend of politics. *TIME*'s annual "Person of the Year" started in 1927 and has become a worldwide phenomenon, as did its "100 Most Influential People" list at the turn of the twentieth century. In many ways, *TIME* created the impression that political leaders may be perceived as celebrities. In addition to drawing focus on pertinent events, *TIME* decided to also explore the personality and character traits of many "people of the year" in its stories. It may be argued that *TIME*'s emphasis on the "individual" has actually prevented the publication from being viewed as an outfit whose sole purpose it is to present events as news. America's desire to read and hear about the intricate aspects of the lives of celebrities has proven to be a distraction from more pressing issues that face the country. Even in *TIME*, a weekly news-magazine, the eating habits of the 2004 Democratic Presidential candidates were revealed. After reading the article, millions of subscribers would know that Senator John Kerry enjoys Hostess cupcakes, Senator John Edwards eats at Applebee's, General Wesley Clark munches on Cheetos and gummi bears, and Dennis Kucinnich is a vegan. In the busy, work-a-day lives of Americans, the question must be posed of whether we truly have the time to read about the politics of elections *and* explore the eating habits of the candidates. Certainly, an article about the diets of the candidates should not be considered news. Human interest story? Perhaps. But since Americans are already pressed for time, news magazines should devote more of their content to the actual issues, rather than the personalities of the candidates.

In recent years, public attention towards movie stars, singers, and other pop culture artists has reached unprecedented levels. Television stations such as *E!*, and programs such as *Entertainment Tonight* have spurned the growth of celebrity culture in the United States. Magazines such as *Entertainment Weekly* and *People* serve as supplemental elements of such a culture. The fact that Americans have a seemingly unquenchable thirst for information pertaining to the lives of their favorite "stars" is, as we shall see, a disturbing component of American culture. As comic actor Ben Stiller recently noted in an interview with *USA Weekend*, "the mania over finding out things about people like Michael Jackson and J. Lo has never been worse." It is certainly strange to see women wearing T-shirts with the words "I'll have your baby, Brad" printed on the front or to hear that a die-hard Yankees fan (who is also evidently a huge fan of Derek Jeter) makes a birthday party for Derek Jeter each year on the date of his birthday, despite the fact that she has never met him.

What is even worse (perhaps even hinging on dangerous) however, is Americans' unrelenting commitment and loyalty toward their favorite celebrities in the face of criminal charges and other wrongdoings. *Sports Illustrated* recently reported, for example, that some NBA fans in Houston shouted "she deserved it" when Kobe Bryant, who allegedly raped a young woman (the criminal case was dismissed), stepped onto the basketball court. These fans evidently believed that Kobe was guilty of rape but still supported their beloved celebrity.

The steroid problem in baseball has created such a media craze not only because it is affecting the sport of baseball but also because it affects the specific baseball *players* that are so endeared by fans. It is the people behind the home runs and stolen bases that people want to know about. The players under investigation for taking steroids should know that they have let down millions of fans across the globe.

The Simpsons, as we shall see, takes a sharp look at America's obsession with celebrities.

Guest Stars on The Simpsons

As noted earlier, *The Simpsons* holds the record for the most guest stars for a television series. On the surface, it would seem as though *The Simpsons* promotes the idea of a celebrity culture. *The Simpsons*, however, simply uses Americans' infatuation with celebrities to achieve high ratings. Even though some guest stars feel as though they become immortalized once they appear on an episode of *The Simpsons*, it is difficult to determine whether or not *The Simpsons* promotes a celebrity culture in America.

In one *Simpsons* episode, Homer approaches the car of actor/director Ron Howard. Howard tells Homer that he is in a hurry to get to the zoo. Homer is impressed that such a big shot celebrity still has time to do the simple things in life, like take his children to see animals in a zoo. Howard tells Homer, however, that the zoo he goes to has animals that *"you've* never seen." Howard's daughter elaborates: "Come on dad. We're missing the fantastapotamus. She only sings twice a day!"

Well, there goes Homer's idea that celebrities are just like regular people. Here we see that stars do often get special treatment. This is satire, of course. Still, this scene helps provide insight into one of the ways that *The Simpsons* addresses celebrity culture.

The Simpsons' Response to Celebrity Culture

"He couldn't do anything illegal. He's a celebrity—he's in show business!" ~ Lisa Simpson

At first glance, *The Simpsons* is fairly lenient in terms of its criticism of America's obsession with celebrities. Bart Simpson's bedroom, for example, is filled with Krusty the Clown memorabilia. Rainier Wolfcastle, the Arnold Schwarzenegger-like character on the show, is, for the most part, portrayed as arrogant but affable. In the episode entitled, "When You Dish upon a Star," however, *The Simpsons* mocks America's obsession with celebrities. In "When You Dish upon a Star," Homer voluntarily—and excitedly—becomes the unpaid personal assistant of guest stars Alec Baldwin and Kim Basinger. Homer performs his job with ebullience—mainly because he is thrilled that the stars treat him with respect. After Homer tells his bar cronies that Alec and Kim are in Springfield, word quickly spreads throughout the town and fans rush to meet the celebrities at their home. Alec and Kim force Homer to leave because he revealed to residents of Springfield that the stars were in town. Homer is angered by the ungratefulness of the stars for the services he had provided and opens a mobile museum filled with items he had stolen from the stars.

The very fact that the residents of Springfield rushed toward Alec and Kim's home demonstrates their desire to meet and greet stars. The following exchange shows that the residents are obsessed with celebrities:

"Homer's Museum of Hollywood Jerks"
Homer: Attention, starstruck fools! Step right up and

see the world's greatest mobile collection of Alec and Ron and Kim-orabilia.

[The fans pay Homer a fee, and enter the mobile.]

Chief Wiggum: Hey, it's Alec Baldwin's Medic Alert bracelet!

Homer: That's right, Mr. Tough Guy can't handle a little penicillin! Oh, and look at this! We can't even pay our bills, and they're drinking [mockingly] "Royal Crown Cola."

Carl: Hey, hey, go easy on the celebrities, eh?

Krusty: Yeah, what gives you the right?

Barney: We love celebrities!

Homer: Oh yeah? What have they ever done for you? When was the last time Barbra Streisand cleaned out your garage? And when it's time to do the dishes, where's Ray Bolger? I'll tell ya! Ray Bolger is looking out for Ray Bolger!

Homer's brilliant commentary at the end of the exchange speaks volumes about America's obsession with celebrities. We are obsessed with their lives, but they have no interest in ours. The effervescence exhibited by Carl, Barney, and Chief Wiggum in the above exchange is a satire of Americans' ridiculous obsession with celebrities. The writers of this episode represent these characters in such a way because they want to show us how foolish we look when our eyes light up upon meeting a celebrity in person.

Later in the episode, Homer switches gears and expresses his true feelings about celebrities:

"I believe that famous people have a debt to everyone. If celebrities didn't want people pawing through their garbage and saying they're gay, they shouldn't have tried to express themselves creatively...In closing, you people must realize that the public owns you for life!"

As usual, Homer's views are a bit misguided, but he speaks for the American people when he argues that the public has a right to "own" celebrities. This episode brilliantly outlined the issue of celebrity culture. We can truly identify with the obsessive nature of the residents of Springfield. "Owning" celebrities in this sense is certainly not a virtue. Caring so much about celebrities can distract us from our own lives. A guest on the *Dr. Phil* television show told millions of viewers about her complete obsession with Tommy Lee. Dr. Phil pointedly observed that such an obsession was distracting her from her own responsibilities and pushing those who loved her out of the picture. All of this was, Dr. Phil correctly argued, because of her infatuation with a man she had never even met.

"Owning" celebrities in the aforementioned manner is clearly quite an unhealthy obsession. But caring about celebrities even in moderation is essentially a fruitless hobby—both for the fan and for the celebrity. Celebrities, though immersed in the public life of show business, like all Americans, do have a right to their privacy. "When You Dish upon a Star" shows us that the stars have lives of their own and often wish to disappear from the public view.

Further satire of celebrity culture may be found in "Treehouse of Horror II." In the segment entitled "The Monkey's Paw," the Simpson family purchases a magic paw that grants them three wishes. They use one of their wishes to become "rich and famous." The family initially enjoys the attention and special courtesy that stars receive:

> **Marge:** Homer, maybe fame and fortune aren't as bad as they say.

Immediately following Marge's approval of fame and fortune, however, fans become sick and tired of hearing about the Simpsons:

> **Woman 1:** If I hear one more thing about the Simpsons, I swear, I'm going to scream.

Woman 2: At first they were cute and funny, but now they are just annoying.

The Simpson family becomes *too* rich and famous. They delve into various types of industries—from music to mammograms:

Otto, after listening to a *Simpsons* music album: "Man, this thing is really getting out of hand."

Bart's image on a billboard: Get a mammogram, man!" Helen Lovejoy complains, "Is there anything [the Simpsons] won't do?!"

Interestingly, this segment highlights and satirizes *The Simpsons*' own pervasiveness in society. While we may not read tabloid papers about Homer's weekly arguments with Marge, *The Simpsons* has achieved the status of celebrity. In this episode, the writers, in a not-so-subtle knock at die-hard *Simpsons* fans, hint that being obsessed with cartoon characters is no better than being obsessed with the lives of Jennifer Lopez or Robert DeNiro.

In this episode, the writers, by placing a limit on the amount of celebrity infiltration the public is willing to handle, also show that the American public will only care about celebrities to a certain extent.

This episode actually tries to show that Americans are not completely obsessed with celebrities and will never fully "buy into" a celebrity culture. The residents of Springfield seem less star struck in this episode and possess a weaker desire to know the intricate details of the lives of celebrities than in "When You Dish upon a Star." *The Simpsons*, therefore, does not seem to influence the growth of a celebrity culture. Instead, the series satirizes our own obsession with celebrities.

Defining Heroes: Celebrities and the

American Dream

In "Radioactive Man," Milhouse is unhappy with his acting role as Fallout Boy and considers how society should define a "hero." Milhouse is right on target in the following exchange with Bart:

> **Bart:** But Milhouse, being a star is every patriotic American's dream.
> **Milhouse:** Not mine. It's a sham, Bart! You get up on that movie screen pretending to be a hero, but you're not. The real heroes are out there, toiling day and night on more important things!
> **Bart:** [dreamy] Television.
> **Milhouse:** No! Curing heart disease and wiping out world hunger.
> **Bart:** But Milhouse, they haven't cured anything! Heart disease and world hunger are still rampant. Those dogooders are all a bunch of pitiful losers...every last one of them. Want results? You have to go to the Schwarzeneggers, the Stallones, and to a lesser extent, the Van Dammes.

Bart's unwillingness to accept the contributions of the "real heroes" serves as a satire on Americans' lack of respect for those who work their hardest to solve societal problems. Milhouse is correct in asserting that the real heroes in society are those who save lives, take care of us, and devote their lives to benefiting mankind. Milhouse's awareness of what constitutes a true hero—as opposed to the action heroes depicted in movies—demonstrates a break from the celebrity-obsessed culture of Springfield. In Springfield, a local television star like Krusty the Clown is generally more glorified than Dr. Hibbert. But to Milhouse, the real heroes are the ones who work hard to make our lives better.

The Simpsons helps to highlight many aspects of our society that perhaps can use some tweaking. The existence of a celebrity culture in contemporary society is an issue that the writers have satirized on the aforementioned occasions. If we wish to avoid becoming like the celebrity-obsessed fans portrayed in "When You Dish upon a Star," perhaps we should take lessons from watching *The Simpsons*.

Gun Control Legislation and "The Cartridge Family"

Homer Simpson: I'd like to buy your deadliest gun, please.
Gun Shop Owner: Aisle six, next to the sympathy cards.
~ At the gun store, "The Cartridge Family"

Gun control has been portrayed on several Simpsons episodes in a number of ways. In a season sixteen episode, Homer notes that "I often get guns and cameras con-fused—once tragically at a wedding." The irresponsible Homer certainly does not seem like the best person to own a handgun. In a "Treehouse of Horror" segment, the townspeople decide to rid the town of all of its handguns. The world initially becomes more peaceful, with the letters on "DANGER" signs being rearranged to spell the word "GARDEN" and the people holding hands with one another. All of these initial positive changes in Springfield would seemingly lend support for the gun control advocates. Later in the segment, however, the series' recurring aliens, Kang and Kodos, notice the dearth of weapons in Springfield and attempt to take over the town. The townspeople are only able to chase away the aliens by resorting to using other sorts of weapons—

like giant wooden boards. Here, we see that weapons are necessary in an imperfect world in order to protect ourselves from aggressors. Still, the episode closes on a more somber note with Kang noting the following: "That board with the nail in it may have defeated us. But the humans won't stop there. They'll make bigger boards and bigger nails. Soon they will make a board with a nail so big it will destroy them all." The possession of weapons may be necessary to protect ourselves from invading forces, but the episode clearly makes the point that we tend to get out of control when stockpiling weapons—or, in the case of the residents of Springfield, building giant wooden boards. With a 2005 U.S. defense budget of a record $417.4 billion, perhaps Kang and Kodos have a point. We may need these weapons as a means of defense, but it's disheartening to consider the fact that we live in a world where we must spend so much money to defend our way of life.

The Simpsons looks at the issue of gun control in the seminal episode entitled, "The Cartridge Family," in which Homer purchases a gun in an effort to provide protection for his family. The episode addresses several important issues within the realm of gun control legislation in the United States. This chapter will examine the references made to gun control laws in this particular episode, while also addressing gun control legislative issues prevalent in contemporary society.

An Introduction to Gun Control Laws: The Second Amendment

Before we delve deeper into "The Cartridge Family," it behooves us to consider the Second Amendment to the United States Constitution. The amendment reads as follows:

"A well-regulated Militia, being necessary to the security of a free State, the right of the people to keep and bear Arms, shall not be infringed."

While a bit vague, the language may, according to gun

advocates, be read from the vantage point of the individual, rather than some collective entity. From the Second Amendment, U.S. citizens have the natural and inalienable right to bear arms for the purpose of their personal defense. In response to gun control laws developed in the late 1990s, Johann Opitz noted the following:

> "One of the arguments often heard from the gun control people is that the Second Amendment to the Constitution really refers to some sort of 'collective' right, not an individual right. If this were true, one would think that the Second Amendment would have been better written to explain that. And if that were true, one would think that the individual states would have expressed a 'collective' right in their own constitutions. Yet, forty-three out of fifty states have their own version of the Second Amendment and none of them, zero, zip, zilch, nada, mention any form of 'collective' right."

Here are some examples of state laws and statements on the right to bear arms. The examples from the thirty-eight other states contain almost identical language:

ALABAMA: "That every citizen has a right to bear arms in defense of himself and the state." Ala. Const. Art.I, Sect. 26
ALASKA: "A well-regulated militia being necessary to the security of a free state, the right of the people to keep and bear arms shall not be infringed. The individual right to keep and bear arms shall not be denied or infringed by the State or a political subdivision of the State." Alaska Const. Art. I, Sect. 19 (second sentence added Nov. 1994)
ARIZONA: "The right of the individual citizen to

bear arms in defense of himself or the State shall not be impaired, but nothing in this section shall be construed as authorizing individuals or corporations to organize, maintain, or employ an armed body of men." Ariz. Const. Art. 2, Sect. 26

ARKANSAS: "The citizens of this state shall have the right to keep and bear arms for their common defense." Ark. Const. Art. II, Sect. 5

COLORADO: "The right of no person to keep and bear arms in defense of his home, person and property, or in aid of the civil power when thereto legally summoned, shall be called in question; but nothing herein contained shall be construed to justify the practice of carrying concealed weapons." Colo. Const. Art. II, Sect. 13

Thus, while individual states certainly place some restrictions on gun ownership, the basic individual right to bear arms is guaranteed by both federal and state constitutions.

Gun Control Advocacy

As with any issue, there are two sides to the gun control debate. As noted by James Incardi in *Elements of Criminal Justice*, "…The Second Amendment…may be the most argued and misunderstood twenty-seven words in the U.S. Constitution."

Gun control advocates have won some important court cases, which have served to limit the consumption of guns in contemporary society. Incardi notes that "the federal courts, in interpreting the Second Amendment, have created a principle of law that says the right to bear arms was not extended to each and every individual but rather was expressly limited to maintaining effective militia." In the 1971 case of *Stevens v. United States*, for example, a federal district court ruled as follows: "Since the Second Amendment applies only to the right of the State to maintain a militia and not to the individual's right to bear arms, there can be no serious claim to any express constitutional right of an individual to possess a firearm." Other court cases have followed stride.

Furthermore, most Americans support gun control. Incardi reports that "in a recent nationwide Harris Poll, 69 percent of all adults and 57 percent of gun owners were in favor of stricter gun laws." In the controversial film, *Bowling for Columbine*, Michael Moore makes the point that the phrase "right to bear arms" is so vague that it is unclear whether or not guns were intended to be included in its definition. Moore sarcastically poses the question of whether or not nuclear weapons should be included within the definition as well.

It is certainly clear that some restrictions on "the right to bear arms" must be established. The question is, of course, where exactly to draw the line. The ongoing debate between gun control advocates and those opposed to such legislative measures influenced the production of "The Cartridge Family."

"NRA4EVER"

The Simpsons has addressed the issue of gun control in a number of Simpsons episodes. In "Mr. Spritz Goes to Washington," for example, Krusty the Clown is elected to Congress and proclaims: "I swear to uphold the Constitution of these United States—so relax, gun nuts, I can't touch ya." In "Who Shot Mr. Burns: Part II," it was revealed that Maggie accidentally shot Mr. Burns. In "Dude, Where's My Ranch," Rich Texan informs us that he is going to jail because he accidentally shot a park ranger while carelessly firing his guns. In another episode, Chief Wiggum realizes that he has left his firearm on a dessert table where it is accessible to children. Here, the writers provide examples of the negative consequences of gun ownership. In the episode "Homer the Vigilante," ten-year-old Bart Simpson, along with other residents, are shown accidentally firing guns off in the Simpson home. In a more recent episode, however, Maggie saves Homer from the mafia by shooting the criminals. In Springfield, as in contemporary society, guns can have both positive and negative consequences.

"The Cartridge Family"

The issue of violence in "The Cartridge Family" first arises at a local soccer game riot in Springfield. To protect his family, Homer decides to purchase a gun at the local gun shop.

In a classic satirical *Simpsons* moment, Homer practices firing an unloaded gun. After pointing the gun at the shop owner's head and pulling the trigger several times, they engage in the following exchange:

> **Gun Shop Owner:** Whoa, be careful there, Annie Oakley.
> **Homer:** I don't have to be careful. I got a gun.

Homer's comment is reflective of the sense of power many individuals feel when armed with a firearm. The comment, also, however, satirizes the lack of precaution certain individuals undertake when operating handguns. Homer's line, while absurd, is certainly not an inaccurate depiction of "unintentional/accidental" murder in contemporary society. As noted earlier, Mr. Burns was accidentally shot by Maggie because a gun was haphazardly placed in an insecure location.

The scene in the gun shop continues on in such a way that virtually every spoken word provides fans with a dose of social commentary. Two of the most memorable exchanges between Homer and the Gun Shop Owner go as follows:

> **Gun Shop Owner:** Sorry, the law requires a five-day waiting period. We've got to run a background check.
> **Homer:** Five days? But I'm mad now!

When Homer returns to the gun shop, he engages in the

following exchange with the Gun Shop Owner:

> **Homer:** Now, I believe you have some sort of firearm for me.
> **Gun Shop Owner:** Well, let's see here. According to your background check, you've been in a mental institution…
> **Homer:** Yeah.
> **Gun Shop Owner:** …frequent problems with alcohol…
> **Homer:** [laughs nervously] Yeah.
> **Gun Shop Owner:** …beat up President Bush!
> **Homer:** *Former* President Bush.
> [The owner slaps a red rubber stamper on Homer's printout.]
> **Homer:** "Potentially dangerous?!"
> **Gun Shop Owner:** Relax, that just limits you to three handguns or less.
> **Homer:** Woo hoo!

The first exchange leads the audience to believe that the law sets strict restrictions on gun ownership. A "background check" certainly sounds like an appropriate—and necessary—step for the gun shop owner to take in such a scenario.

The second exchange, however, provides the satirical social commentary. Indeed, Homer's record causes him to be perceived as a "potentially dangerous" member of society. If society had been the main concern of the gun shop owner, he certainly should not have sold the gun to Homer.

It is here that the writers implicitly state that stricter gun control legislation should be passed. By allowing Homer to purchase a gun, they have certainly built a strong case for such legislative measures. Once Homer does purchase a handgun at the gun shop, he acts quite irresponsibly—even recklessly at times.

The list below outlines some of Homer's inappropriate uses of the gun:
- Points the barrel of the gun at Marge's face
- Shoots dinner plates
- Attempts to turn the safety on, but sets off the gun
- Fires the gun at lights in order to turn them off
- Fires the gun at the TV to change the channel

These points serve as evidence for why Homer definitely should not be allowed to own a gun. The law, however, protects Homer's inherent constitutional right to own a handgun:

> **Marge:** Mmm! No! [pulls gun from Homer] No one's using this gun! The TV said you're 58 percent more likely to shoot a family member than an intruder!
> **Homer:** TV said that…? But I have to have a gun! It's in the Constitution!
> **Lisa:** Dad! The Second Amendment is just a remnant from revolutionary days. It has no meaning today!
> **Homer:** You couldn't be more wrong, Lisa. If I didn't have this gun, the king of England could just walk in here any time he wants and start shoving you around.

From a strictly legal standpoint, Homer most certainly has the right to keep the "king of England" out of his house. From a more practical perspective, however, it is fairly evident that Homer may not be the most appropriate person to own a handgun.

As the episode progresses, the issues explored become increasingly complex. The scene soon cuts to a local NRA meeting.

The NRA Meeting

Homer somehow convinces Marge to attend an NRA meeting with him. At the meeting, the following exchange takes place:

> **Moe:** Yeah, so last night I was closing up the bar,

when some young punk comes in and tries to stick me up. [The crowd gasps.]

Sideshow Mel: Whatever did you do, Moe?

Moe: Well, it coulda been a real ugly situation, but I managed to shoot him in the spine. [Crowd claps and cheers.]

One of the most startling aspects of the meeting was that all of the members came armed with a firearm of some sort. Indeed, the participants later used the guns in a target practice exercise, but the fact that they held the guns while Homer and Moe spoke created an unsettling atmosphere.

After the meeting, the family retreats home, and Homer reluctantly promises Marge that he will dispose of the gun. Homer, seldom regarded as the "clever Simpson," lies to Marge and hides the gun in the vegetable crisper. When Bart finds the gun, he acts recklessly and plans on firing a bullet at an apple located in Milhouse's mouth. Here, the writers utilize an ideology that advocates gun control by showing the danger of keeping a gun in the house.

After Marge leaves Homer as a result of his broken promise to dispose of the gun, Homer holds an NRA meeting at the Simpson home. The NRA regains some respectability in this scene, as Homer makes a complete fool of himself. NRA members are no longer perceived as "gun nuts," but instead outline the proper uses of guns. After Homer fires several bullets at both a beer can and the television, the following exchange takes place:

Agnes: I've never seen such recklessness!

Louie: You mighta hurt someone!

Cleetus: Are you some kind of moron?

A few scenes later, Homer visits the motel where Marge and the kids are staying. The Simpsons are put in danger when Snake attempts to rob the motel's cash register. After duping Homer into giving him bullets for the gun, NRA members Moe, Agnes, Lenny, and Dr. Hibbert appear and point their guns squarely at Snake. This was only made possible because the NRA had the technology in place to be alerted when crimes are being committed. We see therefore that although "The Cartridge Family" was largely in favor of gun control—again, showing a boob like Homer Simpson playing with a gun strongly implies a need for laws prohibiting the individual possession of firearms—the end of the episode showed the positive side of gun ownership. Guns and the NRA ("a wonderful organization," according to Homer) end up saving the day.

After Homer finally agrees to get rid of the gun, Marge, the gun control advocate, places the gun in her purse. Marge ends up being the ultimate hypocrite, as she constantly contends that guns are evil but then keeps the gun for herself. Guns do indeed give people a sense of power, as Marge learns in this final scene.

So what can we take from this episode? First, it was evident from Homer's mishaps with the gun that he was not trained to use it properly (the NRA provided some target practice for gun owners, but it is important to realize that the meetings are optional for gun owners). Perhaps more laws should be passed that can enforce mandatory training for gun owners to use their handguns properly. Homer's careless antics demonstrated the unfortunate—and inevitable—effects of this lack of legislative policy. Secondly, as noted previously, the accuracy of background checks on individuals must be ameliorated. If guns fall into the wrong hands, they can potentially lead to more gun-related injuries and deaths. Finally, it is important to note that "The Cartridge Family" serves as a classic example of the evenhanded episodes (documenting and mocking both sides of the gun control debate) that fans have come to expect from *The Simpsons*.

Homer Simpson and Morality

"Once something has been approved by the government, it is no longer immoral." ~ **Reverend Timothy Lovejoy**

Homer is not exactly a religious man, but he does go to church (it's a great place to listen to the football games on the radio while that "church-guy" is talking) and has pledged his allegiance to "Jebus" on several occasions. Fearing imminent death, Homer once exclaimed, "Jesus, Allah, Buddha, I love you all!," and explained afterward that he was simply covering all of the bases. Funny, yes. But more importantly, this was a classic moment of philosophical inquiry emanating directly from the hectic head of Homer.

Philosophical Thinking and "Homer the Heretic"

In "Homer the Heretic," Homer decides not to go to church with his family on a frigid Sunday and ends up having the greatest day of his life. Alone in the house, Homer finds new expressions of his freedom: he whizzes with the door open, says the word "ass" while taking a shower, strips down to his underwear and dances to "Who Wears Short Shorts?," makes his "patented out-of-this-world space-age Moon Waffles," watches the *Three Stooges* and an incredible football game, eats a bag of potato chips, and, to top everything off, finds a shiny penny underneath the couch. When his family returns, distraught and freezing from the cold, Homer smiles in delight and tells them that he has "been having a wonderful day, and…owes it all to skipping church!"

What can we make of this string of events? Homer initially did not attend church because he was lazy. (Lying in bed, he said that he felt like a "warm, toasty cinnamon bun" and only got out of bed because he needed to go to the bathroom.) So the analysis of Homer's actions could potentially end here: he is just a lazy bum.

While Homer does not hide his penchant for bumming around the house, however, he also provides insight into the importance of living a moral life. He questions the value of going to church and opens up the floor to debate about whether it is better to live a hedonistic life, one in which it is morally acceptable to be obsessed with pleasure, or whether there is some hidden value in going to church. Homer's blatant rejection of organized religion enables us to debate whether or not one could lead a moral life independent of religion, a question posed by philosophers for ages. A deep philosophical question, yes, but, as we shall see, no philosophical question is too complex for Homer to tackle.

Homer attempts to explain his decision not to go to church ever again to Marge:

> "What if we picked the wrong religion? Every week, we're just making God madder and madder!"

Homer's position, while seemingly ludicrous and an obvious attempt to make an excuse for himself to be lazy and enjoy his Sundays at home in a warm house, is a serious one. What would happen if Homer did indeed choose the wrong religion? Would

God be mad at him for indulging in practices that might seem sacrilegious when compared to the actions that God actually wants him to take? Here, Homer, albeit accidentally, provides at least some support for the argument that morality can be—and, in this particular case must be—independent of religion. (Homer never actually mentions the importance of morality in this conversation, but that comes later in the episode during his discussion with God.)

The point here is that if we deem morality to be directly attached to God, we run into a significant problem. Since we can never absolutely know beyond a doubt, however small, that we chose the "right" religion, it is impossible to prove that one's religion preaches the performance of actions that God would absolutely declare to be moral. If Homer chose the wrong religion, then he may indeed be performing some actions that God would deem immoral: some religions, undoubtedly, adhere to certain practices that would be considered immoral by other religions. Homer's argument that he dismisses organized religion because of its lack of certainty is thus a strong one. It is important to note, however, that many argue that contemporary conceptions of morality are a direct result of the influence of religion in general; this idea, if true, would serve to weaken the argument that morality can be formed independently of religion. At least Homer opens up the field for debate.

Homer's Conversation with God

Later in the episode, God, five fingers and all, appears in Homer's dream. Homer has the following conversation with God:

> **God:** Thou hast forsaken My Church!
> **Homer:** [in fear] Uh, kind-of...b-but . . .
> **God:** But what?!
> **Homer:** I'm not a bad guy! I work hard, and I love my

kids. So why should I spend half my Sunday hearing
about how I'm going to Hell?
God: [pauses] Hmm...You've got a point there...You
know, sometimes even I'd rather be watching football...

A lot can be said about this discussion. Homer's declaration
that he's "not a bad guy" provides insight into his conception of
morality. Hard work and being a devoted father, according to
Homer, make him a decent human being. He argues that Sundays
should be spent the way that he wants to spend them. Even God
agrees with this point. God is not depicted as uptight and seems
to appreciate Homer's honesty and sincerity.

Certainly love and hard work could conceivably be part of a
universal conception of morality, so Homer has reached some
standard of goodness. He dismisses the importance of going to
church on the basis that he is able to live a moral life without
hearing the sermons of Reverend Lovejoy. Aside from the criticisms of organized religion, we're left to ask ourselves what exactly constitutes the moral life. Homer's conception seems as good
as any, and, if we turn off the television at this point, we're left to
contemplate the role of morality in our own lives.

Later in the show, Homer fervently dismisses the attempts of
Marge, Flanders, and Reverend Lovejoy to win him back to their
faith. Homer accidentally sets the house on fire, though, and
Springfield's volunteer fire fighters save him from his self-inflicted
disaster. Homer believes that this experience was a result of not
going to church, and, when pressed, notes what lesson he has
taken away from it all: "The Lord is vengeful. [falls to his knees]
Oh Spiteful One, show me who to smite, and he shall be smoten!"

But Homer is immediately set straight by his religious superiors:

Ned: Homer, God didn't set your house on fire.
Rev. Lovejoy: No, but He was working in the hearts

of your friends and neighbors when they came to your
aid, be they [points to Ned] Christian, [Krusty] Jew,
or [Apu]...miscellaneous.

Apu: Hindu! There are seven hundred million of us!

Rev. Lovejoy: Aw, that's super.

Homer eagerly agrees to attend church every Sunday from
that point onward. But the questions about morality and its relationship with organized religion were on par with those posed by
some of the great philosophers of our time. Homer should be
credited with the ability to question authority, a la Socrates, in
search of the truth. The conclusion that we draw from this
episode is that religion helps to bring communities together and
sets ethical standards for people to follow. Homer finds his direct
connection to God without the help of the church. But what he
realizes by the end of the episode is that religion can serve as a
social factor that helps to bridge his community together. By
agreeing to attend church, Homer satisfies both Reverend
Lovejoy and the rest of his family. Homer maintains his direct
link to God, as he continues to speak with him as the episode
comes to a close. But the point is not that going to church pleas-
es God; as noted, Homer's connection to God seems independent of his attending church. Instead, Homer's responsibilities are
to his wife and children, and going to church every Sunday helps
to set a good example for his kids. Going to church is shown to
be a virtue because of the social and ethical benefits it brings to
Springfield.

The Education of Springfield

An Introduction to Springfield's Educational System

T here are two critical aspects of *The Simpsons* opening sequence that help to open viewers' eyes to what it is exactly that *The Simpsons* is all about. Bart is seen writing some particular saying on a chalkboard, presumably as a punishment for something he has done. One chalkboard saying: "Shooting paintballs is not an art form" can be interpreted—especially by artists—as a repression of free and artistic thought, in which virtually *anything* has the potential to be considered an art form. Here the teacher, Edna Krabappel, reinforces the notion that Springfield Elementary prefers its students to engage in ways of conventional thinking, rather than steer off on their own tangents (which may very well lead to progress and benefit society in the long run). By having Bart write sayings that Krabappel deems appropriate on the blackboard, the Springfield educational system—at times—indoctrinates Bart.

Another part of the opening sequence that merits attention occurs when Lisa is kicked out of her band class because of her "unbridled enthusiasm." The band teacher, Mr. Largo, is visibly angered by Lisa's outburst of creativity, which she displays by playing a Jazz tune with improvisations while the other students follow Mr. Largo's commands and play less exciting songs. Lisa, an outspoken activist, is unfazed by her teacher's anger and continues playing her tune even as she leaves the room. She does not conform to the boundaries that Mr. Largo establishes in his classroom. Here, we gain insight into both Lisa's character—we can see the makings of a liberal iconoclast—and the school system's repression of creativity. By examining these aspects of the opening sequence, we can safely assume that *The Simpsons* agenda is to accomplish two related tasks: *subvert* and *attack*.

Students enrolled in Springfield's local elementary school, Springfield Elementary, are not exactly provided a grade-A education (even the meat served in the cafeteria is Grade F). Bart's teacher, Mrs. Krabappel, is a lonely, mildly depressed, heavy smoker who cares more about finding a husband and punishing Bart than teaching students long division. (Despite this, she was nominated by Bart for a prominent national teaching award.) Lisa's teacher, Miss Hoover, similarly lacks the dedication (and perhaps intelligence) required to be a responsible teacher. After Lisa uncharacteristically steals the teacher's editions of all of the school's textbooks, for example, Hoover is unable to teach the material to her class. The school's principal, Seymour Skinner, is uptight, serious, and a staunch supporter of timeliness over tardiness. Skinner believes that field trips to the box factory provide students with an enlightening experience. The school district's superintendent, Chalmers, is a gullible clod who cares more about yelling at Skinner than actually enforcing policies that would strengthen the school's educational system.

But the most conspicuous and egregious problems with Springfield's education system lies within the very culture under which the system operates. In an uncharacteristic moment of apparent dedication to her students, Mrs. Krabappel engages in the following conversation with Principal Skinner:

> **Edna:** Seymour, you have to think of the children's future.
> **Seymour:** Oh, Edna. We all know that these children *have* no future.
> [Everyone stops and stares at Seymour.]
> **Seymour:** Prove me wrong children. Prove me wrong.

Skinner's assertion that the students "have no future" is representative of the very culture present at Springfield Elementary. Why should teachers bust their humps teaching students who have no real chance at future success? Why should students hone their skills when they'll all inevitably end up working at McDonald's?

But perhaps most detrimental to Springfield's children is the idea that independent, innovative thinking by students is dangerous. Such thinking is routinely discouraged. In "Lisa the Vegetarian," for example, Lisa explores the options of vegetarianism and refuses to blindly accept the school's teaching. Agitated and unprepared to handle such a situation, both Miss Hoover and Lunchlady Doris discreetly press the "Independent Thought Alarm." Skinner's response: "That's two independent thought alarms in one day. Willie, the children are over-stimulated. Remove all the colored chalk from the classrooms."

Ideally, independent thinking should be what drives students to engage in mental processes conducive to ways that have the potential to make the world a better place. But, sadly, this is obviously not the case in Springfield.

Whether it's Skinner attempting to eliminate funding for art and music classes, the screening of inane and insipid documentaries starring Troy McClure, or discouraging students from engaging in creative thinking, the Springfield education system is in need of much improvement. What is perhaps most sad about the situation, however, is that it is a fairly accurate—though once again obviously satirized—reflection of the American education system. An analysis of the many flaws with the Springfield education system is of great value because it teaches us not to place blame for our own problems on just one factor—be it funding, dedication, or standards. Instead, a combination of factors has created the problems with the current system in contemporary society. The following highlights some of the major flaws in the Springfield education system.

Before we delve into our analysis of two seminal *Simpsons* episodes pertinent to education, it is valuable to explore the education system in contemporary society. There are certainly a lot of positives we can attribute to public education, and of the U.S. public education system in particular. There are thousands of dedicated teachers, who, unlike Mrs. Krabappel, strive to see their students shine. A recent survey taken by the National Governors Association, however, suggests that a number of students are not satisfied with the way in which their schools operate.

According to a recent article in the *NY Times*, "a large majority of high school students say their class work is not very difficult, and almost two-thirds say they would work harder if courses were more demanding or interesting." A large number of students also feel that they are not being adequately trained academically for college. Instead of requesting easier work and less homework, students seem to be requesting the complete opposite. A majority of students seem to be eager to learn, but because of certain obstacles within the education system, they feel that their needs are going unfulfilled. By studying the education system in Springfield, we can learn a lot about how to improve our own public education system.

"Bart the Genius" and the Value of Standardized Tests

"And how is education supposed to make me feel smarter? Besides, every time I learn something new, it pushes some old stuff out of my brain. Remember when I took that home wine-making course and I forgot how to drive?"
~ **Homer Simpson, on the disadvantages of education**

Any thorough examination of Simpsonian education should include a discussion of the season one episode entitled "Bart the Genius." In this episode, Mrs. Krabappel administers IQ tests to the children in her class. As she hands out the exams, she tells the class the following: "Now I don't want you to worry, class. These tests will have no effect on your grades. They merely determine your future social status and financial success, if any."

Krabappel's statement addresses a fundamental misconception held by persons in contemporary society. For example, the SAT is widely viewed as an indicator of a student's potential for success in college and thereafter. However, the fact that a United States senator (who shall remain nameless) failed to score a combined 800 on the exam (out of a possible 1600 total points) and the success of many other people underscores this idea. The inherent value of the SAT is that virtually all high school students who desire to attend an accredited four-year university must take it (although this trend seems to be slowly shifting). Other standardized tests are suspect as well. As numerous studies have shown, IQ tests in particular provide little insight into future financial and social status.

Krabappel's statement represents the commonly (and falsely) accepted belief that one exam can be the sole factor used to determine a child's future. Later in the episode, Bart switches exams with the class whiz, Martin Prince. When Principal Skinner learns of "Bart's" high score on the exam, he is momentarily skeptical of Bart's intellectual prowess:

Skinner: I think we should re-test him.

Dr. J.: No, I think we should move him to another school.

Skinner: Even better!

Understandably, Skinner would love to rid Springfield Elementary of Bart Simpson's antics. However, the fact that Dr. J. is so easily able to convince Skinner to send Bart to another school (the "Enriched Learning Center for Gifted Children") is revealing of the lack of dedication by teachers and educators in Springfield. Skinner probably did not completely fall for the idea that Bart was actually a genius, but he did not have to be coerced into allowing Bart to transfer into a school that was more geared toward geniuses. Instead, Skinner gleefully exclaims, "Even better!" when Dr. J. mentions the option of transferring Bart.

The complete reliance of the IQ test by Dr. J. in this episode serves to entirely reshape the perceived character traits of Bart Simpson. A quick glance at Bart's horrendous permanent record once made a woman exclaim something to the effect of, "You mean there really is a Bart Simpson?! Dear God!" However, Dr. J. concocts an explanation of Bart's previous school records:

Dr. J.: [measuring Bart's head with calipers] Tell me, Bart, are you ever bored in school?

Bart: Oh, you bet.

Dr. J.: Mm hm. Do you ever feel a little frustrated?

Bart: All the time, sir.

Dr. J.: Uh huh. And do you ever dream of leaving class to pursue your own intellectual development on an independent basis.

Bart: Oh, like you're reading my mind man.

Bart's responses to the first two questions posed by Dr. J. serve as interesting social commentary. Boredom and frustration can be considered characteristics of both "geniuses" and "proud under-achievers." A determination of Bart's intellectual status should thus be considered inconclusive. However, if Dr. J. had bothered to give Bart a history book to read and then tested him on what he had read, he would have quickly realized that Bart must have cheated on the IQ test, as Bart would most certainly have failed the exam.

The issue of reliance on a single examination was similarly examined on an episode of *Saved by the Bell*. In the episode, Zach, who almost invariably received low scores on in-class exams, scored a 1502 on the SAT and was being fervently recruited by the nation's top universities. Jessie, the straight-A student, did not fare as well on the exam. While her GPA was among the highest in her class, she scored only slightly above 1000 on the exam and was rejected by the schools of her choice. In a manner that closely resembles Edna Krabappel's statement pertaining to the importance of an IQ test, *Saved by the Bell* examined the importance and meaning—or lack thereof—of standardized tests. Now, the *Saved by the Bell* episode was not written with a penchant for accuracy. College admissions officers at some of the largest universities in the country utilize a 4800-point scale (out of 6400 total points) for their selection process:

TYPE	VALUE
GPA	2400 points
SAT	1600 points
SAT IIs (3)	2400 points (800 for each exam)

The SAT, while a significant factor in the student selection process, is not the single most important factor for schools that use the above scale. Because college admissions officers are well aware of the possibility that a student "choked" on an exam, other factors play a more prominent role in the selection process.

If the highly touted SAT is not *that* important for high school students, then how could the results of an IQ test from a ten-year-old determine the "future social status and financial status" of the child? Simply put, it cannot. And that is the inherent message behind Krabappel's quote. The episode concludes that standardized tests are often over-used and cannot necessarily determine intelligence or aptitude.

By making us laugh at the ludicrous, *The Simpsons* makes us reconsider our own preconceived misperceptions. And if we think hard enough about what *The Simpsons* presents to us, we often end up laughing at ourselves. In this way, satire can serve as a means by which changes to the inherent structure and ideals of society are conceived.

"Bart Gets an F" and President Bush's "No Child Left Behind" Education Reform Proposal

Further aspects of Simpsonian education can be examined in other episodes of *The Simpsons*.

In the episode entitled "Bart Gets an F," for example, several key aspects of American education are examined. First, the elements of "distraction" and "procrastination" from one's work are thoroughly emphasized by Bart's actions during the first half of the episode. In this particular episode, Bart yields to the enormous appeal of playing video games, as he visits the Noiseland Video Arcade after school. Bart's studies, however, are still at the forefront of his mind. He tells himself that he'll play "a couple more games, then…hit the books." At home later, after being further distracted by the cartoon series, *Itchy and Scratchy*, Bart is called in to eat dinner. Once again, Bart promises that "right after dinner, it's down to business." After dinner, Bart tries to go study, but is yanked into the living room by Homer, who forces Bart to watch *Gorilla the Conqueror* with him. Bart's response:

THE EDUCATION OF SPRINGFIELD 221

"Oh, well, maybe just one more hour [before I study]."

After the show, Bart finally manages to free his mind from distractions and begins to study. His ebullience is expressed as he opens his history book and begins reading. Within a few moments, however, Bart falls asleep. The sequence concludes with the following memorable lines spoken by Homer and Marge, as they observe Bart sleeping at his desk:

> **Homer:** Psst. Marge, come take a look at this.
> **Marge:** Oh...the little tiger tries so hard. Why does he keep failing?
> **Homer:** Just a little dim, I guess.

The brief conversation between Homer and Marge speaks volumes. First, the audience learns that Marge is completely clueless of the fact that Bart had not studied at any point during the day. It becomes obvious to the viewer that Marge should keep a more careful watch on Bart's activities and pay closer attention to how much time he actually devotes to studying. Marge's faults aside, however, it is fair to place most of the blame for Bart's failures on Homer's failures as a respectable role model for his son. In this particular episode, the fact that he forces Bart to watch television instead of encouraging him to study demonstrates a fundamental problem with Homer's parenting techniques.

Sadly, however, Homer's apathy for his son's education is reflective of the attitudes of many fathers in contemporary society. The case can be made such that Homer only dragged Bart to watch television in order to bond with him. This notion, as a matter of fact, was examined on an episode of *Boy Meets World*. In the episode, Alan Matthews (Cory's father) allowed Cory to stay up past his bedtime on a school night and watch an "important" Philadelphia Phillies baseball game. The issue over whether it was more important for Cory to stay up late and bond with his father rather than going to sleep on time was hotly debated throughout the episode. Regardless of one's opinion on the matter at hand, it should be fairly obvious to viewers that Homer's demand that Bart watch television wasn't a "one-time only" request; rather, it was representative of Homer's general apathy for education. Homer seems to instill a sort of procrastination ethic in Bart. Instead of teaching Bart responsibility, Homer effectively reduces his study time by not only tempting Bart with television but also by forcing him to watch. What chance does Bart have to do well in school if his own father does not see the value of responsibility?

Perhaps the most disheartening segment of this episode occurs when Bart is confronted by Mrs. Krabappel, Dr. J. Pryor, and both of his parents after Krabappel calls them all in to discuss Bart's recent failures on class examinations. As Krabappel reveals his grades to the assembled group, Bart exclaims, "Okay, okay! Why are we dancing around the obvious? I know it, you know it. I am dumb, okay? Dumb as a post! Think I'm happy about it?"

Bart then starts to cry and Dr. Pryor recommends that Bart be held back a year in school. Bart adamantly protests the idea: "Look at my eyes! See the sincerity! See the conviction? See the fear?…As God is my witness, I can pass the fourth grade!"

The next day of school is cancelled, and Bart has another opportunity to study. Residents of Springfield enjoy the magnificence of "Snow Day," which Mayor Quimby immediately declares to be "the funnest day in the history of Springfield!" This time, however, Bart fights the immense temptation to engage in activities such as sledding and snowball fights with friends, and instead attempts to study for his exam. Bart is truly determined—and motivated—to do well:

"You wanna be held back a grade? Concentrate, man!" he tells himself.

After Bart completes his exam in school the following day, he slaps himself in the face as a result of his frustration. Krabappel grades the test and informs Bart that he scored a 59. She dully remarks:

"Ugh. Another year together. Ugh, it's going to be hell."

Instead of actually caring about Bart's future, Krabappel is more bothered by the fact that she must spend more time with Bart. She certainly does not demonstrate a great deal of dedication to teaching in this scene. In fact, after noticing that Bart is especially upset after learning of his failure on the exam, she responds:

"I figure you'd be used to failing by now." In a miserably thin effort to sympathize with him, she notes: "Well, a 59 is a high F."

Fortunately for Bart, he is able to recall a highly detailed fact about United States history, and Krabappel passes him with a D-minus. Krabappel's emphasis on test scores serves as a starting point for an examination of the Bush Administration's education reform plan entitled No Child Left Behind.

It is here that several portions of President Bush's No Child Left Behind Act for education reform can be examined within the context of Simpsonian education. Item one of Section 1001 of Bush's proposal reads as follows:

> "...ensuring that high-quality academic assessments, accountability systems, teacher preparation and training, curriculum, and instructional materials are aligned with challenging State academic standards so that students, teachers, parents, and administrators can measure progress against common expectations for student academic achievement."

Unfortunately, no actual techniques or methods for studying are suggested at any point during the episode. Bart was essentially forced to either "pass the test" or "repeat the fourth grade." Thus, it is evident that Bart was not supplied with "appropriate instructional materials" to aid him in his studying habits. If Bush's plan accomplishes what it promises, Bart will have access to more educational resources.

Furthermore, item twelve of Section 1001 states that education reform should afford "parents substantial and meaningful
opportunities to participate in the education of their children..."
Homer and Marge certainly did not exhibit much influence on
Bart's study habits, nor were they encouraged to do so by Mrs.
Krabappel. Bush's aim to encourage parents to become more
involved in the education of their children would, if properly
implemented, serve an important role in education reform. It
should be noted, however, that some parents do not participate at
all in their child's education. Marge and Homer should, at a minimum, be credited with speaking with Mrs. Krabappel about
Bart's poor test scores. Bush's plan also emphasizes the importance of standardized testing in schools. This ideal, however, may
lead to the situation in which a student fails an exam by one point
and is forced to repeat a grade (a la Bart Simpson). In this respect,
Bush's plan does not solve the dilemma of the haphazard creation of
a dividing line between "barely passing" and "completely failing."

The great emphasis that No Child Left Behind places on
standardized test scores has forced some schools to abandon certain subjects and methods of teaching in order to have enough
time to prepare students for the tests. Many educators would be
willing to forego such subjects if doing so would enable students
to improve their test scores. But is No Child Left Behind working? Bart Simpson's peers—fourth-graders—have improved by
one point on math on average and three points in reading since
2003. Eighth-graders scored one point higher in math, but also
scored one point lower in reading. Interestingly, No Child Left
Behind seems to have actually slowed the rate of improvement on
standardized tests in its first few years of operation. Between 2000
and 2003, for example, fourth-graders' math scores improved by
nine points, while eighth-graders' scores jumped five points.
Bart's peers may have been better off before the changes.

Finally, in terms of the episode, it should be mentioned that
Bart was thrilled when he learned he passed the fourth grade.

That is understandable, of course. However, in this particular instance, Bart is thrilled that he earned a D-minus on the exam! While Bart will be able to enter the fifth grade (although the writers will always have him remain in the fourth grade!), there is something humorous about Bart's tremendous delight over his D-minus. Even Homer marvels over Bart's accomplishment:

> **Homer:** We're proud of you, boy!
> **Bart:** Thanks Dad. But part of this D-minus belongs to God…(Bart had previously prayed to God for a day off from school to study; it did indeed snow the following day.)

(The fact that Homer posts Bart's exam next to Lisa's A papers on the refrigerator demonstrates that Bart has made his mark in the Simpson home. This action also demonstrates Homer's penchant for competition among his children.)

Perhaps the writers of *The Simpsons* presented this scene in such a manner to represent a fundamental flaw in the American education system; that being that one point on an exam is often the difference between repeating a grade or moving onto the next. In essence, Bart's effort was rewarded because he was able to memorize a little-known fact. However, based on Bart's earlier test results, most educators would probably consider him a failure in the fourth grade. Still, I for one, am glad Bart passed the test.

The Simpsons: Content with Being Dysfunctional

T*he Simpsons* is a television show that depicts one family's not-so-unique journey through life in a society not entirely dissimilar to our own. I believe that the show's popularity is due in large part to the realness of the Simpson family's place in society: the show chronicles the lives of an "average" middle-class family, and their reactions to the world around them. As noted by London's *Daily Mail*, "The Simpsons are not just cartoon characters; they're real people living the kind of lives we all can identify with." The cumulative experiences of Homer, Bart, Marge, Lisa, and Maggie cover just about every major experience that we have in our daily lives. Whether it's Lisa's qualms with big business, Homer's frustration with the sanitation department, Marge's anger about the violence portrayed in the *Itchy and Scratchy* cartoon series, Bart's quibbles with authority figures (Principal Skinner in particular), or Maggie's relationship with Gerald, the baby with the one eyebrow, the tension that often goes unresolved on *The Simpsons* gives the show a sense of reality unmatched by television shows of lesser quality and depth. Government, big business, the education system, healthcare, consumerism, and celebrity culture are all lampooned on *The Simpsons*. But what truly makes *The Simpsons* special is not its message that authority cannot always be trusted; rather, the representation of one family's reactions and emotions to the way the world works makes *The Simpsons* unique and worthy of serious attention.

If you take only one lesson away from this book, I hope it is the following: Don't mess with *The Simpsons*. Sure, they're "dysfunctional," but that's certainly no reason to ridicule the fab-five. (In fact, as Homer would probably say in regards to comments made about his family: you can't spell "dysfunctional" without "functional.") Barbara Bush and William Bennett learned that lesson the hard way. Barbara Bush, for example, once remarked *"The Simpsons* is the dumbest thing I've ever seen." She later apologized for the comment. Bennett also had his qualms with *The Simpsons*, only to later retract a disparaging statement that he had made. As mentioned earlier, the elder President Bush also made a disparaging statement about *The Simpsons*, only to be criticized by Bart on an episode that aired three days later. The writers of *The Simpsons* aren't afraid of anyone—even Rupert Murdoch, the head of Newscorp (the parent company of Fox).

The Simpson family may not be the ideal family in American society. However, the family is a fairly accurate (although satirized) depiction of the average American family in contemporary culture. Not every family is perfect, and the Simpson family certainly encompasses the flaws that plague many real American families. Most American families have real problems: problems pertaining to ethics, morality, financial status, and family unity. While the Simpson family has many of the same problems that real American families face in their daily lives, and thus can be considered simply a reflection of family life in America, the family truly possesses a keen influence on one important aspect of our family life—that being unity within the classic familial structure. As I have shown, the Simpson family is extremely tight-knit. In fact, during the several instances in which the family seems to move farther apart from each other, episodes invariably conclude with the Simpson familial unit intact. (Recall "Barting Over," the episode in which Bart moves out of the Simpson house but ends up moving back in with the family by the conclusion of the episode.)

Familial values are inherent to the very nature of the Simpson family. While the family may be dysfunctional, the family members are satisfied with their lives and possess true love for one another. To emphasize this important point, please note the following song that the family sang during the Shary Bobbins episode:

> **Homer:** Around the house, I never lift a finger.
> As a husband and father, I'm subpar.
> I'd rather drink a beer
> than win Father of the Year.
> I'm happy with things the way they are.
> **Lisa:** I'm getting used to never getting noticed.
> **Bart:** I'm stuck here till I can steal a car.
> **Marge:** The house is still a mess,
> and I'm going bald from stress—
> **Bart and Lisa:** But we're happy just the way we are.

The Simpsons preaches the ideal of acceptance. Homer once said that "We're all fine the way we are." In the song above, Homer admits that he is not a great father—nor does he care to become one. Bart and Lisa grudgingly accept being ignored by their parents and transform this acceptance into a form of happiness. Bart and Lisa teach us that it is important to be happy with what you have, regardless of how meager a situation you may be in. This is so important because not every family is ideal, and it is a virtue to accept the conditions of your own family and make the best of the situation. Finally, Shary Bobbins's exasperation is certainly understandable. The Simpson clan continues to exist within the family's own unique system. An outsider, such as Shary

Bobbins, however, cannot live within their closed system. She is not part of the Simpson family and would never be able to live with the family for an extended period of time. Further evidence for this point comes from the "Treehouse of Horror" segment entitled "Bad Dream House," in which a haunted house chooses to destroy itself instead of living with the Simpsons. As Lisa pointedly noted:

"It chose to destroy itself rather than live with us. One can't help feeling a little rejected."

The Simpson family teaches us that it doesn't really matter what other people think of you as long as you're happy with who you are as an individual (or in this case, as a familial unit). All in all, the Simpson family is a genuinely decent family. They work as a team to survive the struggles of daily life. They also enjoy being together: it is no accident that the family sits together on the living room couch before each episode begins. The family values togetherness—even though they themselves may not realize it. In the end, fans come to the realization that the Simpson family is just like their own family. In great creative works, it is often difficult to determine whether the work is simply a reflection of society or whether society is a reflection of the work (kind of like the famous chicken and the egg conundrum). While there are certainly many ways in which *The Simpsons* influences society (as outlined in this book), it is sometimes difficult to tell whether the series is a reflection of our own existence or whether our society is merely a reflection of Simpsonian society.

At some point, we come to the following conclusion: the two societies are one and the same. And before you frown, stop and think for a moment. Think about all of the aspects of Simpsonian society that are vital in our lives—from politics to education to healthcare. Then challenge yourself to pick out the character on the series who most defines who you are (everyone *is* essentially a Simpson!). Forget your previous role models: Michael Jordan, the Fonz, Stephen Hawking, Bill Gates…nah…the *Simpsons* character you have just chosen, my friend, is essentially your American idol. And for those critics who *still* believe that Simpsons characters are in some way "dangerous" depictions of real people in contemporary society, Homer has a few words in his own defense:

> **Doctor:** Mr. Simpson, I'm convinced you pose no threat to yourself or others.
> **Homer:** That's the most flattering thing anybody's ever said to me. Can I have it in writing?

Now that we've got that in print, Homer, the world will be much the wiser.

The Pursuit of the Perfect Donut

"Donuts—is there anything they can't do?" ~ **Homer Simpson**

In the closing seconds of "Two Cars in Every Garage, Three Eyes on Every Fish," Mr. Burns tells Homer that he will personally see to it that Homer's dreams "go unfulfilled." Homer does not take the threat with a grain of salt and seeks reassurance from Marge. We know that Homer is a dreamer—in one episode he declared that he has only "one dream in life. To achieve my many goals." Surely, though, Burns would never interfere with Homer's search for his "perfect donut"...or would he?

Let's hear what Marge has to say:

> **Homer:** Oh. My dreams will go unfulfilled? Oh, no! I don't like the sound of that one bit. That means I have nothing to hope for. Marge, make it better please, can't you make it better, huh?
>
> **Marge:** Homer, when a man's biggest dreams include seconds on dessert, occasional snuggling, and sleeping in 'til noon on weekends, no one man can destroy them.

Homer: Hey, you did it! [He then kisses and snuggles with Marge.]

If Homer is seeking the "perfect donut" in the strictly metaphorical sense, whereby the donut is a stand in for everything that he desires to possess in his life, he surely has found it. He has a wonderful wife, three great children (although sometimes he "just wants to choke the boy"), a great home, and a stable job. It is true that we see a lot of things in Homer in which we do not wish to see in ourselves: the beer chugging, the sheer ignorance, the self-centeredness, etc....But at the same time, we can all learn a lot about achieving the ideal of happiness from our favorite cartoon father. It is true that Homer will probably never become wealthy or be able to retire at a young age or achieve great things, but the mark of true success is not necessarily achievement but the ability to go from failure to failure without any real loss of enthusiasm. (And yes, I did get that last part from a fortune cookie!) Homer is happy with the little things in life—and this is something that the wealthy Mr. Burns, who can hardly crack a smile, will never be able to understand. No, Mr. Burns cannot see to it that Homer's dreams go unfulfilled: as long as Homer has great people around him, he will continue to be happy.

I believe that if Homer's biggest influence on our own lives is to force us to look around and be thankful for what we have, *The Simpsons* has accomplished its goal. And, on that note, I really think I should let you close this book and go out and purchase a box of donuts. Just make sure that none of them have that purple fruit stuff inside. Glazed is perfect. Mmm...perfect donut.

The Homer
Simpson
Quiz

Finding Your "Inner Homer": The Homer Simpson Quiz

1. Do you enjoy drinking beer and/or eating donuts? (Score one point if your response is 'Yes.')

2. Do you enjoy watching television? (Score one point if your response is 'Yes.')

3. Do you drool at the dinner table on pork chop night? (Score one point if your response is 'Yes.')

4. Are you a well-intentioned (yet occasionally inconsiderate and absent-minded) husband and father? (Score one point if your response is 'Yes.')

5. Are you a dedicated worker/employee? (Score one point if your response is 'No.')

6. Do you enjoy reading books? (Score one point if your response is 'No.')

7. Do you enjoy reading *TV Guide*? (Score one point if your response is 'Yes.')

8. Are you bald or balding? (Score one point if your response is 'Yes.')

9. Do you enjoy sleeping? (Score one point if your response is 'Yes.')

10. Do you dislike your next-door neighbor? (Score one point if your response is 'Yes.')

Scoring:

0–3 points: You're nothing like the H-man ("D'oh!").

4–6 points: You look a bit like Homer. (You may be in the process of balding or your skin may be gradually changing to yellow, but you can stand to gain a few more pounds!)

7–9 points: You're almost there. You're still slightly more intelligent than Homer.

10 points: Wow, good sir, I salute you. Throw out all of your clothes and purchase one white shirt and one pair of blue pants. This will be your work attire for the rest of your career. And be proud of yourself: not too many Americans exhibit every Homeric characteristic. This is a proud day. You might even want to play golf: you can use your open-faced club sand wedge…"Mmm…open-faced club sandwich."

More on
The Simpsons
and Society

"They have the Internet on computers now?" ~ **Homer**

Please visit my website: www.simpsonsandsociety.com, which includes photos, as well as a list of events, book signings, book festivals, lectures, reviews, and other book information.

My other website is located at:
www.webspawner.com/users/simpsonsandsociety/

If you represent a media outlet who would like to request an interview, a bookstore wishing to schedule a book signing, or if you're a reader who has an inquiry or comment or would just like to drop me a line, you can email me at: homer7422@hotmail.com.

A new website specially created for information regarding *The World According to the Simpsons* is located at: www.stevenkeslowitz.com

Notes

Introduction

1 *A 2003 poll*: Poll results found at:
   http://news.bbc.co.uk/1/hi/world/americas/2985728.stm

2 *Another BBC Internet poll*:
   http://news.bbc.co.uk/1/hi/entertainment/tv_and_radio/2984
   426.stm

3 *As noted by Michael Solomon*: Solomon, Michael, *TV Guide*,
   February 15–21, 2003, 27.

3 *And you know, when you study*: Interview with Matt Groening:
   http://www.snpp.com/other/interviews/groening93.html

3 *Case in point*:
   http://www.nohomers.net/content/info/didyouknow/

5 *The comedy [genre] goes back*: Stated in an interview aired on
   NBC: *Early Today*, April 13, 2004.
   http://wnbc.feedroom.com/iframeset.jsp?ord=721865

9 *As Jonathan Swift notes*: Grossman, Lev, "The Way We Live
   Now," *TIME*, April 26, 2004.

10 *Cultural critic Chris Turner*: Turner, Chris, *Planet Simpson*
    (Cambridge, MA: Da Capo Press, 2004).

10 *In* The Simpsons and Philosophy: *Albany Times-Union*, quoted
    in Henry, Ed, "Heard on the Hill," *Roll Call* 44, no. 81 (May
    13, 1999), quoted in Cantor, Paul A., "The Simpsons:
    Atomistic Politics and the Nuclear Family," in *The Simpsons
    and Philosophy: The D'oh of Homer*, ed. William Irwin,
    (Illinois: Carus Publishing Co., 2001).

10 *So Homer asks*: For an in-depth discussion of gun control and
    The Simpsons, see the gun control essay in Section 3 of this book.

11 *As Michael Starr*: Starr, Michael, "Voice of Treason," *NY
    Post*, August 10, 2004.

Chapter 1: The Simpsons and Society

16   *He goes on to give*: Plato, *The Apology*, trans. Benjamin Jowett, http://www.paganlibrary.com/etext/apology_socrates.php.

17   *In the* Apology: Ibid.

18   *As noted by Elphaba*: Maguire, Gregory, *Wicked: The Life and Times of the Wicked Witch of the West* (New York, NY: Regan Books, 1995).

18   *While admittedly a bleak*: The writers of *The Simpsons* were not the first to explore the idea that power has the potential to breed corruption. This idea, for example, was examined at least as far back as Sophocles' *Antigone*, in which the powerful King Creon makes several key mistakes in judgment as a result of his blindness. Shakespeare also explores the idea that power breeds blindness in tragedies such as *Macbeth*.

20   The Simpsons *shows us*: Biffle, Christopher, *A Guided Tour of John Stuart Mill's Utilitarianism* (New York: McGraw-Hill, 1992).

20   *A line from the fifteenth*: Socrates' notion that people should think for themselves has proved to be a common theme throughout history. Examples of people thinking for themselves include the European Enlightenment, the Renaissance, the development of Lutheranism, and the civil rights movements.

20   *Socrates would surely support*: The idea of "might makes right" is a recurrent theme in Thucydides' *History of the Peloponnesian War*. When the Athenians engage in dialogue with the people of Melos, the Athenians use bullying tactics and claim that the fact that they possess power confers upon them the right to conquer weaker peoples.

20   *In Plato's* Republic: Plato, *The Republic*, trans. Benjamin Jowett, http://classics.mit.edu/Plato/republic.html.

21   *In Carmel, New York*: These laws were culled from a number of internet sources, including http://www.floydpinkerton.net/fun/laws.html

22 *In another, Wiggum*: Other examples of Springfield's silly laws: In "Bart's comet," Homer reminds Bart that, according to the town charter, if "food stuff shall touch the ground, said food stuff shall be turned over to the village idiot." In a season sixteen episode, Homer was arrested for kicking a can on the sidewalk. The evidence is clear: Stupid laws exist both in Springfield and in contemporary society.

22 *He defines the Sleeper Curve*: Johnson, Steven, *Everything Bad Is Good for You* (Riverhead Hardcover, 2005).

24 *We are curious creatures*: There are exceptions to this general idea, of course. In "Lisa the Iconoclast," for example, Lisa stumbles upon some disparaging facts about the revered founder of Springfield, Jebediah Springfield, and decides at the last moment not to come forward with her newly found information. She realizes that the false belief holds a purpose: It unites different generations of Springfield and enables diverse people to form a common bond with one another. By coming forward with the facts about Jebediah, Lisa could have potentially shaken the townspeople's beliefs and disrupted the town's unity.

On a separate note, the fact that the town has so much respect for Jebediah mirrors the respect and adulation we have toward the Founding Fathers of the United States. The Founding Fathers certainly were not perfect people; it serves a purpose though, to hold the belief that they were.

Chapter 2: Is Homer a Good Father?

36 *He prepares her 9 a.m.*: Richmond, Ray, *The Simpsons: A Complete Guide to Our Favorite Family* (HarperCollins, 1997).

40 *In "And Maggie Makes Three,"*: Part of the reason that Homer tries to be a good father towards Maggie is that, as he admitted in the season fifteen episode "Moe Baby Blues," he doesn't want to go "0 for 3" with regards to his children. Maggie, in his mind, serves as a last chance at redemption.

41 *As a moving*: MacGregor, Jeff, "More Than Sight Gags and Subversive Satire," Television/Radio, *New York Times*, June 20, 1999.

Chapter 3: Bart: America's Bad Boy?

44 *Jewish children, for example*: Turner, Chris, *Planet Simpson* (Da Capo Press, 2004).

45 *There was even a black*: Ibid.

46 *Deviancy is easier to*: www.dictionary.com

46 *In "Practicing Deviancy*: Johnston, Daniel, "Practicing Deviancy—The Value of Being Deviant," *Georgia Psychological Association*, http://www.gapsychology.org/dis playcommon.cfm?an=1&subarticlenbr=40.

47 *In his essay "Bart Simpson*: Rushkoff, Douglas, "Bart Simpson: Prince of Irreverence" in *Leaving Springfield*, (Detroit: Wayne State University Press, 2003), 292–301.

47 *While all the Homer*: That is not to say, of course, that Bart is not susceptible to *any* mass media influences: he adores his idol, Krusty the Clown, and in addition to calling the Krusty hotline, has a room full of Krusty paraphernalia. Bart is obviously influenced by different media than Homer, and Krusty may be his one and only weakness. I qualify this point only to show but one exception; for the most part, Bart, as Rushkoff argues, is less complacent—and less influenced by outside media influences—than Homer.

48 *We see here that*: At other times, Bart is also shown to be open to behaving well. In "Separate Vocations," Bart becomes a hall monitor—a figure of authority—and enjoys using his power to promote order and respect throughout Springfield Elementary. Bart is still a deviant, here, however: he is the only student that is given this authority. We see, therefore, that Bart's bad behavior is not a result of his inherent tendency to provoke mayhem and act mischievously. Conversely, Bart will actually behave well if such an oppor-

tunity enables him to be perceived as deviant.

49 *In a June 2004* TIME: Steptoe, Sonja, "Minding Their Manners: A New Breed of Etiquette Classes for the Generation of Kids Raised on Bart Simpsons and Britney Spears," *TIME*, June 7, 2004.

49 *So perhaps bad*: This point, while an important one, must be qualified here. In "Bart's Inner Child," the townspeople attempt to "do what they feel like" a la Bart, and this unequivocally leads to disastrous consequences. Still, the assertion that Goodman sets forth—that is, that exploring society's boundaries and finding one's place within a larger societal social context is important—remains valid. The townspeople get more than a bit carried away with Goodman's ideas, and this extremism is what leads to the disorder in Springfield. Goodman's comments about Bart, while certainly dangerous when acted upon in an extreme manner, can still be considered fundamentally sound when utilized in a proper fashion.

49 *The episode "Bart's Inner Child,"*: The writers of this episode may have had a different agenda than the one discussed in this essay. The main idea behind the episode may very well have been to expose overconfident self-help gurus as purveyors of hogwash. As noted, however, although Goodman's message taken to the extreme leads to disastrous consequences, his main assertion pertaining to exploring and expanding boundaries is interesting to consider, and should not be dismissed as mere hogwash.

50 *As Paul A. Cantor*: Cantor, Paul A, *Gilligan Unbound: Pop Culture in the Age of Globalization* (Rowman & Littlefield Publishers, 2003).

60 *Orwell describes this situation*: http://www.online-literature.com/orwell/887/

60 *Similarly, Bart must keep*: This remains the case despite the fact that Bart has toned down his bad behavior in recent

244 THE WORLD ACCORDING TO *THE SIMPSONS*

years. At times, Bart still does feel pressured to keep up his
"bad boy" image.

Chapter 4: Marge: Holding the Family Together

62–63 *Despite the temptations*: Marge sticks by Homer, despite
being aware of his many, many flaws. In "The War of
the Simpsons," Marge even makes a list of Homer's
imperfections: "He forgets birthdays, anniversaries,
holidays—both religious and secular—he chews with his
mouth open, he gambles, he hangs out in a seedy bar
with bums and lowlifes. He blows his nose on towels and
puts them back in the middle. He drinks out of the carton.
He never changes the baby. When he goes to sleep, he
makes chewing noises. When he wakes up, he makes
honking noises. Oh, oh—and he scratches himself with
his keys. I guess that's it. Oh, no, wait. He kicks me in
his sleep and his toenails are too long...and yellow."

Chapter 6: To Speak or Not to Speak: Maggie Simpson vs. Stewie Griffin

75 *Tao Te Ching*: Irwin, William, *The Simpsons and Philosophy:
The D'oh! Of Homer* (Illinois: Carus Publishing Co., 2001).

Chapter 7: Beyond the Fab Five: A Look at the Supporting Cast

80 *There is no question*: Idato, Michael, "Ready, Set, D'oh!,"
Sydney Morning Herald, February 27, 2003,
http://www.smh.com.au/articles/2003/02/26/1046064102384.h
tml.

81 *Burns's unrequited love*: Indeed, the middle-class industrialized employee, Homer J. Simpson, is viewed as the fortunate man in this situation, as he has successfully won the
heart of Marge. For a more thorough discussion of Homer's
role as the industrialized employee, see the essay on indus-

trialization in this book.

Chapter 8: The Simpsons and Other Television Sitcoms: Politics and the Nuclear Family

94–95 *Ed Bishop of* The Riverfront Times: Bishop, Ed, *The Riverfront Times,* June 3, 1992 quoted in Korte, Dan, "The Simpsons as Quality Television," November 1997, http://www.snpp.com/other/papers/dk.paper.html.

95 *Similarly, Dan Connor's*: Terrace, Vincent, *Television Sitcom Fact Book* (United States: McFarland and Company, Inc., 2000).

96 *Perhaps the balance of*: Also note that Archie Bunker in *All in the Family* often goes to Kelsey's Bar to "escape" from household feuds and his frustrations with the Bunker clan.

97 *Now here's why*: In "The Springfield Connection," Marge becomes a police officer and Homer does seem a bit irritated that she has begun to work outside of the home:

Homer: Oh, you've become such a cop. And not that long ago, you were so much more to me. You were a cleaner of pots, a sewer of buttons, an unplugger of hairy clogs.

Marge: I'm still all of those things. Only now I'm cleaning up the city, sewing together the social fabric, and unplugging the clogs of our legal system.

Homer: You're cooking what for dinner?

Homer does not want to prevent Marge from pursuing her career goals, but he still wants her to be the Marge that he has become accustomed to. Homer acts selfishly, but his intention is not really to control his wife. This episode examines an idea that has arisen a number of times on *The Simpsons* and reflects the trend in contemporary society of shifting roles for men and women.

Chapter 9: Ay Carumba! Simpsonian News and Views

104 *However,* The Simpsons: *The Simpsons'* influence in real-life
politics can also be seen: In the 2005 Brooklyn District
Attorney election, for example, Democratic candidate
Arnie Kriss sent out a mailing with a giant picture of the
Simpson family, and posed the following question to the
voting public: "Really, should we reelect a D.A. who's been
around longer than *The Simpsons*? (He was referring to the
incumbent District Attorney Joe Hynes.)

In a 2005 election campaign in New Zealand, a group
called "the Lisa Simpsons" cast a political opponent as
being similar to Mr. Burns.
(Simpsonschannel.com.)

Chapter 10: The Simpsons and Globalization

109 *Women and Wal-Mart*: Egelko, Bob and Jenny Strasburg,
"US: Wal-Mart Faces Huge Sex Discrimination Suit," *San
Francisco Chronicle*, June 23, 2004, quoted in
http://www.corpwatch.org/article.php?id=11375.

110 *Corporations like Wal-Mart*: Two recent documentaries
address the pros and cons of Wal-Mart: *Why Wal-Mart
Works and Why That Makes Some People Crazy* and *Wal-Mart:
The High Cost of Low Price*.

111 *Corporate culture instills*: The "universalization of sameness"
refers to the globalist push for the sameness of products (a
McDonald's hamburger is designed to taste exactly the
same whether you order it in Brooklyn, New York, or in
Bismarck, North Dakota) and establishments (Target stores
are designed to closely resemble one another).

111 *In 1995, American political*: Barber, Benjamin, *Jihad vs.
McWorld: How Globalism and Tribalism Are Reshaping the
World* (Ballantine Books, 1995, reprinted 2002).

112 *Springfield, the hometown*: In the episode "Lisa's Wedding,"
which is set in the future, the trend toward McWorld and

the penetrance of corporate culture is made even more explicit. In a scene that is often deleted in syndication (presumably because of the need for commercial time), the children at Springfield Elementary learn their lessons via television, rather than being taught by an actual teacher. Corporate culture even dominates in the education system, as can be seen when the children watch "Pepsi Presents Addition and Subtraction." In the Springfield of the future, the intertwined forces of McWorld and corporate culture influence the ways in which children learn lessons in school. Corporations seeking to infiltrate a culture will certainly have a distinct advantage if they can have an impact on the styles in which students learn in school.

We see from this example: Even the local "Mom and Pop Hardware" store in Springfield is "A Subsidiary of Global Dynamics, Inc." (noted by Paul A. Cantor in *Gilligan Unbound*).

113 *A place like Americatown*: Americatown stands in stark contrast to Ethnictown, which is located in Springfield, and, according to Homer, is "where hard-working immigrants dream of becoming lazy, overfed Americans" ("Treehouse of Horror XII").

113 *When Lisa suggests going*: Marge's comment is also a clear dose of social commentary pertaining to the trend of Japanese automakers and electrical designers to design products that are "smaller and more efficient" than products made in the good ol' USA.

116 *In a TIME 27, 2005, article*: Elliott, Dorinda and Powell, Bill, "Wal-Mart Nation," *TIME*, June 27, 2005.

117 *Well, maybe not*: This dialogue is a perfect example of the fact that *Simpsons* quotes can be interpreted in various ways. One may find no deeper meaning in this quote, and simply enjoy the scene for its humor. Others may view the quote as an attempt to criticize McDonald's for covering

up the fact that they use chemicals to produce their food (I'm sure that McDonald's uses something along the lines of "partially gelatinated nondairy gum-based,") but then covertly hide these ingredients by calling the beverage a "shake." *Simpsons* quotes like this one are open to various interpretations, and this is another reason why *The Simpsons* rewards repeat consumption.

118 *As evidenced by Joseph E. Stiglitz*: Stiglitz, Joseph E, *Globalization and Its Discontents* (New York: Norton, 2003), quoted in Papp, Daniel S., *American Foreign Policy: History, Politics, and Policy* (Pearson Education, 2005).

119 *In a July 2005 article*: Quotes about Disney in China excerpted from Schuman, Michael and Jeffrey Ressner, "Disney's Great Leap to China," *TIME*, July 18, 2005.

120 *"Disney has learned,"*: The idea that large corporations cannot successfully impose their will on other nations was examined in the season six episode in which the Simpson family visits Itchy and Scratchy Land, a theme park built in response to the popularity of the children's cartoon series. At the very end of the episode, the scene shifts to Euro Itchy and Scratchy Land, where the gigantic parking lots are shown to be completely empty and the park itself utterly deserted. The idea is that not all elements of popular American culture will be similarly popular in other nations.

121 *Either way, there will always*: On August 3, 2005, it was reported that China has begun to forbid any foreign TV channels from entering the country. This effort, if continued, will curb the expansion of foreign media influence in China. This is but one example of a nation attempting to resist the forces of McWorld. (AOL Business News, August 3, 2005.)

124 *Soft power, as Joseph S. Nye, Jr.*: Nye Jr., Joseph S, *The Paradox of American Power* (New York, Oxford, 2002),

quoted in Papp, Daniel S., *American Foreign Policy: History, Politics, and Policy* (Longman, 2004).

124 *Whether or not soft power*: When considering this question, it is interesting to note that al-Queda leader Osama bin Laden has been known to offer Pepsi to his guests. In videos, he has been shown wearing a Timex watch. Both are products of the West.

124 *Not everyone agrees that*: Friedman, Thomas, *The World Is Flat: A Brief History of the 21st Century* (Farrar, Straus, and Giroux, 2005).

124 *Well, according to a worldwide*: Balko, Radley, "Globalization and Culture: Americanization or Cultural Diversity?," *aworldconnected.org*, www.aworldconnected.org/article.php/486.html.

124–125 *Furthermore, a* Reason *magazine*: Balko, Radley, "Globalization & Culture: Americanization or Cultural Diversity?," *aworldconnected.org*, www.aworldconnected.org/article.php/486.html.

125 *In terms of the argument*: Gray, John, *False Dawn: The Delusions of Global Capitalism* (New Press, 1999), quoted in Beard, Duncan Stuart, *Leaving Springfield* (Detroit: Wayne State University Press, 2003).

125 *The Simpsons: Global Empire*: The Simpson family has visited every continent with the exclusion of Antarctica.

126 *Don't forget: America*: Herskovitz, Jon, "Homer Simpson: Made in Korea," *Reuters*, March 2, 2005, http://www.freerepublic.com/focus/f-news/1354555/posts.

126 *Most people around*: Attempts by certain citizen activist groups have been made in order to suppress airings of *The Simpsons*. In 2005, for example, a resident of Moscow argued that *The Simpsons* promotes violence, drugs, and homosexuality. The claims were dismissed as baseless (Mosnews.com, Simpsonschannel.com).

126   The Wall Street Journal: El-Rashidi, Yasmine, "D'oh! Arabized Simpsons Not Getting Many Laughs," *Wall Street Journal*, October 14, 2005, quoted in http://www.post-gazette.com/pg/05287/588741.stm.

Chapter 11: Television, the Typographic Mind, and Selling the Three-Eyed Fish

130   *In* Amusing Ourselves to Death: Other *Simpsons* episodes have also portrayed the media as presenting gimmicky news. In "Lisa on Ice," for example, Kent Brockman reports on the "Death Toll from Snow." Sounding as though this is a newsworthy story, Channel 6 shows a flashing screen in an attempt to grasp viewers' attention. The actual death toll reported by Brockman? Zero.

130   *High literacy rates spurned*: Postman, Neil, *Amusing Ourselves to Death: Public Discourse in the Age of Show Business* (Penguin Books, 1986).

130–131   *Postman attributes the prodigious*: Ibid. 41.

131   *For example, the* Federalist Papers: Ibid. 38.

131   *Furthermore, he states*: Ibid. 51.

131   *For example, the public*: In contrast to these lengthy debates, even contemporary intellectuals like Lisa find it hard to sit still for such long periods of time. In "And Maggie Makes Three," Homer endeavors to tell his children a story only to be rebuffed by Lisa: "Dad, you can't expect us to sit for thirty minutes straight!"

131   *As Postman states*: Ibid. 47.

133   *In "Two Cars," Mr. Burns'*: Cantor, Paul A., *Gilligan Unbound: Pop Culture in the Age of Globalization* (Rowman & Littlefield Publishers, 2003).

136   *As noted by David Grote*: Grote, David, *The End of Comedy: The Sit-Com and the Comic Tradition* (Hamden: Archon Books, 1983), quoted in Waltonen, Karma, "We're All

Pigs," The Simpsons Archive,
http://snpp.com/other/papers/kw.paper.html.

136–137 *The Simpson family*: Television is such a fundamental part of the life of Homer, for instance, that he notes the following in this conversation:

Marge: We don't think you're slow. But on the other hand, it's not like you go to museums, or read books, or anything.
Homer: You think I don't want to? It's those TV networks, Marge. They won't let me. One quality show after another, each one fresher and more brilliant than the last. If they only stumbled once; just gave us thirty minutes to ourselves! But they won't! They won't let me live! [Sobs]

Television has clearly taken over the life of Homer Simpson.

137 *In fact, as Steven Johnson*: Johnson, Steven, *Everything Bad Is Good for You* (Riverhead Hardcover, 2005).

138 *For example, Neil Postman*: Postman, Neil, *Amusing Ourselves to Death* (Penguin, 1986).

139 *As Postman notes*: Ibid. 128.

139 *Furthermore, Postman correctly states*: Ibid. 134.

139 *The employee, befittingly, turns*: Though not of voting age, Lisa, for one, does not fall victim to Burns's gimmicky political photo opportunity. Upon learning that she must memorize a contrived question to ask Mr. Burns during dinner, she responds initially by asking Burns the following:

Advisor: Little girl, do you think you can memorize this by dinnertime tomorrow?
Lisa: "Mr. Burns: your campaign seems to have the momentum of a runaway freight train. Why are you so popular?"
Advisor: Very good.

> **Lisa:** Mm. Well, as long as I'm asking something,
> can I ask him to assuage my fears that he's contam-
> inating the planet in a manner that may one day
> render it uninhabitable?
> **Advisor:** No, dear. The card question'll be fine.
> **Marge:** Well, I think the non-card question is a
> valid…
> **Homer:** Marge!…Don't worry. My daughter's very
> bright, and I'm sure she'll be able to memorize your
> question by dinnertime tomorrow.

140 *Tricks of the Trade: The Simpsons* has also shown how politicians and the media use gimmicky, disingenuous language
in order to fool their audiences. In "Homer Defined," for
example, Burns argues that his plant is not on the verge of
a "meltdown," but instead is experiencing an "unrequested
fission surplus."

In another *Simpsons* episode, which is set in the future,
Lisa becomes president of the United States, and decides to
raise taxes. But instead of openly stating her proposal, she
notes on national television that she proposes a tax "refund
adjustment." This trick actually works—until the true
intent of her idea comes to the surface.

A quick political gimmick: In "Sideshow Bob Roberts,"
Quimby is sweating during the mayoral debate, and
Channel 6 decides to position a ring of fire around his face
in an attempt to embarrass him further.

141–142 *Postman notes that "today*: Ibid. 131.

142 *Postman also introduces*: Ibid. 107.

142 *As Postman later notes*: Ibid. 141.

144 *Once again, we can*: Television should not be solely blamed
for this tendency. Newspapers and magazines also sometimes attempt to use authoritative voices in order to influence the ideas of their audiences—and in effect, attempt to
block out other media influences. In *Citizen Kane*, Charles

Foster Kane highlights this idea, asserting that "People will tell think what I tell them to think." This famous line, incidentally, was parodied on an episode of *The Simpsons*. When Homer becomes a food critic in "Guess Who's Coming to Criticize Dinner?" he lets the power go to his head and tells Lisa that "People will think what I tell them you think when you tell me what to tell them to think."

Chapter 12: The Simpsons and American Exceptionalism

148 The Simpsons *and American Exceptionalism*: While the following discourse will examine satirical examples of American Exceptionalism found in this episode, one short, but powerful scene in this episode is intended to demonstrate that Americans have a lot to learn from other nations. At a critical point in the episode, the Simpson clan rushes back to the American embassy, which is guarded by a faulty gate, which is, it is made clear, "made in the U.S.A."

150 *The idea of "Exceptionalism,"*: The concept of exceptionalism probably does extend back further—within tribal groups and Biblical settings—but for our purposes, it serves us well to examine its roots in the ancient Greek tradition.

150 *Odysseus notes the following*: Homer, *The Odyssey*, Book IX, http://www.classicauthors.net/Homer/odyssey/odyssey9.html.

151 *In Thucydides'* History: Thucydides', *History of the Peloponnesian War*.

151 *The idea of Exceptionalism*: Herodotus', *The Histories*.

151 *Herodotus, in praising*: Even the ethnocentric Homer Simpson has, at times, been known to express his amazement with the lifestyles of foreigners. In "30 Minutes over Tokyo," Homer, upon seeing an array of colors shooting out of a Japanese toilet, exclaimed "Wha!…They're years ahead of us." This is a rare example of Homer's admiration of other cultures; for once, at least in this regard, he doesn't

view America as superior.

152 *His actions and mindset*: Homer is indeed the "everything" man: he once declared himself a "true Renaissance man" after consuming eight different types of meat. Wow.

153 *In* On Paradise Drive: Brooks, David, *On Paradise Drive: How We Live Now (And Always Have) in the Future Tense* (Simon and Schuster, 2004).

155 *On a grander scale*: Homer Simpson serves as an interesting case-in-point when discussing middle-class America. At times, he seems quite poor—for years he was unable to afford to purchase a $200 air conditioner, for example. At other times, however, Homer and the rest of his family spend money freely on vacations and, as in this episode, lobsters for dinner. The writers show that Homer does struggle with money at times. At many other times, and particularly in "Homer's Enemy," Homer is portrayed as a member of the near-upper middle class.

156 *His upbringing has ingrained*: Again, it's not that Homer actually views himself as "better" than other people. The idea, here, is that Homer accepts the fact that he lives a relatively wealthy lifestyle while there are billions of people starving in the world. Grimes' most important role in this episode is to remind us of this fact.

156 *This is not Homer's*: That is not to say that Homer's life has been absolutely perfect. His mother did leave him twice— once as a child and then, once reunited, again as an adult.

158 *In the controversial season*: In discussing this episode, it is important to note that people from different countries will view this episode from different perspectives. As noted by Duncan Stuart Beard, "While American viewers interpret the show through their worldview, Australians view it through their own distinct set of cultural understandings." *Leaving Springfield* (Wayne State University Press, 2003).

159 *Homer harshly criticizes*: Duncan Stuart Beard (*Leaving*

Springfield, 2003)—notes that this episode referenced the famous Michael Fay capital punishment incident that took place in Singapore during the 1980s.

159–160 *The International Criminal Court*: http://en.wikipedia.org/wiki/International_Criminal_ Court

161 *Paul Cantor, for example*: Cantor, Paul A., *Gilligan Unbound* (Lanham, Maryland: Rowman and Littlefield Publishers, Inc., 2001).

162 *It is true that Larry*: Actually, according to Answers.com, the "Dance of Joy," which is performed by the cousins when they are happy about something, is a cross between the Do-Si-Do, and the hokey pokey with "jazz hands." It was learned by Balki while he lived in Mypos. It is interesting to note that this particular Myposian traditional dance is loosely based on American-style dances.

163 *The writers are thus*: The island Mypos, while fictional, is said to be located in the Greek isles. Balki's accent, according to Answers.com, "was originally based on a Greek accent, but later into the show morphed into more of a Russian dialect."

165 *In "The Crepes of Wrath,"*: The surname "Hoxha" is, as Paul Cantor points out, a reference to the Albanian dictator Enver Hoxha. Cantor, Paul A., *Gilligan Unbound* (Lanham, Maryland: Rowman and Littlefield Publishers, Inc., 2001).

165 *Certainly, one can argue*: Cantor, Paul. A, *Gilligan Unbound* (Lanham, Maryland: Rowman and Littlefield Publishers, Inc. 2001).

167 *While debating the direction*: Lisa is the Simpson whose mindset is most similar to that of Herodotus. She possesses a propensity for knowledge, and while in Australia, even wants to purchase an Australian didgeridoo, an authentic object of Australian culture.

167 *Instead, the message*: Further evidence that the writers' sole

intention here was not simply to portray American children as unaware of the world around them is provided by Homer's reaction to Bart's admission that he is being indicted for fraud in Australia. Homer's response: "Hmm…there it is: Aust-ral-ia. I'll be damned. Look at this country: U-r-uguay—hehehheheheh." Homer, like Bart, is content with knowing his own surroundings, and fails to account for the existence of other nations and cultures. This idea was also examined in the season six episode "The PTA Disbands." In the episode, the teachers go on strike and Marge becomes a substitute teacher. She quickly becomes frustrated:

Marge: It took the kids forty minutes to locate Canada [on the map]!

Homer: Oh, anyone can miss Canada—all tucked away down there.

Once again, we see that Homer knows nothing about geography or the scope of the world. The only place that matters to Homer is Springfield, USA.

168 *Still, Bart's incredulity*: Homer isn't much better: in "Moo Goo Gai Pan," Homer refers to China as a separate "planet."

168 *Bart asked*: Groening, Matt, *The Simpsons Beyond Forever* (New York: HarperCollins Publishers, Inc., 2002).

168 *For one reason or another*: The idea that God pays attention only to America was satirized in an episode of *Family Guy*. In the episode, Chris marries a girl in South Africa, and the following exchange takes place between Chris and his mother, Lois:

Chris: [who has just married a girl in South Africa] We're married.

Lois: Well maybe here, but not in America where God pays attention.

The above exchange clearly outlines the point that Bart

makes: it is implied that America is such a special place that God pays attention only to the affairs and tribulations of Americans, while ignoring whatever is going on in the rest of the world.

169 *The Talmud explicitly states*: Babylonian *Talmud*, Sanhedrin (37a).

169 *The Talmud supports*: The United States' Declaration of Independence similarly dissolves the concept of exceptionalism. For example, Jefferson clearly states that "all men are created equal."

170–171 *The United States, critics*: The U.S. is not the only nation that has taken criticism for its supposedly lackadaisical poverty and disaster relief efforts. The U.N.'s emergency-relief coordinator noted that "[Industrialized nations] were more generous when [they] were less rich, than many of the rich countries. And it is beyond me why [they] are so stingy, really." U.S. Secretary of State Colin Powell defended U.S. efforts, noting that "The United States is not stingy. We are the greatest contributor to international efforts in the world." (Notebook, *TIME*, January 10, 2005.)

172 *Therefore, it is reasonable*: This scenario is loosely based on the famous Prisoner Dilemma, in which an individual prisoner must decide whether or not to tell the truth without knowing the decisions of the others. This creates a paradoxical situation in which various situations lead to strange consequences. The main idea behind this paradox (and the aforementioned Simpsonian example) is that an individual is unable to control fate by herself in situations that demand the decisions of others.

173 *An individual may want*: Mixed Messages: In "Itchy and Scratchy and Marge," Marge's crusades lead to the alteration of content in the immensely violent *Itchy and Scratchy* cartoon

series. Confronted with requests, however, for her to lead
the protests against the exhibition of Michaelangelo's
David, which Marge herself doesn't see as appalling, she
notes that "I guess one person can make a difference, but
most of the time they probably shouldn't."

173   *Just as destroying one*: This line of thinking was used as a
rationale by the Bush Administration in rejecting the Kyoto
Protocol, which created international emission standards.
Since many other nations were excused from signing, and
others still signed the treaty but agreed only to reduce their
emissions slightly, Bush argued that signing the treaty would
a) be unfair to the United States, and b) not solve the problems, since other nations would not cooperate to the extent
that the United States would be required to comply.

Chapter 13: Industrialization and the Worker: Homer Simpson as the Industrialized Employee

176   *These specific instances demonstrate*: One interesting example
of Homer's desire to reap the fruits of his own labor comes
in the episode in which he purchases Pinchy the Lobster.
Homer, in an attempt to fatten up Pinchy before eating
him, is, at least initially, thrilled at the prospect of putting
in the time and labor required to increase Pinchy's girth. In
this sense, Homer acts as the craftsman, who works for
himself and reaps the fruits of his own labor.

177   *For example, John Locke*: Locke, John, *The Second Treatise of
Civil Government*, originally published in 1690. Reprinted
by Macmillan Publishing Company, 1952.

177   *Since men are driven*: King, Margaret L, *Western Civilization
Volume 2: 1500—The Present, 2nd Edition* (New Jersey:
Prentice Hall Inc., 2003).

177   *In the* Wealth of Nations: Smith, Adam, *The Wealth of
Nations* (Reprint, New York: Random House, 1937).

177   *The greediness of corporate*: Katznelson, Ira, *The Politics of*

Power: Fourth Edition (United States: Thomson Learning, 2002).

178   *C. Wright Mills describes*: Ibid. 92–93.

178   *For example, historian Norman Ware*: Dubofsky, Melvyn, *Industrialization and the American Worker* (Illinois: Harlan Davidson, Inc., 1996).

179   Shortly after factory worker: Dubofsky, Melvyn, *Industrialization and the American Worker* (Illinois: Harlan Davidson, Inc., 1996).

179   *As historian Sidney Pollard*: Horowitz, Irving Louis, *The American Working Class: Prospects for the 1980s* (New Jersey: Transaction Books, 1979).

179–180   *Carleton H. Parker supported*: Horowitz, Irving Louis, *The American Working Class: Prospects for the 1980s* (New Jersey: Transaction Books, 1979).

180   *Since the introduction*: A Simpsonian warning: In "Last Exit to Springfield," a scene shifts to a flashback in 1909. A young worker simultaneously warned employers and union officials about the benefits and potential dangers of unions: "You can't treat the working man this way. One day, we'll form a union and get the fair and equitable treatment we deserve! Then we'll go too far, and get corrupt and shiftless, and the Japanese will eat us alive!" The power of unions is depicted in this episode, as Homer heads a union angry over Mr. Burns's abandonment of the company dental plan.

180   *For example, unions have*: Katznelson, Ira, *The Politics of Power* (Wadsworth Publishing, 2005).

180   *For example, factory worker*: Dubreuil, H. *Robots or Men?* (Arno Press, 1977).

180   *Jean Jacques Rousseau stated*: Brooklyn College Department of History, *The Shaping of the Modern World from the Enlightenment to the Present: Third Edition* (New York: Simon & Schuster Custom Publishing, 1998), quoted in Rousseau, Jacques, *The Social Contract*, (Hafner Publishing

Company, 1947).

180 *As Frederick Taylor*: A Freakin' Restriction on Free
Thought: A similar line was used to repress free thought
and creativity on the part of employees in the workplace in
an episode of *Family Guy*. In an episode entitled "Love
Thy Trophy," Peter Griffin's boss said the following:
"We're not paying him to think!" when explaining Peter's
role in the company to the board.

181 *Mills states, "This replacement*: Mills, C. Wright, *White
Collar* (Oxford University Press, 2002).

181 *For example, Leo Lowenthal*: Ibid.

182 *For example, a traditionalist*: Weber, Max, *The Protestant
Ethic and the Spirit of Capitalism* (Republished in New York:
Scribner's Press, 1958).

182 *Factory worker H. Dubreuil*: Dubreuil, H., *Robots or Men?*
(Arno Press, 1977).

184 *One manufacturer's journal sums*: Dubofsky, Melvyn,
Industrialism and the American Worker (Harlan Davidson,
1996).

186 *And he doesn't like*: The idea of employers not knowing the
names of their employees was examined in an episode of
Roseanne. In one episode, Roseanne meets a former boss
who remembers her employee as "Roxanne Conway."
Needless to say, after working for this employer for fifteen
years, Roseanne was disheartened by the fact that her former
employer called her Roxanne.

186 *In "Homer's Enemy,"*: Irwin, William, *The Simpsons and
Philosophy: The D'oh! of Homer* (Open Court Publishing,
2001).

Chapter 14: The Simpsons and Celebrity Culture

187 *People have always been*:
http://encyclopedia.thefreedictionary.com/Time+Magazine

187 *As noted in Wikipedia*:

http://en.wikipedia.org/wiki/Time_magazine

188–189 *Even in* TIME: Fonda, Daren, "Are They Really Fit for Office? What the Candidates Talk about When They Talk about Lunch," *TIME*, February 9th, 2004.

189 *As comic actor Ben Stiller*: Hochman, David, "Stiller: Crazy After All These Years," *USA Weekend*, February 22, 2004.

189 *It is certainly strange*: *TIME*, June 2005. This phenomenon immediately followed Brad Pitt's declaration that he would like to be a father someday.

189 *a die-hard Yankees fan*: Reported on *Good Day, NY*, August 1, 2005.

189–190 Sports Illustrated *recently reported*: Greenfeld, Karl Taro, "Kobe's Two Worlds," *Sports Illustrated*, March 22, 2004.

190 *These fans evidently believed*: Interestingly, Bart's adulation of Krusty the Clown has also led him to having blind faith in his hero, defending him against accusations and criticisms: when Krusty was accused of murder, Bart never lost hope that his hero was not guilty. Bart's undying devotion to Krusty the Clown serves as an interesting parallel to the aforementioned devotion to individual celebrities in contemporary society.

190 *The players under investigation*: Speaking of athletes, *Sports Illustrated* recently developed a new section in their magazine called "The Pop Culture Grid: How Do Sports Stars Fit In?" The significance of such a section is interesting to consider in light of our discussion of celebrity culture. The section includes responses to questions pertaining to aspects of popular culture from athletes (e.g., asking an NFL player what his favorite movie is). Reading this column, it is interesting to pose the question of whether the sports stars are attempting to match their responses to answers they would expect the public to agree with or whether the players' responses are influencing our own ideas about popular

culture. Do the sports stars try to fit in with the public or does the public attempt to fit in with the sports stars?

193   *All of this was*: http://drphil.com/shows/show/602/

194   *In this episode, the writers*: This is not the only instance of *The Simpsons* taking digs at die-hard fans. In "Saddlesore Gallactica," the Simpson family purchases a horse for the second time during the series' run, and Comic Book Guy, the quintessential comic, television, and internet nerd is frustrated by the repetition of this plot:

> **Marge:** Should the Simpsons get a horse?
>
> **Comic Book Guy:** Excuse me, I believe this family already had a horse, and the expense forced Homer to work at the Kwik-E-Mart with hilarious consequences.
>
> **Homer:** Does anyone care what this guy thinks?
>
> **Crowd:** No! (Comic Book Guy walks away).

Later in the episode, he wears a T-shirt bearing the words "Worst Episode Ever," and when Marge mentions her gambling problem (another issue addressed in an earlier episode), Comic Book Guy warns her that: "I'm watching you."

In another episode, Matt Groening guest stars as himself and mocks fans' obsession with him, as he offers them a lock of his hair.

Three quick examples of Simpsonian self-referential humor:

> **Lisa:** It seems like every week something odd happens to the Simpsons.

> **Marge:** A Simpson on a T-shirt—I never thought I'd see the day.

> **Lisa:** If cartoons were meant for adults, they'd put them on in prime time.

195   *Milhouse is right on*: Bart's assertion that many Americans

dream of becoming celebrities is supported by evidence in contemporary society. Dave Price on CBS 2 News reported that a company called "Party Buddies," headed by James King, offers people to pay (costs start at $1,100) to "become" a celebrity for one night. Customers who register for this service are treated like celebrities—they are escorted in limousines and "fans" huddle around them and ask for autographs.

Chapter 15: Gun Control Legislation and "The Cartridge Family"

198 *The amendment reads*: The United States Constitution. (The Bill of Rights).

199 *While a bit vague*: Of course, the Second Amendment does guarantee the militia, a collective entity, the right to bear arms.

199 *In response to gun control*: http://hematite.com/dragon/StateRights.html

199 *Here are some examples*: http://hematite.com/dragon/StateRights.html

200 *As noted by James Incardi*: Incardi, James A, *Elements of Criminal Justice Second Edition* (University of Delaware: Oxford University Press, 2000), quoted in Kruschke, Earl R., *The Right to Keep and Bear Arms: A Continuing American Dilemma* (Springfield, IL: Thomas, 1985).

200 *In the 1971 case*: Ibid. 82–83.

201 *Incardi reports that*: The Harris Poll, May 27, 1998.

202 *"The Cartridge Family"*: *The Simpsons* was not the only series to examine the issue of gun control. In the season three *All in the Family* episode entitled "Archie and the Editorial," the Bunkers take on this controversial issue as well.

Chapter 16: Homer Simpson and Morality

208 *Homer's position, while seemingly*: If Homer truly wanted to make God happy, he probably wouldn't steal (he stole cable in one episode), or cheat. In "Homer Goes to College," he

engages in the following exchange with his tutors
Benjamin, Doug, and Gary:

Nerd 2: Oh, man, I can't believe you failed.

Homer: [whining] Oh, I'm going to lose my job
just 'cause I'm dangerously unqualified!

Nerd 2: Mr. Simpson, there is a way. We could—
well, use a computer to change your grade.

Homer: [surprised] Computers can do that?

Nerd 2: Well, yes…the only problem is the moral
dilemma it raises, which requires—

[Homer kisses one of the computers.]

Homer: Oh, I love—moral whuzzah?

Obviously, Homer cares more about passing his class than
pleasing God.

Furthermore, Homer does not seem to have a problem
with lying. In the season six episode "Homie the Clown,"
for example, Homer receives free products, perks, and services because the townspeople believe that he is Krusty the
Clown. (Homer in clown makeup bears a strikingly similar
resemblance to Krusty.) Homer engages in the following
conversation with Marge:

Marge: I'm not saying [your plan] won't work—
I'm saying it's dishonest.

Homer: If we agree, then why are we arguing?

Chapter 17: The Education of Springfield

213 *By having Bart write*: This point, while an interesting one
for some chalkboard quotes, must be qualified here: the
majority of chalkboard quotes are done just for laughs.
Still, the idea that the chalkboard serves to repress Bart's
creativity merits consideration.

215 *Whether it's Skinner attempting*: Some of McClure's documentaries also serve the purpose of indoctrinating students. In

"Lisa the Vegetarian," Miss Hoover's class is forced to watch *The Meat Council Presents Meat and You: Partners in Freedom.* Dissent from the mainstream idea that eating meat is completely justified is not tolerated in the screening. When the boy in the documentary asks whether his vegetarian friend is crazy, McClure reassures him that the friend is indeed dead wrong. Here is an excerpt from the documentary:

Jimmy: Uhh, Mr. McClure? I have a crazy friend who says its wrong to eat meat. Is he crazy?

Troy: Nooo, just ignorant. You see your crazy friend never heard of "The Food Chain." [Flash to a picture of "Food Chain," with all animals and arrows pointing to a silhouette of a human.] Just ask this scientician.

Scientician: [Looking up from a microscope.] Uhhh...

Troy: He'll tell you that, in nature, one creature invariably eats another creature to survive. [Images of various wild carnivores attacking and eating others appear.] Don't kid yourself Jimmy. If a cow ever got the chance, he'd eat you and everyone you care about! [Image of a cow quietly chewing cud.]

Jimmy: Wow, Mr. McClure. I was a grade-A moron to ever question eating meat.

Troy: [Laughs.] Yes you were Jimmy, yes you were. [Briskly rubs his hand on Jimmy's head.]

Jimmy: [Timid] Uhh...you're hurting me.

The documentary succeeds in brainwashing all of the students in the class, with the exception of Lisa. The students call Lisa a "grade-A moron" for not conforming to the views of the video. Perhaps they should take a hint from Apu and learn to tolerate the beliefs and ideas of others.

216 *According to a recent article*: Janofsky, Michael, *New York*

Times, "Students Say High Schools Let Them Down: Findings of New Survey Made Public During Meeting of Governors" (Survey source: National Governors Association) quoted in AOL News, July 17, 2005.

219 *However, if Dr. J.*: Another interesting *Simpsons* episode that examines the idea that standardized tests can have negative effects on children is the season three episode "Separate Vocations." In the episode, students take the C.A.N.T. aptitude test, which supposedly predicts what their future career will be. This is but another example of the Springfield education system repressing freedom of thought and career choice.

221 *Marge's faults aside*: Award worthy, eh? Homer may have good intentions at times, but he attempts to promote Bart's education in weird ways. In "Lisa on Ice," for example, he carelessly signs Bart's failing school papers and wants to reward him with a present. The reason: Bart did not forge Homer's signature on the papers.

223 *Item one of Section 1001*: http://www.fldoe.org/meetings/Oct02/NoChildLeftBehind Act_10_24_02.pdf

225 *Bart Simpson's peers*: Gajilan, Arlyn Tobias, "School Reform: Difficult Lessons," *TIME*, October 31, 2005.

Conclusion

227 *As noted by London's*: *London's Daily Mail* quoted in Turner, Chris, *Planet Simpson* (Da Capo Press, 2004).

228 *If you take only one lesson*: Another important lesson courtesy of Homer: "You can't depend on me all of your life. You have to learn that there's a little Homer Simpson in all of us." Yes, Homer, that puts us at ease!

228 Barbara Bush, for example: Pinsky, Mark, *The Gospel According to The Simpsons* (John Westknox Press, 2001).

Author's Note

Unless otherwise noted, all quotes found in this book were found in the sources listed in the bibliography or directly from the episodes via my own memory. I have made every attempt possible to find exact word-for-word quotes, but several quotes have been paraphrased. I can assure readers that any minor changes in the wording of specific quotes have not changed the meaning behind the quotes. Similarly, readers may occasionally find slight alterations of plot situations within this book. I apologize in advance for any slight (and accidental) modifications of *Simpsons* episodes discussed in this book. Remember, like Lisa's cap says, "Pobody's Nerfect."

Websites/Published Web Articles:

- Answers.com
- The Simpsons Archive (www.snpp.com) for quotes, plot summaries, and an excerpt from Ed Bishop of *The Riverfront Times*.
- Interview with Matt Groening:
  http://www.snpp.com/other/interviews/groening93.html
- BBC Simpsons polls:
  http://newsvote.bbc.co.uk/1/hi/programmes/wtwta/2959462.stm
  http://news.bbc.co.uk/1/hi/entertainment/tv_and_radio/29844
  26.stm
- Many of Homer's quotes were found at:
  http://www.angelfire.com/comics/pearly/homer/homer-quotes1.html

- Homer Simpson: Made in Korea:
  http://www.freerepublic.com/focus/f-news/1354555/posts
- Bart's Prank Phone Calls:
  http://moes.virtualave.net percent2Fpranks.html
- American medicine quotation found at:
  http://www.snpp.com/other/papers/bv.paper.html
- Idato, Michael. "Ready, Set, D'oh!" February 27, 2003,
  http://www.smh.com.au/articles/2003/02/26/1046064102384.html
- *The Cosby Show* quotes:
  http://www.imdb.com/Quotes?0086687
- Bush's speech on the war with Iraq:
  http://www.atour.com/government/usa/20030116b.html
- The International Criminal Court:
  http://en.wikipedia.org/wiki/International_Criminal_Court
- *Dr. Phil*: http://drphil.com/shows/show/602/
- Walmart Lawsuit information:
  http://www.corpwatch.org/article.php?id=11375
- Balko, Radley. "Globalization and Culture: Americanization or Cultural Diversity?"
  www.aworldconnected.org/article.php/486.html.
- *TIME* magazine history—Luce:
  http://encyclopedia.thefreedictionary.com/Time%20Magazine
- *TIME* magazine information—Wikipedia:
  http://en.wikipedia.org/wiki/Time_magazine
- Johnston, Daniel. *Practicing Deviancy—The Value of Being Deviant*, Georgia Psychological Association:
  http://www.gapsychology.org/displaycommon.cfm?an=1&subarticlenbr=40.
- Funny Laws: http://www.floydpinkerton.net/fun/laws.html
  Mosnews.com
- FOX News Report on Gun Control:
  http://www.foxnews.com/story/0,2933,90037,00.html
- Orwell's "Shooting the Elephant" story:

http://www.online-literature.com/orwell/887/
- Tufts University website:
  http://www.excollege.tufts.edu/coursesS04_frame.htm
- Ohio State University: http://ohioline.osu.edu
- President Bush's No Child Left Behind Proposal:
  http://www.fldoe.org/meetings/Oct02/NoChildLeftBehindA
  ct_10_24_02.pdf
- Gun Control State Legislature:
  http://hematite.com/dragon/StateRights.html
- Homer. *Odyssey*. (Book 9):
  http://www.classicauthors.net/Homer/odyssey/odyssey9.html
- Plato. *The Apology*.
  http://www.paganlibrary.com/etext/apology_socrates.php.
  Translated by Benjamin Jowett.
- Plato. *The Republic*.
  http://classics.mit.edu/Plato/republic.html. Translated by
  Benjamin Jowett.
- Father's Network:
  http://www.fathersnetwork.org
- *We're All Pigs* (Academic Paper):
  Waltonen, Karma. *We're All Pigs*, The Simpsons Archive,
  http://snpp.com/other/papers/kw.paper.html.
  http://www.scoop.co.nz/stories/PO0509/S00067.htm (Sept.
  7, 2005)
- Westbrook, Bruce. "*The Simpsons* Enters its 17th Season,"
  Houston Chronicle, September 8, 2005,
  http://www.chron.com/cs/CDA/ssistory.mpl/headline/enter
  tainment/3343405.
- Dictionary.com
- Mosnews.com
- http://www.post-gazette.com/pg/05287/588741.stm
- http://www.nohomers.net/content/info/didyouknow/

Books:

- Alberti, John et. al. *Leaving Springfield.* Detroit, Michigan: Wayne State University Press, 2003.
- Aristotle. *Metaphysics.*
- Essays cited from this volume include Douglas Rushkoff's "Bart Simpson: Prince of Irreverence," Mick Broderick's "Releasing the Hounds," and Duncan Stuart Beard's "Local Satire with a Global Reach."
- *Babylonian Talmud*, Sanhedrin 37a.
- Barber, Benjamin. *McWorld vs. Jihad: How Globalism and Tribalism Are Reshaping the World.* Ballantine Books. (This is the newest edition, published in 1996.)
- Biffle, Christopher. *A Guided Tour of John Stuart Mill's Utilitarianism.* McGraw Hill, 1992.
- Brooklyn College Department of History. *The Shaping of the Modern World from the Enlightenment to the Present: Third Edition.* New York: Simon & Schuster Custom Publishing, 1998.
- Brooks, David. *On Paradise Drive: How We Live Now (and Always Have) in the Future Tense.* Simon and Schuster, 2004.
- Cantor, Paul A. *Gilligan Unbound: Pop Culture in the Age of Globalization.* Lanham, Maryland: Rowman and Littlefield Publishers, Inc. 2001.
- Clausen, Alf. *The Simpsons Songbook.* United States: Warner Brothers Publications, 2002.
- Descartes, Rene. *Meditations on First Philosophy: Meditation I,* 1641. Reprinted: Pojman, Louis P. *Introduction to Philosophy* (2nd edition) CA: Wadsworth, 2000.
- Dubofsky, Melvyn. *Industrialization and the American Worker.* Illinois: Harlan Davidson, Inc. 1996.
- Dubreuil, H. *Robots or Men?* New York: Harper & Brothers, 1930.
- Foucault, Michael. *The History of Sexuality.* Reprinted by

Vintage Books, 1990.

- Friedman, Thomas. *The World Is Flat: A Brief History of the 21st Century*. Farrar, Straus, and Giroux, 2005.
- Gimple, Scott M. *The Simpsons Forever: A Complete Guide to Our Favorite Family Continued*. New York: Harper Perennial Publications, 1999.
- Glassner, Barry. *The Culture of Fear*. Basic Books, 2000.
- Gray, John. *False Dawn: The Delusions of Global Capitalism*. New Press, 2000.
- Grote, David. *The End of Comedy: The Sit-Com and the Comic Tradition*. Hamden: Archon Books, 1983.
- Herodotus. *The Histories*. Penguin Classics, 1996 Reprint. Translated by Aubrey de Selincourt, edited by John M. Marincola.
- Hooker, Michael. *Descartes' Critical and Interpretative Essays*. London: The Johns Hopkins University Press, 1978. (Quoted Section: Marlies, Mike: *Doubt, Reason, and Cartesian Theory*).
- Homer. *The Iliad of Homer*. University of Chicago Press, 1961 Reprint. Translated by Richard Lattimore.
- Homer. *The Odyssey of Homer*. Perennial Classics, 1999 Reprint. Translated by Richard Lattimore.
- Irwin, William. *The Simpsons and Philosophy: The D'oh! Of Homer*. Illinois: Carus Publishing Co., 2001.
- Joachim, Harold H. *Descartes' Rules for the Direction of the Mind*. London: George Allen & Unwin Ltd., 1957.
- Johnson, Steven. *Everything Bad Is Good for You*. New York: Riverhead Books, 2005.
- Katznelson, Ira. *The Politics of Power: Fourth Edition*. United States: Thomson Learning, 2002.
- King, Margaret L. *Western Civilization—Volume 2: 1500—The Present (2nd edition)*. New Jersey: Prentice Hall Inc., 2003.
- Kruschke, Earl R. *The Right to Keep and Bear Arms: A Continuing American Dilemma*. Springfield, Ill.: Thomas,

1985, quoted in Incardi, James A. *Elements of Criminal Justice* (Second Edition). University of Delaware: Oxford University Press, 2000.
- Locke, John. *The Second Treatise of Civil Government.* Originally published in 1690. Reprinted by Macmillan Publishing Company, 1952.
- Maguire, Gregory. *Wicked: The Life and Times of the Wicked Witch of the West.* New York, NY: Regan Books, 1995.
- McCann, Jesse L. *The Simpsons Beyond Forever: A Complete Guide to Our Favorite Family Still Continued.* New York: Perennial, 2002.
- Mills, C. Wright. *White Collar.* England: Oxford University Press, 1951.
- Nye Jr., Joseph S. *The Paradox of American Power.* New York, Oxford, 2002.
- Papp, Daniel S. *American Foreign Policy: History, Politics, and Policy.* Pearson Education, 2005.
- Pinsky, Mark I. *The Gospel According to* The Simpsons. Kentucky: Westminster John Knox Press, 2001.
- Plato. *Plato Five Dialogues: Euthyphro, Apology, Crito, Meno, Phaedo.* Hackett Publishing Company, 1981 Reprint.
- Plato. *The Republic.* Hackett Publishing Company, 1992 Reprint (2nd edition). Translated by G.M.A. Grube, C.D.C. Reeve.
- Postman, Neil. *Amusing Ourselves to Death: Public Discourse in the Age of Show Business* (Ch. 4: *The Typographic Mind*), Penguin Books, 1986.
- Richmond, Ray. *The Simpsons: A Complete Guide to Our Favorite Family.* New York: Harper Collins Publications, 1997.
- Rousseau, Jacques. *The Social Contract.* Reprinted by Hafner Publishing Company, 1947.
- Sachs, Jeffrey D. *The End of Poverty.* United States: Penguin Books, 2005.

- Shakespeare, William. *Macbeth*. Reprinted in the United States: Washington Square Press, 2003. Originally written in 1606.
- Smith, Adam. *The Wealth of Nations*. Reprint, New York: Random House, 1937.
- Sophocles. *Antigone*. New York: Dover Publications, 1993 Reprint. Originally written in 441 BC.
- Stiglitz, Joseph E. *Globalization and Its Discontents*. New York: Norton, 2003.
- Terrace, Vincent. *Television Sitcom Fact Book*. United States: McFarland & Company, Inc., Publishers, 2000.
- Thucydides, *History of the Peloponnesian War*. Indianapolis: Hackett, 1998. Translated by Steven Lattimore.
- Turner, Chris. *Planet Simpson*. Cambridge, MA: Da Capo Press, 2004.
- Weber, Max. *The Protestant Ethic and the Spirit of Capitalism*. Republished in New York: Scribner's Press, 1958.

Published Articles (Print):

- "American Idol," *TIME*, June 7, pg. 22.
- Notebook. *TIME*, January 10, 2005.
- People. *TIME*, June 13, 2005.
- *TIME*, March 28, 2005.
- *TIME*, March 14, 2005.
- El-Rashidi, Yasmine. "D'oh! Arabized Simpsons Not Getting Many Laughs," *Wall Street Journal*, October 14, 2005.
- Elliott, Dorinda and Bill Powell. "Wal-Mart Nation," *TIME*, June 27, 2005.
- The Harris Poll, May 27, 1998.
- Fonda, Daren. "Are They Really Fit for Office? What the Candidates Talk about When They Talk about Lunch." *TIME*, February. 9, 2004.
- Gajilan, Arlyn Tobias. "School Reform: Difficult Lessons," *TIME*, October 31, 2005.

- Greenfeld, Karl Taro. "Kobe's Two Worlds," *Sports Illustrated*, March 22, 2004, 48–51.
- Grossman, Lev. "The Way We Live Now," *TIME*, April 26, 2004.
- Hochman, David. "Stiller: Crazy after All These Years," *USA Weekend*, February. 22, 2004.
- Janofsky, Michael. "Students Say High Schools Let Them Down: Findings of New Survey Made Public During Meeting of Governors," *New York Times*, quoted in AOL News, July 17, 2005.
- MacGregor, Jeff. "More Than Sight Gags and Subversive Satire," *New York Times*, June 20, 1999.
- Schuman, Michael and Ressner, Jeffrey. "Disney's Great Leap to China," *TIME*, July 18, 2005.
- Slouka, Mark. Review, *New York Times*, June 20, 1999: Television/Radio 27. Excerpted in *Harper's Magazine*, September, 2002.
- Solomon, Michael. "They're Yellow, But They're Not Chicken," *TV Guide*, February 15–21, 2003, 27.
- Steptoe, Sonja. "Minding Their Manners: A New Breed of Etiquette Classes for the Generation of Kids Raised on Bart Simpsons and Britney Spears," *TIME*, June 7, 2004.

Documents:
- The United States Declaration of Independence. 1776.
- The United States Constitution, 1787.

TV References:
- *20/20*
- *24*
- *The Tonight Show with Jay Leno*
- *The Late Show with David Letterman*
- *The Cosby Show*
- *Family Guy*

- *Father Knows Best*
- *Roseanne*
- *I Love Lucy*
- *The Flintstones*
- *The Honeymooners*
- *Leave it to Beaver*
- *Married with Children*
- *The Tracey Ullman Show*
- *The View*
- *All in the Family*
- *Dr. Phil*
- *Boy Meets World*
- *Saved by the Bell*
- *American Idol*
- *Good Day New York*
- FOX News Channel
- NBC's *Early Today*
- CBS 2 News
- *Perfect Strangers*
- *Gilligan's Island*

Movie References:
- *Patch Adams*
- *Bowling for Columbine*
- *Pulp Fiction*
- *Citizen Kane*
- *Fiddler on the Roof*
- *Finding Nemo*
- *Why Wal-Mart Works and Why That Makes Some People Crazy*
- *Wal-Mart: The High Cost of Low Price*

TV Interviews:
- Paul Levinson: Interview aired on NBC: *Early Today*, April 13, 2004, http://wnbc.feedroom.com/iframeset.jsp?ord=721865.

The Simpsons Shorts

Season One: 1987

Season Two: 1987–1988

This list includes all of the episodes aired before *The World According to The Simpsons* went to press. For updated episode information, please visit *The Simpsons* Archive at www.snpp.com.

The Simpsons from The Tracey Ullman Show

Season One (1987)—7 Shorts

1. MG01 Good Night
2. MG02 Watching Television
3. MG03 Bart Jumps
4. MG04 Babysitting Maggie
5. MG05 The Pacifier
6. MG06 Burp Contest
7. MG07 Eating Dinner

Season Two (1987–1988)—22 Shorts

8. MG09 Making Faces
9. MG14 The Funeral
10. MG10 Maggie's Brain
11. MG08 Football
12. MG12 House of Cards

13. MG15 Bart & Dad Eat Dinner
14. MG13 Space Patrol
15. MG18 Bart's Haircut
16. MG20 World War III
17. MG16 The Perfect Crime
18. MG17 Scary Stories
19. MG19 Grandpa & The Kids
20. MG11 Gone Fishin'
21. MG21 Skateboarding
22. MG22 The Pagans
23. MG23 The Closet
24. MG24 The Aquarium
25. MG25 Family Portrait
26. MG26 Bart's Hiccups
27. MG27 The Money Jar
28. MG29 The Art Museum
29. MG28 Zoo Story

Season Three (1988–1989)–19 Shorts

30. MG30 Shut up Simpsons
31. MG35 The Shell Game
32. MG38 The Bart Simpson Show
33. MG33 Punching Bag
34. MG40 Simpson Christmas
35. MG39 The Krusty the Clown Show
36. MG34 Bart the Hero
37. MG41 Bart's Little Fantasy
38. MG37 Scary Movie
39. MG32 Home Hypnotism
40. MG31 Shoplifting
41. MG36 Echo Canyon
42. MG44 Bathtime
43. MG45 Bart's Nightmare
44. MG46 Bart of the Jungle

45. MG47 Family Therapy
46. MG42 Maggie in Peril—Chapter One
47. MG43 Maggie in Peril—The Thrilling Conclusion
48. MG48 TV Simpsons

The Simpsons

Season One (1989–1990)–13 Episodes

1. 7G08 (SI-108 / S01E01) Simpsons Roasting on an Open Fire
2. 7G02 (SI-102 / S01E02) Bart the Genius
3. 7G03 (SI-103 / S01E03) Homer's Odyssey
4. 7G04 (SI-104 / S01E04) There's No Disgrace Like Home
5. 7G05 (SI-105 / S01E05) Bart the General
6. 7G06 (SI-106 / S01E06) Moaning Lisa
7. 7G09 (SI-109 / S01E07) Call of the Simpsons
8. 7G07 (SI-107 / S01E08) The Tell-Tale Head
9. 7G11 (SI-111 / S01E09) Life on the Fast Lane
10. 7G10 (SI-110 / S01E10) Homer's Night Out
11. 7G13 (SI-113 / S01E11) The Crepes of Wrath
12. 7G12 (SI-112 / S01E12) Krusty Gets Busted
13. 7G01 (SI-101 / S01E13) Some Enchanted Evening

Season Two (1990–1991)–22 Episodes + 2 Music Videos

14. 7F03 (SI-203 / S02E01) Bart Gets an F
15. 7F02 (SI-202 / S02E02) Simpson and Delilah
16. 7F04 (SI-204 / S02E03) Treehouse of Horror
17. 7F01 (SI-201 / S02E04) Two Cars in Every Garage and Three Eyes on Every Fish
18. 7F05 (SI-205 / S02E05) Dancin' Homer
19. 7F08 (SI-208 / S02E06) Dead Putting Society
20. 7F07 (SI-207 / S02E07) Bart vs. Thanksgiving
21. 7F06 (SI-206 / S02E08) Bart the Daredevil
22. 7F09 (SI-209 / S02E09) Itchy & Scratchy & Marge

23. 7F10 (SI-210 / S02E10) Bart Gets Hit by a Car
24. 7F11 (SI-211 / S02E11) One Fish, Two Fish, Blowfish, Blue Fish
25. 7F12 (SI-212 / S02E12) The Way We Was
26. 7F13 (SI-213 / S02E13) Homer vs. Lisa and the 8th Commandment
27. 7F15 (SI-215 / S02E14) Principal Charming
28. 7F16 (SI-216 / S02E15) Oh Brother, Where Art Thou?
29. 7F14 (SI-214 / S02E16) Bart's Dog Gets an F
30. 7F17 (SI-217 / S02E17) Old Money
31. 7F18 (SI-218 / S02E18) Brush with Greatness
32. 7F19 (SI-219 / S02E19) Lisa's Substitute
33. 7F20 (SI-220 / S02E20) The War of the Simpsons
34. 7F21 (SI-221 / S02E21) Three Men and a Comic Book
35. 7F22 (SI-222 / S02E22) Blood Feud
    7F75 (—/—) "Do the Bartman"
    7F76 (—/—) "Deep, Deep Trouble"

Season Three (1991–1992)–24 Episodes

36. 7F24 (SI-224 / S03E01) Stark Raving Dad
37. 8F01 (SI-301 / S03E02) Mr. Lisa Goes to Washington
38. 7F23 (SI-223 / S03E03) When Flanders Failed
39. 8F03 (SI-303 / S03E04) Bart the Murderer
40. 8F04 (SI-304 / S03E05) Homer Defined
41. 8F05 (SI-305 / S03E06) Like Father, Like Clown
42. 8F02 (SI-302 / S03E07) Treehouse of Horror II
43. 8F06 (SI-306 / S03E08) Lisa's Pony
44. 8F07 (SI-307 / S03E09) Saturdays of Thunder
45. 8F08 (SI-308 / S03E10) Flaming Moe's
46. 8F09 (SI-309 / S03E11) Burns Verkaufen der Kraftwerk
47. 8F10 (SI-310 / S03E12) I Married Marge
48. 8F11 (SI-311 / S03E13) Radio Bart
49. 8F12 (SI-312 / S03E14) Lisa the Greek
50. 8F14 (SI-314 / S03E15) Homer Alone

51. 8F16 (SI-316 / S03E16) Bart the Lover
52. 8F13 (SI-313 / S03E17) Homer at the Bat
53. 8F15 (SI-315 / S03E18) Separate Vocations
54. 8F17 (SI-317 / S03E19) Dog of Death
55. 8F19 (SI-319 / S03E20) Colonel Homer
56. 8F20 (SI-320 / S03E21) Black Widower
57. 8F21 (SI-321 / S03E22) The Otto Show
58. 8F22 (SI-322 / S03E23) Bart's Friend Falls in Love
59. 8F23 (SI-323 / S03E24) Brother, Can You Spare Two Dimes?

Season Four (1992–1993)–22 Episodes

60. 8F24 (SI-324 / S04E01) Kamp Krusty
61. 8F18 (SI-318 / S04E02) A Streetcar Named Marge
62. 9F01 (SI-401 / S04E03) Homer the Heretic
63. 9F02 (SI-402 / S04E04) Lisa the Beauty Queen
64. 9F04 (SI-404 / S04E05) Treehouse of Horror III
65. 9F03 (SI-403 / S04E06) Itchy & Scratchy: The Movie
66. 9F05 (SI-405 / S04E07) Marge Gets a Job
67. 9F06 (SI-406 / S04E08) New Kid on the Block
68. 9F07 (SI-407 / S04E09) Mr. Plow
69. 9F08 (SI-408 / S04E10) Lisa's First Word
70. 9F09 (SI-409 / S04E11) Homer's Triple Bypass
71. 9F10 (SI-410 / S04E12) Marge vs. the Monorail
72. 9F11 (SI-411 / S04E13) Selma's Choice
73. 9F12 (SI-412 / S04E14) Brother from the Same Planet
74. 9F13 (SI-413 / S04E15) I Love Lisa
75. 9F14 (SI-414 / S04E16) Duffless
76. 9F15 (SI-415 / S04E17) Last Exit to Springfield
77. 9F17 (SI-417 / S04E18) So It's Come to This: A Simpsons
    Clip Show
78. 9F16 (SI-416 / S04E19) The Front
79. 9F18 (SI-418 / S04E20) Whacking Day
80. 9F20 (SI-420 / S04E21) Marge in Chains
81. 9F19 (SI-419 / S04E22) Krusty Gets Kancelled

Season Five (1993–1994)–22 Episodes

82. 9F21 (SI-421 / S05E01) Homer's Barbershop Quartet

83. 9F22 (SI-422 / S05E02) Cape Feare

84. 1F02 (SI-502 / S05E03) Homer Goes to College

85. 1F01 (SI-501 / S05E04) Rosebud

86. 1F04 (SI-504 / S05E05) Treehouse of Horror IV

87. 1F03 (SI-503 / S05E06) Marge on the Lam

88. 1F05 (SI-505 / S05E07) Bart's Inner Child

89. 1F06 (SI-506 / S05E08) Boy-Scoutz N the Hood

90. 1F07 (SI-507 / S05E09) The Last Temptation of Homer

91. 1F08 (SI-508 / S05E10) $pringfield (Or, How I Learned to Stop Worrying and Love Legalized Gambling)

92. 1F09 (SI-509 / S05E11) Homer the Vigilante

93. 1F11 (SI-511 / S05E12) Bart Gets Famous

94. 1F10 (SI-510 / S05E13) Homer and Apu

95. 1F12 (SI-512 / S05E14) Lisa vs. Malibu Stacy

96. 1F13 (SI-513 / S05E15) Deep Space Homer

97. 1F14 (SI-514 / S05E16) Homer Loves Flanders

98. 1F15 (SI-515 / S05E17) Bart Gets an Elephant

99. 1F16 (SI-516 / S05E18) Burns's Heir

100. 1F18 (SI-518 / S05E19) Sweet Seymour Skinner's Baadasssss Song

101. 1F19 (SI-519 / S05E20) The Boy Who Knew Too Much

102. 1F21 (SI-521 / S05E21) Lady Bouvier's Lover

103. 1F20 (SI-520 / S05E22) Secrets of a Successful Marriage

Season Six (1994–1995)–25 Episodes

104. 1F22 (SI-522 / S06E01) Bart of Darkness

105. 1F17 (SI-517 / S06E02) Lisa's Rival

106. 2F33 (SI-633 / S06E03) Another Simpsons Clip Show

107. 2F01 (SI-601 / S06E04) Itchy & Scratchy Land

108. 2F02 (SI-602 / S06E05) Sideshow Bob Roberts

109. 2F03 (SI-603 / S06E06) Treehouse of Horror V

110. 2F04 (SI-604 / S06E07) Bart's Girlfriend

111. 2F05 (SI-605 / S06E08) Lisa on Ice
112. 2F06 (SI-606 / S06E09) Homer Badman
113. 2F07 (SI-607 / S06E10) Grampa vs. Sexual Inadequacy
114. 2F08 (SI-608 / S06E11) Fear of Flying
115. 2F09 (SI-609 / S06E12) Homer the Great
116. 2F10 (SI-610 / S06E13) And Maggie Makes Three
117. 2F11 (SI-611 / S06E14) Bart's Comet
118. 2F12 (SI-612 / S06E15) Homie the Clown
119. 2F13 (SI-613 / S06E16) Bart vs. Australia
120. 2F14 (SI-614 / S06E17) Homer vs. Patty and Selma
121. 2F31 (SI-631 / S06E18) A Star Is Burns
122. 2F15 (SI-615 / S06E19) Lisa's Wedding
123. 2F18 (SI-618 / S06E20) Two Dozen and One Greyhounds
124. 2F19 (SI-619 / S06E21) The PTA Disbands
125. 2F32 (SI-632 / S06E22) 'Round Springfield
126. 2F21 (SI-621 / S06E23) The Springfield Connection
127. 2F22 (SI-622 / S06E24) Lemon of Troy
128. 2F16 (SI-616 / S06E25) Who Shot Mr. Burns? (Part One)

Season Seven (1995–1996)–25 Episodes

129. 2F20 (SI-620 / S07E01) Who Shot Mr. Burns? (Part Two)
130. 2F17 (SI-617 / S07E02) Radioactive Man
131. 3F01 (SI-701 / S07E03) Home Sweet Homediddly-Dum-Doodily
132. 3F02 (SI-702 / S07E04) Bart Sells His Soul
133. 3F03 (SI-703 / S07E05) Lisa the Vegetarian
134. 3F04 (SI-704 / S07E06) Treehouse of Horror VI
135. 3F05 (SI-705 / S07E07) King-Size Homer
136. 3F06 (SI-706 / S07E08) Mother Simpson
137. 3F08 (SI-708 / S07E09) Sideshow Bob's Last Gleaming
138. 3F31 (SI-731 / S07E10) The Simpsons 138th Episode Spectacular
139. 3F07 (SI-707 / S07E11) Marge Be Not Proud
140. 3F10 (SI-710 / S07E12) Team Homer

141. 3F09 (SI-709 / S07E13) Two Bad Neighbors
142. 3F11 (SI-711 / S07E14) Scenes from the Class Struggle in Springfield
143. 3F12 (SI-712 / S07E15) Bart the Fink
144. 3F13 (SI-713 / S07E16) Lisa the Iconoclast
145. 3F14 (SI-714 / S07E17) Homer the Smithers
146. 3F16 (SI-716 / S07E18) The Day the Violence Died
147. 3F15 (SI-715 / S07E19) A Fish Called Selma
148. 3F17 (SI-717 / S07E20) Bart on the Road
149. 3F18 (SI-718 / S07E21) 22 Short Films about Springfield
150. 3F19 (SI-719 / S07E22) Raging Abe Simpson and His Grumbling Grandson in "The Curse of the Flying Hellfish"
151. 3F20 (SI-720 / S07E23) Much Apu about Nothing
152. 3F21 (SI-721 / S07E24) Homerpalooza
153. 3F22 (SI-722 / S07E25) Summer of 4 Ft. 2

Season Eight (1996–1997)–25 Episodes

154. 4F02 (SI-802 / S08E01) Treehouse of Horror VII
155. 3F23 (SI-723 / S08E02) You Only Move Twice
156. 4F03 (SI-803 / S08E03) The Homer They Fall
157. 4F05 (SI-805 / S08E04) Burns, Baby Burns
158. 4F06 (SI-806 / S08E05) Bart after Dark
159. 4F04 (SI-804 / S08E06) A Milhouse Divided
160. 4F01 (SI-801 / S08E07) Lisa's Date with Density
161. 4F07 (SI-807 / S08E08) Hurricane Neddy
162. 3F24 (SI-724 / S08E09) El Viaje Misterioso de Nuestro Jomer (The Mysterious Voyage of Homer)
163. 3G01 (SI-825 / S08E10) The Springfield Files
164. 4F08 (SI-808 / S08E11) The Twisted World of Marge Simpson
165. 4F10 (SI-810 / S08E12) Mountain of Madness
166. 3G03 (SI-827 / S08E13) Simpsoncalifragilisticexpiala(ANNOYED GRUNT)cious
167. 4F12 (SI-812 / S08E14) The Itchy & Scratchy & Poochie

Show

168. 4F11 (SI-811 / S08E15) Homer's Phobia

169. 4F14 (SI-814 / S08E16) Brother from Another Series

170. 4F13 (SI-813 / S08E17) My Sister, My Sitter

171. 4F15 (SI-815 / S08E18) Homer vs. the Eighteenth Amendment

172. 4F09 (SI-809 / S08E19) Grade School Confidential

173. 4F16 (SI-816 / S08E20) The Canine Mutiny

174. 4F17 (SI-817 / S08E21) The Old Man and the Lisa

175. 4F18 (SI-818 / S08E22) In Marge We Trust

176. 4F19 (SI-819 / S08E23) Homer's Enemy

177. 4F20 (SI-820 / S08E24) The Simpsons Spin-off Showcase

178. 4F21 (SI-821 / S08E25) The Secret War of Lisa Simpson

Season Nine (1997–1998)–25 Episodes

179. 4F22 (SI-822 / S09E01) The City of New York vs. Homer Simpson

180. 4F23 (SI-823 / S09E02) The Principal and The Pauper

181. 3G02 (SI-826 / S09E03) Lisa's Sax

182. 5F02 (SI-902 / S09E04) Treehouse of Horror VIII

183. 5F01 (SI-901 / S09E05) The Cartridge Family

184. 5F03 (SI-903 / S09E06) Bart Star

185. 5F04 (SI-904 / S09E07) The Two Mrs. Nahasapeemapetilons

186. 5F05 (SI-905 / S09E08) Lisa the Skeptic

187. 5F06 (SI-906 / S09E09) Realty Bites

188. 5F07 (SI-907 / S09E10) Miracle on Evergreen Terrace

189. 5F24 (SI-924 / S09E11) All Singing, All Dancing

190. 5F08 (SI-908 / S09E12) Bart Carny

191. 5F23 (SI-923 / S09E13) The Joy of Sect

192. 5F11 (SI-911 / S09E14) Das Bus

193. 5F10 (SI-910 / S09E15) The Last Temptation of Krust

194. 5F12 (SI-912 / S09E16) Dumbbell Indemnity

195. 4F24 (SI-824 / S09E17) Lisa, the Simpson

286 THE WORLD ACCORDING TO *THE SIMPSONS*

196. 5F13 (SI-913 / S09E18) This Little Wiggy
197. 3G04 (SI-828 / S09E19) Simpson Tide
198. 5F14 (SI-914 / S09E20) The Trouble with Trillions
199. 5F15 (SI-915 / S09E21) Girly Edition
200. 5F09 (SI-909 / S09E22) Trash of the Titans
201. 5F16 (SI-916 / S09E23) King of the Hill
202. 5F17 (SI-917 / S09E24) Lost Our Lisa
203. 5F18 (SI-918 / S09E25) Natural Born Kissers

Season Ten (1998–1999)–23 Episodes

204. 5F20 (SI-920 / S10E01) Lard of the Dance
205. 5F21 (SI-921 / S10E02) The Wizard of Evergreen Terrace
206. 5F22 (SI-922 / S10E03) Bart, the Mother
207. AABF01 (SI-1001 / S10E04) Treehouse of Horror IX
208. 5F19 (SI-919 / S10E05) When You Dish upon a Star
209. AABF02 (SI-1002 / S10E06) D'oh-in' in the Wind
210. AABF03 (SI-1003 / S10E07) Lisa Gets an "A"
211. AABF04 (SI-1004 / S10E08) Homer Simpson In: "Kidney Trouble"
212. AABF05 (SI-1005 / S10E09) Mayored to the Mob
213. AABF06 (SI-1006 / S10E10) Viva Ned Flanders
214. AABF07 (SI-1007 / S10E11) Wild Barts Can't Be Broken
215. AABF08 (SI-1008 / S10E12) Sunday, Cruddy Sunday
216. AABF09 (SI-1009 / S10E13) Homer to the Max
217. AABF11 (SI-1011 / S10E14) I'm with Cupid
218. AABF10 (SI-1010 / S10E15) Marge Simpson In: "Screaming Yellow Honkers"
219. AABF12 (SI-1012 / S10E16) Make Room for Lisa
220. AABF13 (SI-1013 / S10E17) Maximum Homerdrive
221. AABF14 (SI-1014 / S10E18) Simpsons Bible Stories
222. AABF15 (SI-1015 / S10E19) Mom and Pop Art
223. AABF16 (SI-1016 / S10E20) The Old Man and the "C" Student
224. AABF17 (SI-1017 / S10E21) Monty Can't Buy Me Love

225. AABF18 (SI-1018 / S10E22) They Saved Lisa's Brain
226. AABF20 (SI-1020 / S10E23) Thirty Minutes over Tokyo

Season Eleven (1999–2000)–22 Episodes

227. AABF23 (SI-1023 / S11E01) Beyond Blunderdome
228. AABF22 (SI-1022 / S11E02) Brother's Little Helper
229. AABF21 (SI-1021 / S11E03) Guess Who's Coming to Criticize Dinner?
230. BABF01 (SI-1101 / S11E04) Treehouse of Horror X
231. AABF19 (SI-1019 / S11E05) E-I-E-I-(ANNOYED GRUNT)
232. BABF02 (SI-1102 / S11E06) Hello Gutter, Hello Fadder
233. BABF03 (SI-1103 / S11E07) Eight Misbehavin'
234. BABF05 (SI-1105 / S11E08) Take My Wife, Sleaze
235. BABF07 (SI-1107 / S11E09) Grift of the Magi
236. BABF04 (SI-1104 / S11E10) Little Big Mom
237. BABF06 (SI-1106 / S11E11) Faith Off
238. BABF08 (SI-1108 / S11E12) The Mansion Family
239. BABF09 (SI-1109 / S11E13) Saddlesore Galactica
240. BABF10 (SI-1110 / S11E14) Alone Again, Natura-Diddly
241. BABF11 (SI-1111 / S11E15) Missionary: Impossible
242. BABF12 (SI-1112 / S11E16) Pygmoelian
243. BABF13 (SI-1113 / S11E17) Bart to the Future
244. BABF14 (SI-1114 / S11E18) Days of Wine and D'oh'ses
245. BABF16 (SI-1116 / S11E19) Kill the Alligator and Run
246. BABF15 (SI-1115 / S11E20) Last Tap Dance in Springfield
247. BABF18 (SI-1118 / S11E21) It's A Mad, Mad, Mad, Mad Marge
248. BABF19 (SI-1119 / S11E22) Behind the Laughter

Season Twelve (2000–2001)–21 Episodes

249. BABF21 (SI-1121 / S12E01) Treehouse of Horror XI
250. BABF20 (SI-1120 / S12E02) A Tale of Two Springfields
251. BABF17 (SI-1117 / S12E03) Insane Clown Poppy

252. CABF01 (SI-1201 / S12E04) Lisa the Tree Hugger
253. CABF04 (SI-1204 / S12E05) Homer vs. Dignity
254. CABF02 (SI-1202 / S12E06) The Computer Wore Menace Shoes
255. CABF03 (SI-1203 / S12E07) The Great Money Caper
256. CABF06 (SI-1206 / S12E08) Skinner's Sense of Snow
257. BABF22 (SI-1122 / S12E09) HOMR
258. CABF05 (SI-1205 / S12E10) Pokey Mom
259. CABF08 (SI-1208 / S12E11) The Worst Episode Ever
260. CABF07 (SI-1207 / S12E12) Tennis the Menace
261. CABF10 (SI-1210 / S12E13) Day of the Jackanapes
262. CABF12 (SI-1212 / S12E14) New Kids on the Blecch
263. CABF09 (SI-1209 / S12E15) Hungry, Hungry Homer
264. CABF11 (SI-1211 / S12E16) Bye Bye Nerdie
265. CABF13 (SI-1213 / S12E17) Simpson Safari
266. CABF14 (SI-1214 / S12E18) Trilogy of Error
267. CABF15 (SI-1215 / S12E19) I'm Goin' to Praiseland
268. CABF16 (SI-1216 / S12E20) Children of a Lesser Clod
269. CABF17 (SI-1217 / S12E21) Simpsons Tall Tales

Season 13 (2001–2002)
270. CABF19 (SI-1219 / S13E01) Treehouse of Horror XII
271. CABF22 (SI-1222 / S13E02) The Parent Rap
272. CABF20 (SI-1220 / S13E03) Homer the Moe
273. CABF18 (SI-1218 / S13E04) A Hunka Hunka Burns in Love
274. CABF21 (SI-1221 / S13E05) The Blunder Years
275. DABF02 (SI-1302 / S13E06) She of Little Faith
276. DABF01 (SI-1301 / S13E07) Brawl in the Family
277. DABF03 (SI-1303 / S13E08) Sweets and Sour Marge
278. DABF05 (SI-1305 / S13E09) Jaws Wired Shut
279. DABF04 (SI-1304 / S13E10) Half-Decent Proposal
280. DABF06 (SI-1306 / S13E11) The Bart Wants What It Wants
281. DABF07 (SI-1307 / S13E12) The Lastest Gun in the West

282. DABF09 (SI-1309 / S13E13) The Old Man and the Key
283. DABF08 (SI-1308 / S13E14) Tales from the Public Domain
284. DABF10 (SI-1310 / S13E15) Blame It on Lisa
285. DABF11 (SI-1311 / S13E16) Weekend at Burnsie's
286. DABF12 (SI-1312 / S13E17) Gump Roast
287. DABF13 (SI-1313 / S13E18) I Am Furious (Yellow)
288. DABF14 (SI-1314 / S13E19) The Sweetest Apu
289. DABF15 (SI-1315 / S13E20) Little Girl in the Big Ten
290. DABF16 (SI-1316 / S13E21) The Frying Game
291. DABF17 (SI-1317 / S13E22) Poppa's Got a Brand New Badge

Season Fourteen (2002–2003)–22 Episodes

292. DABF19 (SI-1319 / S14E01) Treehouse of Horror XIII
293. DABF22 (SI-1322 / S14E02) How I Spent My Strummer Vacation
294. DABF20 (SI-1320 / S14E03) Bart vs. Lisa vs. 3rd Grade
295. DABF18 (SI-1318 / S14E04) Large Marge
296. DABF21 (SI-1321 / S14E05) Helter Shelter
297. EABF01 (SI-1401 / S14E06) The Great Louse Detective
298. EABF02 (SI-1402 / S14E07) Special Edna
299. EABF03 (SI-1403 / S14E08) The Dad Who Knew Too Little
300. EABF04 (SI-1404 / S14E09) The Strong Arms of the Ma
301. EABF06 (SI-1406 / S14E10) Pray Anything
302. EABF05 (SI-1405 / S14E11) Barting Over
303. EABF07 (SI-1407 / S14E12) I'm Spelling as Fast as I Can
304. EABF08 (SI-1408 / S14E13) A Star Is Born-Again
305. EABF09 (SI-1409 / S14E14) Mr. Spritz Goes to Washington
306. EABF10 (SI-1410 / S14E15) C.E. D'oh.
307. EABF11 (SI-1411 / S14E16) 'Scuse Me While I Miss the Sky
308. EABF12 (SI-1412 / S14E17) Three Gays of the Condo

309. EABF13 (SI-1413 / S14E18) Dude, Where's My Ranch?
310. EABF14 (SI-1414 / S14E19) Old Yeller-Belly
311. EABF15 (SI-1415 / S14E20) Brake My Wife, Please
312. EABF16 (SI-1416 / S14E21) The Bart of War
313. EABF17 (SI-1417 / S14E22) Moe Baby Blues

Season Fifteen (2003–2004)–22 Episodes
314. EABF21 (SI-1421 / S15E01) Treehouse of Horror XIV
315. EABF18 (SI-1418 / S15E02) My Mother the Carjacker
316. EABF20 (SI-1420 / S15E03) The President Wore Pearls
317. EABF22 (SI-1422 / S15E04) The Regina Monologues
318. EABF19 (SI-1419 / S15E05) The Fat and the Furriest
319. FABF01 (SI-1501 / S15E06) Today I am a Clown
320. FABF02 (SI-1502 / S15E07) 'Tis the Fifteenth Season
321. FABF03 (SI-1503 / S15E08) Marge vs. Singles, Seniors, Childless Couples and Teens, and Gays
322. FABF04 (SI-1504 / S15E09) I, (Annoyed Grunt)-Bot
323. FABF05 (SI-1505 / S15E10) Diatribe of a Mad Housewife
324. FABF06 (SI-1506 / S15E11) Margical History Tour
325. FABF07 (SI-1507 / S15E12) Milhouse Doesn't Live Here Anymore
326. FABF09 (SI-1509 / S15E13) Smart and Smarter
327. FABF08 (SI-1508 / S15E14) The Ziff Who Came to Dinner
328. FABF10 (SI-1510 / S15E15) Co-Dependent's Day
329. FABF11 (SI-1511 / S15E16) The Wandering Juvie
330. FABF12 (SI-1512 / S15E17) My Big Fat Geek Wedding
331. FABF14 (SI-1514 / S15E18) Catch 'Em If You Can
332. FABF15 (SI-1515 / S15E19) Simple Simpson
333. FABF13 (SI-1513 / S15E20) The Way We Weren't
334. FABF17 (SI-1517 / S15E21) Bart-Mangled Banner
335. FABF18 (SI-1518 / S15E22) Fraudcast News

Season Sixteen (2004–2005)–21 episodes

336. FABF23 (SI-1523 / S16E01) Treehouse of Horror XV
337. FABF20 (SI-1520 / S16E02) All's Fair in Oven War
338. FABF19 (SI-1519 / S16E03) Sleeping with the Enemy
339. FABF22 (SI-1522 / S16E04) She Used to Be My Girl
340. FABF21 (SI-1521 / S16E05) Fat Man and Little Boy
341. FABF16 (SI-1516 / S16E06) Midnight Rx
342. GABF01 (SI-1601 / S16E07) Mommie Beerest
343. GABF02 (SI-1602 / S16E08) Homer and Ned's Hail Mary Pass
344. GABF03 (SI-1603 / S16E09) Pranksta Rap
345. GABF04 (SI-1604 / S16E10) There's Something about Marrying
346. GABF05 (SI-1605 / S16E11) On a Clear Day I Can't See My Sister
347. GABF06 (SI-1606 / S16E12) Goo Goo Gai Pan
348. GABF07 (SI-1607 / S16E13) Mobile Homer
349. GABF08 (SI-1608 / S16E14) The Seven-Beer Snitch
350. GABF12 (SI-1612 / S16E15) Future-Drama
351. GABF10 (SI-1610 / S16E16) Don't Fear the Roofer
352. GABF11 (SI-1611 / S16E17) The Heartbroke Kid
353. GABF13 (SI-1613 / S16E18) A Star Is Torn
354. GABF14 (SI-1614 / S16E19) Thank God, It's Doomsday
355. GABF15 (SI-1615 / S16E20) Home Away from Homer
356. GABF09 (SI-1609 / S16E21) The Father, the Son, and the Holy Guest Star

Season Seventeen (2005–2006)

357. GABF18 (SI-1618 / S17E—) The Bonfire of the Manatees
358. GABF16 (SI-1616 / S17E—) The Girl Who Slept Too Little
359. GABF19 (SI-1619 / S17E—) Milhouse of Sand and Fog
360. GABF17 (SI-1617 / S17E—) Treehouse of Horror XVI
361. GABF20 (SI-1620 / S17E—) Marge's Son Poisoning

A Special Message to My Nuclear Family

"As far as anyone knows, we're a nice, normal family."
~ Homer J. Simpson

Mom, Dad, and Justin: You have always encouraged me to pursue my goals. I'm sure you didn't think watching *The Simpsons* would amount to anything, but alas, here's a book based on America's favorite family. Despite the fact that *The Simpsons* are America's favorite family, the three of you comprise my favorite family. And don't think for a moment that I didn't have each of you in mind while writing this book:

Mom: The polls say that Marge is the world's greatest mother, but the people voting must have never met you—you are truly the best. It's hard to pin down what you've given me in just a few words. To say that you've always been there for me is clearly an understatement. We're a lot alike—except when it comes to M&Ms. (Next time I buy a bag, I'll save you the brown ones, but the green ones are mine.) Also, *The Simpsons* is better than *I Love Lucy*. I promised myself that I wouldn't reveal in this book that your real hair color isn't blue (oops).

Dad: Well, I can't say that you're like Homer. For one thing, you're smart. Secondly, you don't drink beer. Thirdly, Homer does not usually rank toward the top of the "greatest dad" polls—but you're always # 1. Still, you've been known to eat your fair share of donuts, given the chance. Thank you for your encouragement and for always being there to talk to. Don't take a second job at the Kwik-E-Mart.

Justin: You're as smart as Lisa. We've spent countless hours watching *The Simpsons* and discussing quotes from the show. It would be easy to say that I keep you around just so you could give me quotes to use in my book, but that's not the case. You're a really cool guy, and I'm lucky to have such a great brother. Thanks for keeping down that "infernal racket" while I wrote this book. (World's Best Brother Rank: #1)

Acknowledgments

I would like to acknowledge and thank many of the great people in my life:

My grandfather, Poppy Leon, with whom I speak about politics, play chess, and always learn a lot from; Nana, who taught me how to bake rugelach, and with whom I have shared many good times; my grandmother, Florence, who has always supported everything I have attempted; my other family members, with whom I've spent many fun times.

My close friend, John, who cofounded Backrow Inc., walked around with *Simpsons* poster boards to advertise my first book signing, laughed for five minutes straight after I put on the oversized nerd glasses, and with whom I have engaged in countless conversations about *The Simpsons*; Daniel, who has been one of my closest friends since high school; Dmitriy, who has been one of my closest friends, despite the fact that he doesn't think *The Simpsons* are the "shiznit"; Chris, who still believes that rough drawings of Africa look similar to Kirk Van Houten's depiction of "dignity," and constantly misses the "chili cook-off"; my basketball buddies, who I've spent countless hours shooting hoops with; my friends in the CUNY Honors College; my literary agents, Stacey Glick and Michael Bourret of Dystel and Goderich Literary Management, for having confidence in the value of this project; Dr. Duncan Dobbelmann, for his invaluable guidance and advice; Joe Fodor, who, from the *The Simpsons and Society*'s original publication, helped tremendously in getting the book noticed; Bruce Bobbins and Andrea Greif, for their supreme efforts in getting *The Simpsons and Society* serious media attention; the CUNY Honors College; the editors of *The Excelsior*; my friends in the Brooklyn College student body; my friends and coworkers in the BC Learning Center; and *The Simpsons* Archive, for their wealth of resource material. Thanks also to all of the readers and fans of *The Simpsons* who have emailed or called me with inquiries regarding the show.

I'd also like to thank Rick Miller, Jouni Paakkinen, Robert Thompson, Sam Henrie, Meredith Hayes, Summer Mullins, Lori Sellstrom, Hats Off Books, Dr. Laura Schor, Dr. Kimberly Brodsky, Malcolm Farley, and everyone else I've worked with in the publishing and media fields. Thanks also to all those who I've spoken to about *The Simpsons* throughout the duration of writing this book. The experience has been unforgettable.

A great, big thanks is owed to Sourcebooks for their fortitude and desire to publish this book. Huge thanks also to my editors at Sourcebooks, Peter Lynch and Rachel Jay, whose enthusiasm, dedication, suggestions, and encouragement made writing this book even more enjoyable than sitting on my couch with a bag of popcorn and watching an episode of *The Simpsons*. (Then again, writing this book sort of entailed that kind of research!) Thanks also to my publicist at Sourcebooks Whitney Lehman, and Stephanie Wheatley and Anne LoCascio of the Production department.

And, of course, a super shout-out to Homer Simpson: without you, good sir, there simply would be no book. (Well, duh...)

Finally, a nod to the mysterious "Mr. X," whose pursuit of the truth—at least initially—would have made Socrates proud.

Inspiration for *The World According to The Simpsons*

During my senior year at James Madison High School in Brooklyn, New York, my friends and I formed a club entitled "Backrow Inc." We created the club because we all sat in the back row in our band class. In many ways, we were the heart and soul of the band: we wore goofy glasses without lenses to make everyone laugh, made our official "Backrow Inc." sign, held up flags that read "Go Percussion" when the drummers played well, and even had an official mascot. Soon, other members of the band (those not seated in the back row) began to join our club. Above all else, the common link that all club members shared was our infatuation with *The Simpsons*. Between us, we knew *everything* there was to know about the series. Every day, we quoted different lines from the series, and invariably burst into laughter. Our senior year in high school was amazing because of the fun we had in band. While we also spoke about basketball, school, and playing music, our friendship was initially formed based on our shared interest in *The Simpsons*. Were we fanatics? Maybe—but there's nothing wrong with knowing everything there is to know about what you love. *The Simpsons* made our senior year memorable.

One of my friends once remarked, "We remember quotes from *The Simpsons*, but don't remember what we learned in history class. We'll be telling *Simpsons* quotes to our grandchildren." All of us hope that *The Simpsons* will always live on.

—Steven Keslowitz (also known in Backrow Inc. as Robert Douglas)

....The legacy of *The Simpsons* will live on, and..."They'll Never Stop *The Simpsons*."

B.R.I.

Index

S teven Keslowitz, a University Scholar in the CUNY Honors College at Brooklyn College, is the author of two books, *The Simpsons and Society*, and *The World According to The Simpsons*. *The World According to The Simpsons* is, in large part, an updated and expanded version of *The Simpsons and Society*.

Keslowitz, twenty-one, was recently deemed a "*Simpsons* Expert" by FOX 5 News, NY. He has presented a number of lectures on *The Simpsons* and has appeared on NBC's *Early Today*, Fox 5 News, and *Kobra*, a popular culture program on Swedish National Television. Steven's writings on *The Simpsons* have received international recognition, as he has given interviews with radio stations in the United States, Canada, and Ireland. He was also asked to appear on the Discovery Channel. His views on the political and social significance of *The Simpsons* have been featured in more than five hundred newspapers and other media outlets across four continents, including the *Washington Post*, *NY Daily News*, *Miami Herald*, *Toronto Star*, CNN.com, Yahoo! Asia, and MSNBC.com.

His writing on *The Simpsons* is required reading for English, writing, sociology, and *Simpsons* courses taught at Tufts University, Carnegie Mellon University, Drury University, Montana State University, and the University of Colorado at Denver, among others.

Steven is a two-time prizewinner of the National Kaplun Essay Contest, taking home awards in both 2000 and 2002. He also tutors Greek Classics at the Brooklyn College Learning Center. He continues to write a weekly *Simpsons* column for the Brooklyn College newspaper, *The Excelsior*. Steven is a political science major and plans to pursue a career as a lawyer.

...Steven also hopes to follow his true dream of becoming the safety inspector of the Springfield Nuclear Power Plant. In his spare time, he enjoys drinking Duff beer at Moe's Tavern. He has made a guest appearance on the *Itchy and Scratchy* show, in which he provided the voice for Poochie, the rockin' dog. He is also full of neighborly love ("Shut up, Flanders").

"If it's in a book, it's gotta be true." ~ Milhouse Van Houten

We need to cover one last thing before we're done here. I know what everyone is thinking: how could you write an entire book about fictional characters without ever even mentioning *The Muppets*? Well, I would have devoted a section to the topic, but I wasn't quite sure how exactly to define a "muppet." Give it a shot, Homer:

> **Lisa Simpson:** Dad, what's a Muppet?
> **Homer:** Well, it's not quite a mop, it's not quite a puppet, but man...[laughs hysterically] So to answer your question, I don't know.

Well, anyway, it was worth a shot . . .

So *now* you've reached the end of this book. I suppose you have better things to do anyway. May I suggest watching a famous movie entitled...er...well, maybe Homer has a recommendation:

> "I saw this movie about a bus that had to SPEED around a city, keeping its SPEED over fifty, and if its SPEED dropped, it would explode! I think it was called, *The Bus That Couldn't Slow Down*."

(And I had always thought the title of the movie was *Speed*! Boy, I was *way* off!)

Or perhaps you'd rather read another book. May I suggest Homer's *Odyssey?*

Homer: "Hmm...Homer's *Odyssey?* Is this about that minivan I rented once?"

And finally, in the words of Homer J. Simpson: "That's my cue to exit."

Note: You Have Finally Reached the End of This Book (Woo-hoo!) Bart has just one more comment and follow-up question for you:
"You read a book all the way through. Why?"
~ **Bart Simpson, "The Girl Who Slept Too Little"**